Contents

Acknowledgements

The editors would first like to thank the contributors to this volume for their good-natured response to many requests over a very short timescale and their support in making this book a truly collective enterprise. We would also like to thank our anonymous referees and reviewer, particularly 'referee 2' (who, we hope, will know who s/he is), for giving encouragement to pursue this slightly 'offbeat' project, providing several extremely valuable suggestions as to how it could be rendered manageable, and also raising several important questions in relation to its rationale and coherence. We hope that readers will find our answers to these questions clear and present in the contents of the book. Our thanks also go to all those involved in the book's production at The Policy Press, it has been a pleasure to work with them. Finally, we would like to thank Richard Jenkins who had the initial idea for a book which 'problematised' the concept of 'policy'. We liked the idea of a book that brought together academics from the area of 'culture and identity' and those from more traditional policy interested disciplines, and thus we have acted in loco parentis for Richard's baby and have nurtured it as our own. In view of this, any omissions, errors and inaccuracies are our own and we take full responsibility for these.

Notes on the contributors

Kathy Boxall is a lecturer in the Department of Sociological Studies, University of Sheffield. She works closely with health and social care service users in teaching and research and also has experience as a service user herself.

Joanne Britton is Lecturer in Applied Sociology at the University of Sheffield. Her research interests and publications centre on the study of race and ethnic relations and social identity, and currently on the social construction of 'whiteness' and also the development of British Muslim identity.

Ruby C.M. Chau is Lecturer in Social Work at the University of Sheffield. She has worked with health and social service users from ethnic minorities since 1995. She specialises in participatory methodologies and user perspectives.

Malcolm Cowburn is a senior lecturer in social work, and Director of the Research Unit on Men and Masculinities at the University of Bradford.

Bob Deacon is Professor of International Social Policy at the University of Sheffield. He is founding editor of *Global Social Policy*, Director of the Globalism and Social Policy Programme, and advises UN agencies on global and regional social policy. His most recent book is *Global Social Policy and Governance* (2007) published by Sage.

Kevin Farnsworth is Lecturer in Social Policy at the University of Sheffield. He has published widely on business power and business influence on social and public policy. His first book, *Corporate Power and Social Policy*, was published by The Policy Press in 2004. He is currently working on a second book which examines the impact of business on international social policy development and implementation.

Marilyn Gregory is a lecturer in social work at the University of Sheffield where she teaches qualifying and post-qualifying students. Before entering the academic field she worked for 16 years as a probation officer and court welfare officer. She is currently completing a PhD study on the critical history of probation practice.

Susan M. Hodgson works in the field of science studies and her research is primarily concerned with processes of knowledge production and the reproduction of scientific communities. She is Director of Research Training in the Faculty of Social Sciences at the University of Sheffield.

Zoë Irving is Lecturer in Comparative Social Policy at the University of Sheffield, and has published in the areas of gender and employment and the teaching of social policy. She convenes the 'Policy' module on the MA Sociological Research at Sheffield and is currently researching the development of social rights in small island states.

Richard Jenkins is a social anthropologist and has been Professor of Sociology at the University of Sheffield since 1995. Among his books are *Foundations of Sociology* (2002), *Social Identity* (2nd edn, 2004), *Rethinking Ethnicity* (2nd edn, 2008) and *Being Danish* (2008).

Noémi Lendvai's current research interest is EU integration and the transformation of post-communist welfare. She is currently a research fellow at the Institute of Social and European Studies, Hungary. She has also worked as a policy consultant for various organisations, such as the Hungarian Ministry for Social Affairs and the European Commission.

David Phillips is Reader in Social Policy at the University of Sheffield. He has written widely on quality of life and social quality in both a European and global context, and is on the editorial board of *The International Journal of Social Quality*.

Paul Stubbs is a senior research fellow at the Institute of Economics in Zagreb, Croatia and Honorary Senior Research Fellow at the University of Sheffield. His main research interests include: international actors and social policy; policy translation and the role of intermediaries; and transnational governmentality.

Lorna Warren is a lecturer in the Department of Sociological Studies, University of Sheffield. She has been doing research on and increasingly with older people for over 25 years.

ONE

Policy and its exploration

Susan M. Hodgson and Zoë Irving

This book, about policy, aims to disturb some of the comfortable ground upon which the study of policy, for the most part, rests. In this first chapter we aim to assess the ways in which the study of policy has so far been approached. This involves an element of description but also some analysis of the directions in which scholarship in this field has travelled and some explanation of why the need for a rethink of policy has arisen at this time. Judged by title alone, this book may symbolise an unwelcome diversion to both those who are more concerned with the pressing matters of the real world of policy, either by impact or process, and those who are more concerned with abstract, meta-developments within which policy represents a small piece of the jigsaw. The book's aims and contents do not sit comfortably within any of the existing literatures around 'policy analysis', the 'policy process', 'public administration' or even 'social policy', and they certainly do not feature in wider systemic accounts of human development. In fact, this awkwardness is deliberate and, we suggest, crucial to the book's contribution to debate and study within the field of what we will refer to as 'policy studies'.

The chapters in this collection represent a spectrum of both conventional and less conventional ways of thinking around policy, its research and practice. They are intended to bridge theoretical and disciplinary divides, to identify commonalities and shared interests and to insist that different perspectives from both policy-interested disciplines (such as social work, social policy and public administration, as well as the sociology of welfare), and policy-interested scholars from outside these traditional domains, can be brought together as a means to engender dialogue, as much as to demonstrate contrasts.

Policy provides the practical framework for the expression of political messages and the achievement of social goals. The use of policy as a governmental device is central in maintaining social, political and economic relationships:

- between states
- within states
- between states and citizens
- within organisations
- between the providers and users of services.

But policy is also a non-governmental construct and practice, as contributions to the 'policy studies' literature have argued and explored (for example, Walker, 1981; Rhodes, 1997). There are three reasons why, given this prominence in social and political life, and centrality within social scientific endeavour, the idea, process, custom and performance of policy need to be reassessed. First, at an abstract level, because the relationship between meanings, process and practice is highly illustrative of the intellectual divide which has broadly separated political scientists, policy analysts and social administration empiricists from theoretical sociologists, and both of these groups from practitioners. Second, because at a concrete level, the policy arena has undergone significant change both in process and practice: the range of actors, location of power and form of policy implementation has altered radically since the 1960s and 1970s when much of the thinking around policy studies was crystallised. And third, the manner in which policy is informed has also been subject to change with the official privileging of 'evidence' produced via natural scientific method occurring at the same time as more inventive and revealing research tools are developed in qualitative social science.

We begin this introductory chapter with some discussion of intellectual divides, partly because, in this volume, we hope to expose some of the artificiality of these divisions and partly because it is important in understanding why the exploration of policy provides a vehicle for undertaking an attempt at reconciliation. We then present an account of changes in the policy landscape, which necessitate the reinspection of established frameworks of understanding and explanation. Linked to these broader, contextual changes, we consider the extent to which an altered policy terrain has coincided with movement in the more abstract realm of knowledge production. Finally, in the context of these discussions, we set out the structure of the book and explain its role in reconsidering policy.

Family feuds and partnership potential

To some extent the division of meanings, politics and practices of policy reflects an intellectual or theoretical divide between analytical perspectives which foreground structure, such as is found in materialist and institutional accounts, and those which are considered (by their proponents and opponents) to be 'post' meta-narrative, whether termed post-modern, post-structural, post-positivist, post-empiricist, or post-whatever. In its crudest, binary form, this intellectual divide can be thought of in the sense of two opposing families, such as the Montagues and Capulets in Shakespeare's *Romeo and Juliet*. The members of each 'family' present analyses from a range of perspectives, which are subject to considerable variation, but at the same time there are fundamental ties that bind them in terms of their position around the starting point for both description and explanation. These ties tend to prevent interfamilial communication, other than at the level of critique, and 'stepping out' with members of the opposition can be a potentially vilifiable activity.

In policy studies, a sense of the impact of such a division, can be drawn from Fischer's (2003, p x) concern that the dominant neopositivist policy community regard the development of constructivist or interpretivist approaches as some kind of sinister subversive movement with a secret ideological agenda of its own. Whether the nature of the divide is focused on objectivity versus subjectivity, universalism versus relativism or what people say compared with what they do, is, for the purposes of this chapter, perhaps not so important as the impact its acceptance has had upon policy and its exploration.

With regard to issues of disciplinary interests and positions, we can now briefly map out some of the family trees and family feuds that make up the field of 'policy studies', a term which we use here to describe a field of academic interest, rather than in the US sense, where it implies a sub-discipline of political science. Many disciplines have an interest in policy and it is important to identify intellectual cleavages where they impact on the development of knowledge or the information and execution of social action.

'Policy analysis' is a historically well-established aspect of academic research and debate, which overlaps with the study of 'public policy' and the 'policy process'. In Colebatch's (2002, p 83) view, the formative years of disciplinary development (particularly in the US) saw a 'struggle for the soul' of policy studies between political science and economics, the outcome of which was that 'political science won on the campus but economics won in the corridors of power' (2002, p 84). The traditional domain of policy studies, then, has tended to be formed and re-formed around these areas, with a particular focus on politics and a certain disregard for both understandings and meanings, and also the 'social'. Partly as a result of the manner in which academic departments and subject areas have evolved in different national contexts, there is clearly a 'transatlantic effect' on how policy studies has come to be understood.

In the US, policy studies is indeed far removed from analysis of the 'social' – in Fischer's (2003) words, it is 'empiricist' and 'technocratic' and draws from the methodological tools of mainstream political science and the theory of 'organisations'. In contrast, UK understandings of the field of policy studies are likely to demonstrate a much more developed sense of the social – mainly due to the historical co-development of public and *social* administration and the reformist current present in the latter. However, Rhodes (1997, p 170) remarks that 'British policy studies is all periphery and no core', and similar arguments have been directed at social policy as a subject that has become 'hollowed out' or, as Paul Spicker has (informally) termed it, 'deracinated'. Rhodes's criticism concerns what he sees as a lack of genericism in the study of policy, while Spicker's bemoans a general lack of practice-oriented collective endeavour. With no hierarchical arrangement implied, Figure 1.1 provides a representation of how the academic policy studies 'family' currently maps out. It is undeniable that specialist study of areas such as housing, health and urbanism has gained ground from earlier, all-purpose analysis of policy, but this specialisation has in fact also contributed much to the strengthening of interest and understanding in the process and practice of policy. Nevertheless, there remains a need for a reconsideration of policy that attempts to locate and explore its enduring and universal problematics.

Figure 1.1: The policy studies family

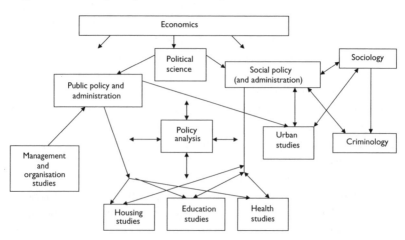

Despite the greater recognition of the 'social' in policy analysis originating in the UK, there has, at the same time, been a long-standing 'divide' between sociology and social policy, which was particularly apparent in the 1960s when social policy had not yet evolved from the more commonly studied 'social administration'. As Townsend observes:

> The separation of the study of social policy from sociology … arises in part because the concept of social policy, perhaps unconsciously for political reasons, has been confined narrowly by many scholars and others to that of welfare administration: in part because the pursuit of sociology has been wrongly believed by many to be 'value-free'; and in part because many sociologists have adopted unduly optimistic and facile theories of social change. (Townsend, 1976, p 1)

Four decades after the period to which Townsend is alluding, there are continuing, if less explicit, antagonisms between social policy and sociology that remain focused on the dismissal of navel-gazing on the one hand or 'counting lamp-posts' on the other (Mann, 1998), depending on who is doing the dismissing. In putting together this collection, this low-intensity or 'subcutaneous' rancour has been apparent with social policy scholars mildly chastised for their lack of reflection on the fundamental tool of their trade while sociologists are teasingly derided for their need to undertake such reflection in the face of the need to act. In a discussion of the importance of words, meaning and context in the analysis of policy, Robert Walker has rather more elegantly described the 'normative' predilection of social policy as resulting from it being 'ideographic rather than nomothetic' (Walker, 2004, p 10).

It is certainly the case that social policy study in Britain has developed within the context of its imperialist history (Irving et al., 2005), but, since the 1960s, social policy has, nevertheless, taken a 'theoretical turn' in relation to the framing of empirical 'facts' within analyses of structures of power and the politics of progress (Gough, 1979; Taylor-Gooby, 1981; Williams, 1989), and more recently (relatively late in comparison to other disciplines) has ventured into the space opened up by the cultural turn in sociology. The first 'turn', which situated the practice of welfare within political economy and structural relations of patriarchy and racialisation, has been more comfortably accommodated than the second, which challenges the entire architecture and essential characteristics and assumptions of universal welfare. The questioning of 'the universal' and the role of 'culture' continue to symbolise the struggle to connect social policy's concern with the redistribution of resources with post-modernism's proposed diversity and relativism (Taylor-Gooby, 1994, 1997; Hillyard and Watson, 1996; Penna and O'Brien, 1996; Thompson and Hoggett, 1996). Scholarship has mostly come to terms with and, to some extent, embraced particularism and diversity as a means to 'differentiated' universalism. This brings an overdue recognition of the significance of social identity and brings about an amplification of previously silenced voices (Williams, 1992; Fitzpatrick, 1996; Taylor, 1998; Lister, 2003). 'Culture', however, remains problematic to many within social policy, who reject its utility because it is associated with everything and nothing (in contrast to seeing it, as proponents do, as a route into 'everything'). In addition, despite valiant efforts to assist social policy in 'coming to terms with culture' (Clarke, 1999), official recourse to 'culture' as an excuse to pathologise capitalism's losers renders the concept immediately suspect within a field essentially concerned with 'who gets what'. Even where the role of 'culture' in social policy has made headway (in, for example, the area of gender and cross-national analysis, see for example Chamberlayne and King, 2000; Pfau-Effinger, 2005), there remains little to attract social policy scholars to the individualistic accounts in more generalised post-modernist writing (Mann, 1998).

Subject maturation in social policy has taken place amid some robust academic discussion, and debates continue around the nature of 'social policy', its separation from 'economic policy', its relationship to 'public policy' and its meaning or meaninglessness in a more individualised, consumerised, globalised era. These concerns and the encounter between post-modern theory and mainstream political science have become established in recent literature as central to policy analysis and theories on governance (Colebatch, 2002; Newman, 2002; Hudson and Lowe, 2004). It is interesting then that both Hudson and Lowe (2004, p 254) and Newman (2002) argue for putting 'policy' back into 'social policy', the former (2004, p 253) from a belief that the 'sociological agenda has squeezed the other disciplines to the margins' of social policy enquiry, and the latter (2002, p 353) from a concern that in the UK under New Labour, policy making requires some re-engagement with 'theories of governance, power and the state'. Despite the multifaceted shift of theoretical and political attention towards the individual, it is undeniably the collective that is inherent in any understanding or practice of 'policy'. For this reason it is fitting that the idea and reality of policy should be subject to a critical evaluation, while recognising the continuing significance of past debates.

If post-modern perspectives have found limited acceptance in social policy, this reaction is considerably amplified in public administration, where they are assumed to have even less to offer in the way of intellectual progress. The debate around policy network analysis, for example, offers a clear illustration of how epistemological divisions tend to close down rather than open up avenues of intellectual exchange (for a useful summary of network theory, its development and critique, see Hudson and Lowe, 2004, ch 8). Thus while Dowding (2001) calls for an end to 'pointless theorising', Fischer (2003, p vii) observes that 'The dominant neopositivist/empiricist approach [in political/policy studies] has given rise to a methodological orientation – some say "methodological fetish" – that brings ever more rigorous quantitative analysis to bear on topics of narrower and narrower import.' Fischer's work represents one of a small number of exceptions to the outright rejection of non-empiricist approaches, and it is worth identifying these and their place in relation to this book in a little detail here. For the most part, the ground-breaking literature and standard textbooks in the discipline of public administration adopt a traditional approach that considers the exercise of political power and its empirical observation and measurement as the key to understanding policy. Some authors suggest that this is now lacking in the study of social policy, while others suggest that its dominance in the study of public policy is ill-fitting in the face of fundamental social, political and economic change.

In the preface to his restatement of an alternative approach to policy analysis, *Reframing Public Policy*, Fischer (2003, p x) suggests that the critique of his 'discursive approach' (or interpretivist or social constructionist depending on how it is categorised – see Chapter Four), based on its alleged relativist downplaying of power and power relations, is outdated and that 'politics in a democratic society ... is a struggle for power played out in significant part through arguments about the "best story"'. Colebatch (2002, p 80) also identifies himself as writing from a 'post' perspective. Although he does not specify which 'post' label he prefers, he suggests that his position means that 'there are multiple ways of mapping social action' and what is important is not which is correct but how they are used. He argues that policy should be understood as a way of explaining and validating action rather than simply as a product of organisational behaviour or governance. There are other important contributions to public administration (for example, Rhodes, 1997; Stone, 2002) which deviate from the traditional frameworks of analysis, and this work suggests that, as several contributors to this volume discuss, the contests which inhere in policy are played out in the whole gamut of theoretical and observable spaces.

At a time when numerous disciplines are chasing 'interdisciplinary' exchange, it seems appropriate to consider the partnership potential of perspectives and methodologies drawn from all sides of the epistemological debate as well as the various members of the policy studies' (multi)disciplinary immediate family, and also some more distant cousins whose disciplinary 'home' lies in geography or anthropology or planning (although not all are represented in this volume). If disciplines, as Moran (2006, p 74) argues, 'are about power, hierarchy and control in the organisation of knowledge' then any attempt to revisit the study of policy has to challenge traditional notions of what can be studied, how, and in whose academic domain. Policy is especially interesting in this venture since its application in the 'real world' has no respect for or interest in the boundaries of social science.

Contextualising policy

To return to the second element of our rationale for reconsidering policy, the context for policy making has changed radically since the closing years of the twentieth century. This change has occurred at all levels of politics and practice from the internationalisation of policy making and the ascendance of global and transnational policy arenas, to shifts in the status of and relationships between the agents of policy design and delivery and policy's intended subjects. The shift has been described as one of 'government' to 'governance' (Rhodes, 1997; Colebatch, 2002; Hudson and Lowe, 2004), and signifies a fundamentally altered policy environment. The impact of globalisation reverberates not only through the design and content of policy, which is reformed to comply with the demands of global economic strictures (albeit via regional, national and local interpretations of reform), but also within the practice of policy, the patterns of administrative and political 'implementation' that are evolving. This means that both the players involved in the policy-making game and the rules under which they participate no longer conform to the patterns identified or models developed in established policy studies. What is more, the populations on whom policy is targeted are far less static and passive than hitherto assumed. Categorising, for the purpose of resource allocation or any other kind of purposive action, is increasingly problematic as concepts of 'family', 'nationality' and 'work' are subject to greater scrutiny and disagreement in an era of intensifying demographic, migratory and economic complexity. These particular configurations of social change present a fundamental challenge to policy study, which, for the most part, has tended to seek simplicity and linearity in explanatory endeavours.

More related to the meanings of policy and the intellectual basis on which it is constructed in Europe, and especially the UK, the 'third way' political project demonstrates the unprecedented influence of sociological theory in underpinning its practical developments (Giddens, 1998, 2000; Etzioni, 1995, 1997, 2000). Notwithstanding academic critique of its principles, this project has somehow slipped past the economic gatekeepers to refocus attention on social change, and 'the social' more generally. Britain under New Labour has seen a much higher degree of governmental engagement with the academic social scientific community than under previous governments, both in terms of the 'traceability' of ideas and in the government's demand that social scientists should put up (or otherwise, no doubt, shut up) the evidence to support policy development (see Young et al's [2002] opening discussion for an early expression of this desired relationship). It is to discussion of the novel elements of political concern with evidence and objectivity that we now turn.

Changing forms of knowledge

It is not just the superficial, structural or even social processes that have altered in the contemporary policy arena: underlying knowledge generation processes have also shifted. While analysis of the productive aspects of policy has traditionally formed the key component of scholarship, it is equally as important to investigate the link between *generative* and *productive* aspects of policy making in order to better explain the 'how' as well as the 'why'. Changes in the context of the 'production' of policy have been outlined in the previous sections. In terms of the generation (or in many cases 'regeneration') of policy, it is argued that it is the manner in which it is informed that has changed.

It is interesting that as political attention is refocused on social goals, support for claims to 'knowledge' of the social has come down firmly on the side of empiricist natural science. 'Evidence-based policy', or 'evidence-informed policy' or even 'evidence-inspired policy'[1] as a mantra for government and non-governmental agencies, now operates to frame what knowledge can and cannot be considered worthy enough to inform policy. Indeed, it is not only the approaches, questions and methods of an empiricist science that increasingly frame what counts as a valid research pursuit, the disciplines of science are also beginning to stake claims to the territory of the social. The shift to 'evidence-based' policy which began in the late 1990s rather begs the question of what policy is assumed to have been based upon prior to the ascendance of a techno-rational, pseudo-neutral approach to managing the 'social'. One contribution of policy analysis to our understanding of policy making has been to explore the significance of political values in determining the policy agenda. How ideas are propelled to the centre or the margins of policy debates and how different forms of power are exercised in order to ensure that the game is played according to the rules of dominant interests has been well exposed, and demonstrates the ideological basis of policy. Notwithstanding the economic constraints, other assumed bases for policy are hard to imagine, although undoubtedly policies have originated from the whims of civil servants or as injudicious and hasty responses to specific events. However, it seems that in the current political climate, governments (and international actors such as the OECD and WHO) are keen to demonstrate that in policy making they are no longer ideologically driven in the way that the hard-line New Right model characterised developments in the 1980s, but rather seek the best fitting policy available, based on 'evidence' of the efficacy of particular solutions.

In the UK context, New Labour's dictum that 'what matters is what works' can thus be seen in contrast to the memorable claim made by a previous Conservative Home Secretary that 'prison works'. The former was intended to be symbolic of a new politics of rationality, moderation and openness, an intellectual glasnost for a new millennium, while the latter would be seen to represent the ill-founded, monovisionist, ideological fervour of a bygone age. In practice, the policy outcomes may not be any different – for example, sending more people to prisons has emerged as both the 1980s' ideologically preferred solution and the 2000s' path of least resistance, regardless of the evidence base.

As Black (2001) has observed, not only do competing political and economic influences impact on the decisions of policy makers, and the extent to which 'evidence' is deemed important as a basis for these decisions, but the nature of the 'evidence' to which they are exposed is also subject to human interference, whether this be through the mediation of 'knowledge purveyors' (civil servants, for example) or the interpretations of the policy makers themselves (see for example Marmot's [2004] summary of evidence and subsequent policy making in relation to alcohol and health). In the context of healthcare, Black even goes so far as to suggest that 'many researchers are politically naïve' (2001, p 277) and assume that if they can uncover and present objective 'facts', then these will be unquestioningly accepted by policy makers.

Many scientists, especially in the field of public health are concerned about what they regard as the problem of 'policy-based evidence' (Davey Smith et al., 2001; Marmot, 2004; Choi et al., 2005). Black's view is that the level of existing consensus on an issue determines the extent to which 'evidence' is required; the greater the agreement the less need for evidence to support the proponents' and opponents' cases. Comparing governmental attention to the evidence for health inequalities in the Black Report (produced in the 1970s) and the Acheson Report (released in 1998), Marmot (2004) discusses the policy research relationship in the context of a 'willingness to act', such that 'evidence' will have an impact only where it fits pre-existing policy aspirations, what Choi et al. (2005) refer to as 'systematic bias' (see Naughton, 2005 for an example of how this has occurred in the field of criminal justice policy). To assume that recourse to an 'evidence' base signified the 'end of ideology' in policy making would thus be foolish, particularly given that where it is commissioned, the type of research evidence favoured belies an ideological twist in itself, and one which the biomedical community does not necessarily recognise.

The 'evidence' preferred by governments and research-funding organisations is that established through the use of natural scientific methods or methods as close to these as can be employed where people are involved. Methods of evaluation as Pawson (2002a, 2002b) identifies have evolved, he argues, into the more quantitative forms of meta-analysis where previous research findings are 'classified, tallied and compared', and the more qualitative 'narrative review' which classifies but also introduces value judgements regarding the 'best' or most 'successful' social interventions. Meta-analysis, Pawson's (2002a) critique suggests, lacks adequate focus on context and subjects, while narrative review is like herding cats. Pawson's (2002b) way forward is to adopt a 'realist synthesis' of the two forms, a more nuanced approach which recognises that both the subjects of intervention and the intervention itself are situated in time and place and that, as a consequence, 'effectiveness' is neither universal nor guaranteed. While it is difficult to argue against the need for 'evidence', we also have to question its basis, as any claims-making activity must be viewed as just that. Fischer (2003) suggests that, for this reason, the empiricist policy community is uncomfortable with 'post-empiricist' interpretivism – because it challenges their claims to scientific knowledge, and thus the validity of the 'evidence' produced.

Despite governmental preference for the objective rational model of research, this does not imply that policy makers are more favourably disposed to natural scientists than they are social scientists, or that scientists are favourably disposed to politicians (see for example Rosenstock and Lee, 2002; Choi et al., 2005). Choi et al. (2005) argue for example that (natural) scientists and policy makers inhabit different worlds where (stereotypically speaking) narrowly conceived but highly in-depth expert knowledge, subject to open peer review, is the domain of the former, while the latter exist in the domain of the electorally acceptable quick-fix, cobbled together on a need-to-know basis. Importantly, then, they note that the two sets of actors speak a different language and there is a need for translation or a 'knowledge broker' to facilitate communication and understanding (see Lendvai and Stubbs, Chapter Ten, for further discussion of this idea).

In social science, the evidence-based policy movement has been influenced by the biomedical model but, as would be expected, has collided with not only conflicting research paradigms but also an array of unforgiving critics. A key problem for many is that evidence-based assessment concerns individualised interventions (Davey Smith et al., 2001), the personal 'risk factors' involved in being the subject of policy (for example being unemployed, a young offender or a heart attack or obesity sufferer), at the expense of any attention to structural and environmental conditions. In this sense, the rise of evidence-based policy can be regarded as another dimension of what Ferge (1997) has termed 'the individualisation of the social'. Writing as the UK Economic and Social Research Council's 'Centre for Evidence Based Policy and Practice', Young et al. (2002, p 223) suggest that rather than evidence-based policy, the ultimate aim should be an 'evidence-informed society', but perhaps an 'evidence-base-aware' society might be preferable. This compels us to consider the origins and purpose of the questions being asked, the nature of data gathered and, more importantly, the ways in which data are and can be manipulated.

The book

One of the aims of this book is to prompt some reconsideration of the nature of the intellectual divisions described earlier. Collectively, the chapters map out both traditional and more pioneering excursions into the field of 'policy studies' and in this way we hope also to challenge some of the accepted, and sometimes unhelpful and artificial, boundaries that separate the realist/constructivist 'families' and disciplinary family 'members', and lead to rigid distinctions between the 'public' and the 'social' for example. The overarching theme of the collection is thus to emphasise the gains to be made from studying policy through a lens made up of multiple perspectives. Historically, disciplinary concerns in the academic study of policy have tended to engender somewhat constrained analyses, that focus on a particular aspect such as 'mechanics' or 'outcomes', in which theorising is insufficiently linked to the work of practitioners and actors. Today, those whose interests lie 'out in the field' and those whose interests are more 'abstract' are still rarely found in conversation with one another, and more often regard each other's concerns as belonging to different worlds. The range of authors represented here work within the perhaps predictable disciplines of social work, social policy and sociology, disciplines which would be expected to have an interest in 'policy', and those from which it is assumed that much policy-related theorising and research is generated. Sociology, however, is home to a range of very different approaches and our 'sociological' contributors are not by any means sociologists of welfare, for example. A clash of ideas between disciplines itself, however, is not the focus of the book although it is important to establish what these disciplines and the basis of this clash might be. Our interest in cross-disciplinarity is simply in terms of encounters between the abstract and the applied, in the importance of the generation of questions that these encounters entail, and in the dialogue that is opened up within this process. As editors of this collection, we are ourselves engaged in an interesting encounter between perspectives drawn from a traditional structural-institutionalist social policy and a sociology of science tradition born of the post-structural turn.

Working from a cross-disciplinary perspective, the book identifies key topics within the policy arena, from conceptualisation to operationalisation, presenting a critical and reflective engagement with the theory and practice of policy at all levels of political organisation and within a range of contexts. It explores the development of the meaning and language of policy and examines the practice of policy from the local to the supranational levels, using a collection of illustrative case studies to demonstrate how contemporary policy is contested, shaped and accounted for. The key thinking, developed across each of the contributing chapters is that given the significance of policy as a means by which social, economic and political life is organised and directed, there is a need for a critical restatement of its genealogy, development and form. To this end, a focus on both the genesis and production of policy is provided, with attention to conceptual as well as practical concerns. By drawing on different disciplinary perspectives, issues of analytical perspective and method come to the fore. Therefore, the contributions, overall, also present an opportunity to interrogate the research–policy interface in terms of the problems of standpoints and evidence discussed here.

A keyword search for 'policy' in any academic library catalogue will demonstrate the scope of general usage of the term (18,159 titles in University of Sheffield library), where it is employed to describe formalised courses of action established to address particular problems or to facilitate the pursuit of particular strategies or goals. In designing the structure of a book which intends to reconsider policy, it is important to begin with some analysis and discussion of meanings, because the idea of policy and its study is mundane yet ill-defined, academically ubiquitous yet coveted by separate disciplines. The book then turns to politics because 'policy' and 'politics' are terms that in many languages, and in practice, are inseparable. However, this does not suggest that the relationship between politics and policy is in any sense straightforward, and the absence of uniformity leads to the reconsideration of practices, with the emphasis on plurality, in the final section.

Part One, Meanings, provides analysis and discussion of conceptual issues – ranging from how we know what policy is to matters of discourse and ontology, symbolic politics and categorisation. This part explores the notion of policy at a conceptual level, introducing readers to theoretical frameworks and tools which can be used to understand the evolution and understandings of policy, its relationship to political and social development and how it is interpreted and expressed through and within practices. In Chapter Two, Richard Jenkins questions, from an anthropological standpoint, received wisdoms around the nature and purpose of policy in modernity, and argues for its recognition as more than the frame within which lives are lived. He makes the case for greater appreciation of the centrality of policy in ethnographic research. Developing further the theme of 'symbolic politics' raised by Jenkins, David Phillips, in Chapter Three, explores the manner in which policy is used to represent visions of 'the good society', how this usage travels between national and supranational arenas and the extent to which visions can become reality. Jo Britton (Chapter Four) examines processes of categorisation and their meaning in relation to policy development and policy outcomes. Using the example of categories based on 'race' and ethnicity, Britton illustrates the ways in which categorisation is both politically constructed and socially constructive, a process whereby in the abstract, identity and membership are ascribed and contested, with concrete implications for practice in issues of distribution and access to resources, which are themselves both abstract and material.

All three chapters in Part One also lead to the generation of questions regarding the political faces of policy, which is the focus of Part Two. These questions centre around matters of values and power, how structural and social relations govern acts of representation, symbolism and categorisation. Part Two is thus concerned with the relationship between policy and politics through examination of the influences that determine the policy process and policy outcomes. The chapters in this section situate policy as a contested domain where the interests of actors are proclaimed, negotiated, compromised and reinvented as policy, in ways that reflect the specific interplay of national and international forces. The chapters cohere around the interrogation of 'politics' at multiple levels, but the discussions are all also illustrated by 'practices' in one way or another, in pursuit of reconciliation between the abstract and the applied. Developing the idea of policy as 'meaning-making' introduced in Part One, Chapter Five, by Marilyn Gregory, charts the impact of changing policy discourse as an example of the relationship between meaning and action. Using the example of probation work, Gregory demonstrates how the politically dependent language of policy alters both policy approach and policy practice. Kevin Farnsworth (Chapter Six) takes a different approach to the analysis of politics in policy, examining the contemporary alignment of agents of power and the different ways in which structural power and power of agency is exercised. His analysis draws attention to the limitations of both established theoretical explanations of power in the policy-making process and, in the realm of practice, the continuing significance of conflict and consensus in determining policy directions. Following Farnsworth's discussion of changes in 'horizontal' power relationships between capital and state, Bob Deacon (Chapter Seven) provides an insight into some of the evolving 'vertical', or 'scalar', relationships, between policy actors operating at multiple levels of governance and across national borders. The discussion here presents a picture of a political landscape where policy is largely determined by processes of contestation occurring outside the agencies and institutions traditionally the subject of policy analysis.

Part Three applies a conceptual and methodological appraisal to the level of practice; the chapters here provide a critical review of the knowledge and methods used to inform policy making and the impact of policy assumptions on the manner in which policy objectives are set, achievable and achieved. In all cases, the relations between research informing policy and practice, and policy informing research and practice, are addressed. Malcolm Cowburn (Chapter Eight) begins with a cautionary tale regarding the basis of policy research and consequent policy practice. Combining an analysis of the role of ethics in the research process with a critique of method in relation to research on male sex offenders, Cowburn's analysis reminds us that the (potentially shaky) foundations of policy practices run deeper than statements at the level of formulation. Continuing the questioning of the research–policy interface and its implications for practice, Kathy Boxall, Lorna Warren and Ruby C.M. Chau (Chapter Nine) describe the evolution of user involvement in policy research and examine some of the issues arising from the convergence of the interests of academic social science and those of previously marginalised social groups around 'research' and its outcomes. Both their chapter and Cowburn's highlight challenges to 'objectivity' and the significance of resistance to dominant research paradigms, and both suggest that policy subjects are as important as policy providers in the realm of practice. The final chapter in Part Three advances analysis of issues of communication among contemporary collections of policy actors and informants. In Chapter Ten, Noémi Lendvai and Paul Stubbs present a worked example of the kind of methodology advocated by Richard Jenkins in Chapter Two, demonstrating that meaning and practice are intimately related. Having established 'translation' as central to a theoretical framework for policy analysis in the context of global governance and exchange, Lendvai and Stubbs examine the practice of policy as played out by international actors in a political terrain, which defies the logic of welfare settlements in the traditional sense. With an emphasis on the players rather than the game, Lendvai and Stubbs thus provide an alternative view of policy processes as they unfold along a far from predictable route towards ends which are themselves evolving.

The chapters in this section cannot capture the myriad policy practices in their entirety. What they serve to illustrate are ways of opening out our understandings of policy in practice to reflect the view that rather than representing a simple end point in the policy process, 'practices' can be identified and explored at every level and in all aspects of policy development and delivery. These analyses thus promote depth of understanding of the wider themes of the book rather than breadth of knowledge of practice in policy areas, organisations or professions. Questions of 'ethics', the role of policy 'subjects' and processes of communication in the design and implementation of policy are enduring problems for the operation of policy bureaucracy and actors as well as more generally for all of us in our lived reality.

Inevitably, in a collection such as this, different styles of writing are evident, different forms of argument are presented and differing norms emerge. Some of the chapters require case studies to illustrate the kind of reconsideration of policy that is being undertaken, and from these it is intended that the reader may take and apply the arguments presented to her or his own policy areas of interest. In the final chapter we attempt a synthesis of standpoints and conclusions which foregrounds recurrent themes, in order to explore a way forward for policy studies which problematises territories and boundaries, revisits the 'how' of policy making and emerges from a changing world.

Note
[1] We are grateful to Richard Jenkins for bringing to our attention a UK Economic and Social Research Council poster using this term.

Part One
Meanings

Introduction

This first part of the book is oriented around the concept of meanings. Meanings operate at all levels, whether you are interested in what policies mean to us as individuals as we go about our daily lives; or your concern is more with national or international policy intents. Meanings are important because policy is an organising principle, not just a product or outcome.

One purpose of these chapters is to lay out some ground that readers can identify as foundational in all policy work, although the ground may not have been previously approached in this manner. The terrain to be covered includes, how policy makes sense of the world (and how the world makes sense of policy), how policy puts the world into categories (and how categories allow policies to be made) and how we might want to change it all, through visions of imagined futures, through symbolic politics.

In this section the authors adhere to the dictum of 'questioning the taken for granted'. Jenkins begins the section by addressing the twin concerns of what ethnography can do for policy and what policy can do for ethnography. His answer is 'quite a lot', on both counts, provided we are willing to reframe what we currently accept as 'policy analysis' and to explore policy as an interactive process rather than a backdrop to everyday life. Phillips uses the process of EU enlargement as a lens to view relations between policies and values; that is, relations between how we might like the world to be and the forces that may work for and against this. He presents policy as representing a vision, an expression of the fundamental aspirations of collectivities. In the process he raises key matters of competition and dialogue; elements of policy work that are of increasing importance in our globalising world. Britton pushes us to face up to our categorising practices and the political sense-making of 'who is who'. Her chapter raises issues of identity that remain too marginal in the policy field at the current time. If we continue to ignore matters of 'representation' (in an ontological sense), how are we meant to progress the understanding of the dynamics between policy and representation (in a political sense)?

All three chapters lead us to reconsider how we position 'policy' as an object of study and provide a reminder that 'policy' cannot be studied as a confined entity, rather that it is constitutive of everyday life. To appreciate this fully, these chapters emphasise that we need to pose different, sometimes radical and sometimes obvious, questions. Only by drawing non-conventional voices into discussions of policy can we really challenge the field. One way to force this introduction of non-conventional voices is to draw on other disciplines in an attempt to be adventurous. Readers are asked to question whether 'policy' is the same as or different from any other subject of social scientific study and, in turn, whether this requires different action on our behalf as policy analysts. The questions that these authors pose suggest that the field of policy studies is *more* important than many working within the wider social sciences currently realise.

TWO

The meaning of policy/policy as meaning

Richard Jenkins

In this chapter I am not specifically concerned with welfare policy, or even with social policy more generally. I am, rather, interested in policy and policy making as a generic institution of modern governmentality, in the Foucauldian sense of power/knowledge, the intellectual technology of power and its exercise. I want to approach the generic concept of 'policy' as if it were at least a little anthropologically strange. In other words, I intend to treat the notion of 'policy' as something to be interrogated, rather than taken for granted; to ask, 'what *is* policy, what does it *do*, what does it *mean*?' Rather than simply accepting policy and policy making as established aspects of the contemporary human world that everybody, in some senses, knows about and understands, I will attempt to look at them from the naive perspective of a stranger. While this is, of course, impossible in any thoroughgoing sense, it does, at least, offer a point of view from which to engage in critical inquiry.

Talking about 'anthropological strangeness' as an epistemological stance that might offer useful insights does not, however, imply that there is anything specifically anthropological, in a narrow disciplinary sense, about what follows. With an intellectual pedigree running through from Alfred Schutz (1944, p 500) to Harold Garfinkel (1967, p 9), and beyond, there is a long-standing perspective within sociology – reiterated by Zygmunt Bauman (1990, p 15) – that recognises one of sociology's core tasks, and most useful epistemological tactics, as the defamiliarisation of the familiar. This is what I hope to do, even if only tentatively and partially.

That aside, there are other good reasons to distance this discussion from anthropology. As an anthropologist by training, and even more particularly as one who has studied policies and their consequences for nearly thirty years, I am convinced that we should be sceptical about the recurrent invention of new 'anthropologies of this or that', in this case the relatively recent 'anthropology of policy' (for example, Shore and Wright, 1997). That some anthropologists write about policy and policy-related matters does not, in itself, make for an 'anthropology of policy'. This minor disciplinary imperialism – and professional opportunism – implies that there is something genuinely distinctive that one can define and defend as a peculiarly anthropological point of view, which will shed new and better light on whatever 'this or that' is at stake. Such an approach is at least an overstatement, given the long-standing, mutually fruitful two-way traffic between anthropology and sociology (not to mention other related disciplines). It is certainly immodest and, perhaps most important, it is unwise: anthropologists who go down that road are apt to neglect the hard-won cumulative insights of generations of scholars who have toiled before them in the academic vineyard. In the process, they risk being seen naively to reinvent the wheel, to encourage intellectual fragmentation, and to inhibit rather than encourage critical inquiry. On balance, I prefer the challenges and demands of interdisciplinarity, within the open intellectual terrain of a broad social science approach that I have elsewhere called 'generic sociology' (Jenkins, 2002, pp 15–38).

What is policy?

In one sense, in our everyday lives we all know what 'policy' is. We recognise policies when we read them, hear others talking about them, or encounter them in action. If nothing else they are often called this, that, or the other *policy*, just so we should not be in doubt. But, much as we do not generally question the ontology of law, for example, we tend not to spend much time thinking about what 'a policy' amounts to, or what the history of policy as a distinctive approach to government or decision making might be.

The axiomatic inattention of everyday life aside, there is a completely understandable tendency for policy analysts – and, indeed, a wide range of other social scientists – to take for granted what 'policy' is, and to take for granted that we *know* what policy is. There are at least three, closely related, reasons for this. First, working within any 'normal science' intellectual community, the common assumption is that everybody pretty much knows what everyone else is talking about when it comes to the conceptual basics of the field. Second, working in applied contexts, necessarily close to government, corporations, non-governmental organisations (NGOs) or social movements, and with the aim of getting things done, heads are down and people are dealing with the specifics and details of particular, substantive policies. Third, compared to sociology, for example, or political science, the academic fields that have become established as 'social policy' or 'public policy' possess very little in the way of distinctive meta-theory and, specifically, very little towards the ontological end of the theoretical spectrum. This may simply be due to the definitively applied nature of these activities. It may, however, also be because these subject areas are, historically if nothing else, intellectually derivative of sociology, political science and political economy. These three factors taken together mean that in the everyday business of social or public policy analysis, whether in or outside the academy, fundamental conceptual discussion is unlikely to be common.

This tacit, practical working consensus may be understandable, but it does not help us to clarify our thinking, should we be moved to ask, as I do here, 'what, *actually*, is policy?'. Fortunately, however, not everyone concerned with social and public policy takes the conceptual foundations for granted, and there are interesting and sophisticated discussions of the nature of policy. That many of these are to be found in introductory textbooks is unsurprising: where else, after all, is discussion of the conceptual basics more appropriate and necessary? It is also, however, a timely reminder that writing of this kind, which demands clarity in meta-conceptualisation, and offers unusual opportunities for constructive ground clearing and reflection, is generally insufficiently acknowledged as a site of serious intellectual work. Introductory texts are certainly extremely useful when thinking about topics outside one's own disciplinary patch.

Before looking at some introductory policy studies texts, however, I want to start with an even more basic view of policy, which locates it within a model of human cognition and decision making. This comes from a relatively early, and still somewhat unusual, collection of essays problematising policy and the policy process:

> Various labels are applied to decisions and actions we take, depending in general on the breadth of their implications. If they are trivial and repetitive and demand little cogitation, they may be called routine actions. If they are more complex, have wider ramifications, and demand more thought, we may refer to them as tactical decisions. For those which have the widest ramifications and the longest time perspective, and which generally require the most information and contemplation, we tend to reserve the word *policy*. (Bauer, 1968, pp 1–2)

We have here a cognitive and practical hierarchy, from routine actions, to tactical decisions, to policy; incrementally moving from the habitual, axiomatic procedures and assumptions of everyday time through to a deeper prospect that shades into the long run of historical time. Bauer goes on to describe policy as 'parameter-shaping acts'. By this he seems to mean that policy creates the frames of meaning within which the contingencies of everyday life play out. So, in this context, the distinctiveness of 'policy' is partly a matter of perceived complexity, partly a matter of the time frames that are involved, and partly a matter of significance (which is not to suggest that complexity, time and significance are easy to tease apart).

Turning now to one of the founders of British social policy analysis, Richard Titmuss is also concerned with fairly basic matters, and with decision making. He defines generic policy as:

> the principles that govern action directed towards given ends. The concept denotes action about means as well as ends and it, therefore, implies change … [it] is only meaningful if we … believe that we can effect change in some form or another. (Titmuss, 1974, pp 23–4)

Today, in a more sceptical, even cynical, age than the optimistic decades of post-war welfare reform to which Titmuss contributed so much, we might want to dissent from the definitional centrality of change. After all, any given policy may be as easily oriented to preserving a conservative or reactionary status quo as to promoting change. But the rest is clear enough: policy is a matter of defining means and ends and the relationship between them. Despite his commitment to change, Titmuss's example could be described as a strikingly simple, almost apolitical definition of policy.

By contrast, Colebatch (2002, pp 8–10) has recently developed something a little more complex and nuanced. For him, the notion of policy emerges out of three axiomatic assumptions about the modern world: *instrumentality* means that all organisations are goal-oriented, *hierarchy* that government works in a 'top-down' fashion, and *coherence* that everything fits together into some kind of system. Given these axioms, policy, in Colebatch's definition, is about the maintenance of order through the exercise of legitimate authority, whether delegated or direct, informed by appropriate expertise. In its mission to maintain order, policy attempts to avoid 'arbitrary and capricious' decision making and to constrain courses of action that may run counter to that principle. The reliance upon expertise – 'expert knowledge' in Giddens's formulation (1990, pp 83–92), an 'evidence base' in recent political terms – is part of this mission, and is one of the reasons why policy is often specialised and devoted to distinct fields or issues. It is also fundamental to the principle of legitimacy.

One last excursion into the textbooks should be sufficient. Michael Hill's standard introduction for undergraduates offers several additional observations about the complexities of policy (2005, pp 6–10). He suggests that policy may often be difficult to identify as a specific phenomenon, in that it may be broad ranging, implicit rather than explicit, and embedded in multi-stranded ongoing processes in many different contexts. In as much as policy is bound up with networks of decision making over time, it is not fixed but can, at least in principle, be changed. Nor is policy simply a matter of discourse: in the first place, it is definitively a matter of what people do as well, and, in the second, it may be as much a matter of non-decisions as decisions, of public silences as well as public statements. Policy may be at least as much aimed at the production of an appearance of coherence and order, as actual coherence and order; being seen to have a policy – as opposed to actually effecting the outcomes specified by policy – may be the most important end in any given situation.

Finally, Hill points out that policy may emerge as an ex post facto rationalisation of emergent trends and practices, rather than as the product of any deliberative policy process. At the very least, it is often the case that the practical implications and meanings of policy only emerge as the unintended cumulative consequence of a range of uncoordinated actions. In this sense, the tacit improvisation of outcomes at 'street-level' (Lipsky, 1980) is as much a part of the policy process as self-conscious policy making higher up the organisational hierarchy.

It would be too much to suggest that the above definitions and observations agree with each other exactly. They do, however, converge on a number of core propositions that, taken together, begin to offer a fairly comprehensive ideal typical model of policy:

- Policy is an attempt to define, shape and steer orderly courses of action, not least in situations of complexity and uncertainty.
- Policy involves the specification and prioritisation of ends and means, and the relationships between competing ends and means.
- Policy is best regarded as a process, and as such it is ongoing and open-ended.
- The policy process is, by definition, an organisational practice.
- The policy process is embedded in and is not distinct from other aspects of organisational life.

- Policy appeals to, and is intended to foster, organisational trust – that is, external trust of organisations, and trust within organisations – based upon knowledge claims and expertise.
- Policy appeals to, and is intended to foster, organisational trust based on legitimate authority.
- Policy is about absences as well as presences, about what is not said as much as what is said.
- Policy may be implicit as well as explicit.

One final point has only been hinted at so far: policy formulation and policy implementation, although they are often talked about as distinct processes, are to a considerable extent implicated in each other (Hill, 2005). Looking at studies of organisational policy (for example, Jenkins, 1986, pp 207–8), it becomes clear that, rather than being sequential processes – first one, then the other – policy formulation and implementation typically inform and shape each other in ways that are hard to disentangle. It is, indeed, difficult to see how it could be otherwise: policy initiatives are shaped by the experience of managing previous, related, policies and, ideally at least, the review and monitoring of policy in practice produces refinement, re-evaluation and development. As Wenger (1998) has argued, organisations can be understood as 'communities of practice' that are, among other things, environments within which practical learning takes place. In this light, we should, perhaps, talk about a single process of policy formulation and implementation.

Policy, politics ... and culture

A strong implication of the discussion so far is that 'whatever it is that we call policy' is a diverse phenomenon, encompassing a variety of institutional forms and practices, in a range of settings. Policy is certainly not, for example, an organisational practice or device that is peculiar to the state and its delegates. What is more, precisely because of the centrality of policy to government, and because of its massive consequences for everyday life, even *public* policy cannot accurately be described as being confined to, or contained within, the organisational ambit of the state. Public policy processes are as much characteristic of civil society – the media, political parties, NGOs, interest groups, think tanks, academics, business interests, lobbyists, and so on – as of the formal institutions of the state.

This, conveniently, brings me to the relationship between policy and politics. According to Therborn, English and Dutch are the only

European languages to distinguish between politics (*politiek*) and policy (*beleid*).[1] Therborn appears to approve of this distinction: politics, according to him, is about deciding the nature of the governmental game, its objectives and its rules (or, put another way, how things should be run and who should run them). Policy, however, he sees as a matter of how to achieve objectives within the rules and nature of the political game: 'Politics, then, precedes and wraps up policy' (Therborn, 2001, p 19).

The discussion above of the relationship of reciprocal implication, one in the other, which exists between policy formulation and implementation suggests that there are good grounds for arguing that Therborn's argument about the separation of politics and policy does not hold much water. In the first place, to persist with his own metaphor of 'the game', policy processes are an essential part of the nature and rules of the modern political game: they are simultaneously ends and means, both objective and plan. Having a policy – and being *seen* to have a policy – is, as has already been suggested, a significant political objective in its own right. Less cynically, politics depends on policy as one of its chief instruments for getting things done, while policy formulation and implementation are, for their part, deeply politicised. Interactionally, the policy process is, almost by definition, a matter of negotiation: compromise, imposition, deal making and arm-twisting may all have their place, and these can all accurately be described as political (albeit with a small 'p'). Nor is the temporal sequence *first* politics, *then* policy: the relationship between them is, rather, a matter of feedback loops that may not be that easy to disentangle in practice.

Furthermore, this apparently objective distinction between politics and policy is actually likely to be deeply political in its own right; in this sense, the other European languages have definitely got it right. The technocratic illusion of 'rational' policy – derived from an objective knowledge base and somehow above the fray of sectional interests and ideologies – is certainly powerful. It is, however, just that, an illusion; which may, of course, be its entire political point. Thus the policy process is deeply implicated in the modern exercise of rational authority, and its legitimation (Weber, 1978, pp 215–26). It is politically important that decisions should be *seen* to be founded in proper, rational processes. The policy process is a very close cousin of planning in this respect, although the latter may claim even more strongly that it is a technical or managerial discipline rather than a political practice (and that claim is no less an illusion).

With this in mind, it cannot be said too often or with too much emphasis that precisely because policy is political it is also a matter of values and ideology. All those authors whose definitions of policy I have referred to above agree about this. Policy is not simply concerned with rationality, knowledge and efficient means–ends relationships. It is as much about ends as means, and ends are generally specified, at least in part, by values and ideology. Policy formulation and implementation is also a prime medium in modern nation states for the packaging, communication and promotion of values and ideology.

Finally, to return to a complex set of issues that has been alluded to in a number of places above, policy as a device that allows an organisation or actor to be *seen* to do something, while perhaps doing something else or effectively nothing at all, has a long history. This can perhaps best, and most charitably, be described as the art of 'symbolic politics' (see, for example, Solomos, 1988). All of which suggests another direction from which we should, perhaps, look a little more closely and sceptically at the distinction between ends and means. In other words, means may be ends in their own right (and often are). Nor is the qualitative nature of an 'end' self-evident from the language in which it is specified or the way in which it is presented; it is, rather, necessarily bound up with the proposed means of its achievement as well.

Whether we are talking about huge organisations or small, in the public or the private sectors, the complete implication in each other of politics and policy seems to be an inescapable conclusion (and, to be fair, the rest of the Therborn paper to which I have just referred would seem to bear this out in the EU context). Something similar can probably be said about planning, about the law as a means of social control, and about bureaucracy as a form of organising human activity. Our understanding of all of these cannot easily be separated from how we understand either the policy process or politics.

Nor can our understanding of policy and politics – or, indeed, planning, law and bureaucracy – be divorced from our understanding of 'culture'. In one respect or another, policy and politics are in the business of producing and reproducing the shared meanings that are at the heart of culture and cultural differences. If nothing else, this is one implication of the earlier discussion about the differences in terminology between different European languages (Heidenheimer, 1986; Therborn, 2001). Sticking with the focus of this collection, shared meanings are crucial in that policy has, ideally, to make sense, if nothing else. Decisions should be meaningful to those who make them and, in principle at least, to those about whom they are made. Policies should be able to be communicated and sold to those who may have to carry them out and even – once again in principle at least – to those whose lives are affected by them. So culture, in the broad sense that I am using the word here, is an important aspect of policy, and policy is also an important dimension of culture.

Culture is also a matter of values and ideology. If we accept a working definition of ideology as bodies of knowledge that make claims about how the world is and about how it ought to be (Jenkins, 1997, p 84), then *all* policy is probably, by definition, ideological. In this ideological sense, policy processes either reproduce existing meanings or create and disseminate new meanings, whether these be moral values, specifications of legitimate or illegitimate action, categories of individuals or collectivities, estimations of the relative value of resources, and so on.

So policy, of whatever sort, constitutes and is constituted by meaningful practices, codes and categories, on the one hand, and may reiterate the status quo or call into being new or modified meaningful practices, codes and categories, on the other. To return to 'culture', it may not be too much to say that, in the modern world, policy processes are among the most important vehicles and instruments – along, perhaps, with socialisation and mass communications – for the production and reproduction of the shared meanings which frame and imbue everyday life (Clarke, 2004, pp 31–51).

This argument is not intended to imply a definitively top-down model, whether of policy or culture: there is also resistance, and policy can, and is, made in all sorts of places. The argument also begins to suggest an interesting, and perhaps insufficiently recognised, avenue of further inquiry. Policy processes contribute to the imagining of collectivities, of whatever size or character. This is said, of course, with a conscious nod in the direction of Benedict Anderson (1983), and in the belief that although collectivities are imagined they are not imaginary (Jenkins, 2004). In the human worlds of modernity, policy – and not just social policy, incidentally – contributes massively to the shaping of whatever it is that we call 'the social' (Lewis et al., 2000). Not the least important sense in which this happens is that policy formulation and implementation often, whether explicitly or implicitly, identifies and defines human beings and the relationships that ought to exist between them – as populations, as groups, as categories of individuals, or as individuals – in ways that are necessarily consequential, even if those consequences may be unintended (Clarke, 2004, pp 52–71).

Changing meanings of policy

The meaning of 'policy' has not been fixed and constant. The very notion itself has been constituted and reconstituted over time. For the English language, *The Oxford English Dictionary* (OED)[2] offers us a survey of its historical uses, as follows:

- *from the late 1300s onwards (now obsolete)*: an organised or established system of government, such as a constitution or a state;
- *from the late 1300s onwards (now obsolete)*: government, administration and, in general, the conduct of public affairs;
- *from the early 1400s onwards*: political wisdom, skill, statecraft and diplomacy; used in a negative sense, there may also be the implication of political cunning;
- *from the 1400s onwards*: prudent or expedient conduct or action in general, wisdom and shrewdness; used in a negative sense, there may also be the implication of craftiness and cunning;
- *from the 1400s onwards (now obsolete)*: a contrivance, device, crafty stratagem or trick;
- *from the mid-1400s onwards*: a particular course of action that is adopted by a government, party, ruler, politician or their representative; more generally, any particular course of action that is adopted as advantageous or expedient.

In addition, there is a set of very specific, although much less common, meanings of 'policy', as a noun relating to insurance, gambling and social control. I am not going to discuss those here – other than to say that each invokes, whether implicitly or explicitly, the attempt to minimise or mitigate uncertainty.

Thus, the notion of 'policy' appears to enter the English language during the late medieval period. By the beginning of the early modern period the word was in established, recurrent use, referring to a complex of related meanings that clustered around the sensible conduct of public and private business. Arguably, all of these historical meanings of policy find at least an echo – and often much more than that – in the word's modern uses: government, orderly action, prudence, strategy, even a degree of deceit. No less to the point of the present discussion, however, the OED's detailed exploration of patterns of English usage demonstrates conclusively that the last meaning described – 'any particular course of action that is adopted as advantageous or expedient' – has been the dominant meaning of the word since the nineteenth century.

During the twentieth century, in the shape of things, people and processes such as policy documents, policy makers and policy making, that dominant notion of policy acquired increasingly powerful overtones of science, social science and rationality. The development within higher education of domains of study and research called 'social policy' and 'public policy' has been both end and means in this respect, both consequence and cause. These developments had a great deal to do with the more general expansion of science as a frame of reference during this period, but they also reflected and contributed to the growing intimacy of the relationship between trust and expertise that characterises modern politics.

'Culture' and modernity

Future-oriented courses of action are always uncertain. While policy making is always intentional and has objectives, what is intended may or may not happen, the unintended consequences of actions are always lurking in the wings as major, sometimes even determinate, influences on outcomes (Merton, 1957, pp 19–84). What Harold Macmillan called 'events' are an ever-present and unpredictable factor. This means that the effectiveness with which policy processes produce their stated outcomes is always compromised by contingencies. As a result, policy cannot be regarded as a definitive and reliable guide to 'what is to be done' (let alone what is, or has been, done). However, the role of policy in the creation, under conditions of complexity and uncertainty and within large geopolitical territories, of acceptable or good-enough representations of past, present and future action is certainly important. Policy, in other words, may belong most definitively to the realm of the collective imagination: the domain of symbolic politics. This is also the domain of 'culture'.

Another reason why policy is not a good guide to what actually happens is bound up with the intrinsic nature of government in the modern world. I have argued elsewhere (Jenkins, 2004, pp 179–83) that an unintended but unavoidable consequence of the modern development of formally organised public affairs and economic life is – and only apparently paradoxically – the creation of bureaucracy's antitheses: informality, non-rule-governed discretion and even subversion. This is in part because formal policies and procedures can never be sufficiently detailed enough to allow for every eventuality, and in part because it is impossible to ignore, bypass or subvert a policy that does not exist.

There is, however, something more profound going on, too, in that concepts such as 'informality' and 'discretion' actually make no sense, either logically or in everyday practice, without formality and rules as their counterpoints. To put this in another way, informality is not a relic of pre-modern or pre-bureaucratic ways of life; it is, rather, a way of doing things that is characteristic of modernity and bureaucracy. Thus, in much the same way as the criminal justice system can be said to produce crime, policy formulation and implementation, those constitutive and definitive processes of modern bureaucracy, are likely to sow the seeds of their own subversion (creating in the process, of course, a perceived need to make further policy). Much the same can be said about the law and planning: all regulation is, in this respect, uncertain and potentially counterproductive.

Everything that I have said in this chapter so far adds up to an argument that policy and policy making, as ways of organising human life, are fundamental features of the rational pursuit of efficiency and the iron-caged bureaucratisation of the world that Weber believed to be at the heart of modernity (Hill, 1993, pp 103–52), an insight that was subsequently developed in other directions by Foucault (Watson, 2000). Whether or not modernity is actually as constrained and constraining as either of these perspectives would have us believe is a discussion for another place and time. Suffice it to say that, for reasons which have already been summarised, the policy process is uncertain in its outcomes, limited in its vision, partial in its scope, as inefficient as one might expect of any organisational process, and to some extent self-defeating: it is neither iron cage nor panopticon.

Policy and policy making are, however, discourses and practices that are deeply dyed in the warp and weft of modernity, without which the modern world as we know it would be unthinkable. Furthermore, policy and policy processes are definitive aspects of modernity that have largely been neglected, if not completely ignored, by recent social theorists of modernity. Policy is arguably the most fundamental of the intellectual technologies that produce and reproduce the institutional charters of the modern state and other organisations. Policy formulation and implementation contributes in important ways to how public and private organisations operate, to their self-image, and to their identity in the eyes of their crucial audiences. Policy processes are inescapably implicated in the constitution of individuals and collectivities and the distribution to them of rewards and penalties. No less than capitalism or industrialism, bureaucracy or science, the policy process is right at the centre of modernity.

Ethnography and policy

Theorising, especially in fields such as public and social policy, is of little value unless it can be operationalised in systematic empirical research. So, how might we best investigate the reciprocal relationships between the formulation and implementation of policy, on the one hand, and the production and reproduction of shared meanings, on the other? In principle, any of the established approaches to policy analysis and research have potential in this respect. However, if we take seriously the emphasis in the discussion so far on policy as process – on formulation and implementation, production and reproduction – then some approaches might appear to be more useful than others.

Ethnography is perhaps the most processual approach to investigating the shared meanings that we summarise in the shorthand notion of 'culture'. Ethnography is also the research approach that is most suited to, or at least most closely identified with, the attempt to view the world as 'anthropologically strange' (Hammersley and Atkinson, 1995, pp 8–9). It can be defined concisely as systematic inquiry into everyday life that depends, at least in large part, on the observation of ordinary social activity, paying close attention to what people do as well as what they say, and problematising the relationship between the two (Holy and Stuchlik, 1983). There is not an ethnographer working anywhere in the world today whose informants' everyday domestic, neighbourhood and institutional environments are not massively constituted by policy processes. Policies shape people's lives everywhere; and ethnographers, whether anthropologists or sociologists, have increasingly been working in fields and on topics that are, in whatever senses, 'policy-related' or 'policy-focused'. This is a trend in basic and applied research that is only likely to grow in the future.

However, and not least to resist the temptation to call into being an 'ethnography of policy' that would be only marginally preferable to an 'anthropology of policy', I want to go further, to insist that *all* ethnographic research, no matter what its focus, topic or context might be, should be thoroughly mindful of policy and policy processes. Nor should they be treated merely as 'background' or 'context'. In other words, rather than keeping the ethnographic nose firmly to the immediate micro-empirical grindstone – and there is still too much ethnographic research to which this metaphorical characterisation applies – a wider ethnographic vision is required, albeit retaining the local perspective that is the approach's hallmark (Jenkins, 2006). As is also argued by Lendvai and Stubbs in Chapter Ten, policy and policy processes, and their short-, medium- and long-term consequences, need to be brought to ethnographic life.

If we accept this premise, it is obviously better that ethnographic research should be informed by maximum possible conceptual clarity with respect to what policy is and how policy processes work. So, what is the relevance for ethnographers – who typically undertake short-to medium-term participatory research with people who live, work or otherwise interact together in spatially relatively compact settings – of my discussion in this chapter of policy and policy processes? To reiterate, perhaps the most important implication is that *ethnographic researchers should never treat policy as just part of the backdrop, merely as the frame within which the really interesting stuff happens.* To do so will lead to interesting questions and issues being overlooked, and a lopsided view of human experience in the modern world.

As part of this greater awareness, it needs to be emphasised that policy processes are utterly amenable to ethnographic investigation:

- Policy processes are processes of representation and of the production and reproduction of meaning. Representations and processes can be investigated locally, as can the articulation between national and local representations and frameworks of meaning.
- Policy processes are, at least in large part, a matter of the relationship between doctrine and representations, on the one hand, and practices or courses of action, on the other. As already suggested, ethnography is a particularly good approach to understanding the complex, and not always obvious, relationships between what people say and what they do.
- Given that national or supra-local policy processes resonate at local level – they are generally meant to, anyway – very often national policy means the creation of local policy, a process which can be investigated at first hand and in face-to-face detail.
- Policy formulation and implementation are, as argued earlier, thoroughly implicated in each other and should be treated as such. As a complex iterative process, policy formulation and implementation can, and should, be studied ethnographically.
- Policies are worked out and realised during interaction, through interpretation, resource allocation, evasion, subversion, and so on. These can all be researched ethnographically.
- Policy may be tacit as well as explicit, or an emergent outcome rather than an intentional goal. Ethnography, with its appreciation of the importance of the doing as well as the saying, is perhaps the best method we have for studying tacit and emergent aspects of human experience and practice.

We live in a modern world that has been and continues to be shaped, in about every way that we can imagine, by policy and policy processes. So do our informants, whether they are the few remaining hunter-gatherers, the urban unemployed, small farmers, middle-ranking bureaucrats, older people living on pensions, cash-rich drug dealers, millionaire financiers or politicians. Policy processes are not an optional extra, in our lives or theirs. If we are to do justice to those lives – and it is arguably both a scientific or epistemological obligation and an ethical imperative that we should do so, or at least *attempt* to do so – investigating those processes is not an optional extra for ethnographers, either.

Meaning, modernity and policy

Policy is that aspect of the intellectual technology of modern governance – whether public or private – that attempts to make explicit desired means and appropriate ends and the relationships between them. Policy processes are concerned with where we want to go and how we intend to get there, and with explaining and justifying both objectives and methods. Policy and politics are not distinct aspects of modern governance, but are so deeply implicated in each other as to be difficult to distinguish, both conceptually and empirically. In this respect, policy processes bring together two kinds of Weberian social action, *wertrational* (derived from values) and *zweckrational* (derived from rational means–ends considerations), in the exercise of rational-legal legitimate authority. In addition to maintaining and changing values, policy formulation and implementation also produces and reproduces shared categories. In both of these respects, if no others, policy processes are hugely significant in the making of everyday life, for everyone. Policy is thus 'cultural' through and through.

Combining governance and the exercise of legitimate authority with the production and reproduction of shared meanings, policy processes have been, and still are, constitutive, and in important senses definitive, of the modern era. Given that they shape and pervade all aspects of the modern human world, from the supranational to the most intimate, the study of policy processes is not really an 'optional extra' for any of the social sciences. It is certainly much too important to be left solely to specialists in public and social policy.

Notes
This chapter owes much to my teaching on the MA in Sociological Research at Sheffield. It was first delivered in something like its present form to the research seminar on 'Investigating Welfare from an Anthropological Perspective', at the University of Aarhus, Denmark, in November 2005. I am grateful to the workshop participants for their helpful comments. A version of that presentation was published

as *Arbejdspapir* 138–06 of the *Center fur Kulturforskning*, Aarhus. I am also grateful to Bob Deacon, Susan Hodgson, Zoë Irving and Jenny Owen for their comments on earlier drafts.

[1] In a long historical discussion of the difference between what he calls 'English' and 'continental' concepts of policy, Heidenheimer (1986), although he ignores the Dutch example, argues that the linguistic differences reflect the very different evolutions of the state in England and in the countries of continental Europe. In the latter, 'stateness' is, apparently, more institutionalised.

[2] I have drawn upon the second edition of *The Oxford English Dictionary*, updated to 2006, available as an electronic database through the University of Sheffield Library.

THREE

Policy and 'the good society'

David Phillips

Introduction

A central theme underpinning all the chapters in this book relates to the 'meaning' of policy in the context of policy studies. Part of the context for this relates to the tensions between representations of policy as a technical process and as a facet of 'the Social' – here explicitly capitalised in its reference to the ways people realise themselves collectively as interactive human beings in a societal setting. This chapter sets this debate within a discourse about values and ideology.

Over the past few decades there has been fierce debate among politicians and policy makers about what constitutes 'the good society', ranging from a social democrat vision of an all-encompassing universalist and collectivist welfare state through to a market liberal vision of a minimalist state, merely providing a safe social environment in which individuals and families can freely pursue their own interests. Central to this range of visions are sets of values. This chapter explores these themes not at a national level, but in the context of the enlarging European Union (EU) where, from its very inception, a debate has taken place between what can be broadly identified as a social versus an economic vision of its identity. At the turn of the twenty-first century the battle lines have been drawn under the banners of, on the one hand, *Social Europe* in the guise of the European Social Model (ESM) and, on the other, the goal of the Lisbon accord of the EU becoming the world's most dynamic and competitive knowledge-based economy. Central to this debate is the question of whether the ESM is still viable (if it ever was) or whether the enlarged EU – nudged by the World Bank – is moving inexorably towards a regional 'race to the bottom' with the dismantling of social benefits in the liberal market-oriented political economy of an unstoppable globalisation.

This debate is particularly pertinent at the present time with the enlarged EU 27 contemplating its identity and how different it is from that of the EU 15 and how it might be even further affected if Turkey were ever to join. The process of enlargement not only affects the practicalities of harmonisation and compatibility between institutions, policies and procedures but also the extent to which there are common values, or even a vision of what such values might actually be.

All these themes are central to EU policy making: and 'policy' is seen here as deeply imbued with values and ideology and is, at least partly, an attempt to present and produce what can be seen as orderly actions in situations of complexity and uncertainty (see Jenkins, Chapter Two). This perspective on policy is explored below in relation to the long-term EU goal of achieving a progressive convergence of policy objectives based on an agreed set of values. It is argued that there is at best a tension, and at worst a contradiction, among these wide-ranging policy goals. This tension is explored in the context of the differing welfare regimes within Europe, utilising Paul Bernard's *democratic dialectic* framework of the good society (Bernard, 1999).

Values and policies at national level: welfare regimes

Worlds of welfare in the EU

Gospa Esping-Andersen's influential book, *The Three Worlds of Welfare Capitalism* (1990), initiated a vigorous and still ongoing debate about different national approaches to the 'good society'. He produced a threefold typology of welfare regimes in capitalist nations – conservative, liberal and social democratic – and claimed that each of the most developed Western nations approximated to one of these types. Although historical and political factors are central in determining which typology a country will most closely resemble, Esping-Andersen (1990) classifies the regimes in terms of the extent to which they decommodify labour, and of their social stratification. Following Arts and Gelissen (2002), his typology can be summarised as follows (with names of Esping-Andersen's European exemplars in square brackets):

*   *Social democratic* [Austria, Netherlands, Belgium, Denmark, Norway, Sweden]: here there is high decommodification and strong universalism. Social security is redistributive and not determined by contributions; in effect it 'crowds out' the market and results in universalistic solidarity. Social policy maximises capacities for individual independence, there is a national commitment to full employment among men, and women are encouraged to participate in employment, particularly in the public sector.
*   *Liberal* [the UK and Ireland]: these nations have low decommodification and strongly encourage individualism and self-

reliance. The state intervenes actively or passively to support the market. There are means-tested benefits, little redistribution and limited social rights. Women are encouraged to participate in the labour force particularly in the service sector

- *Conservative* [Italy, France, Germany, Finland, Switzerland]: these are modestly decommodifying and are supported by the twin pillars of Catholic social policy and corporatism. The state provides income maintenance related to occupational status and has a policy of subsidiarity so it will only intervene when family resources are exhausted. Women's labour market participation is strongly discouraged in order to maintain the integrity and supportive role of the family.

While some commentators have supported Esping-Andersen (for example Powell and Barrientos, 2004) others have sought to modify or add to his typology, and a few have doubted its usefulness at all (Scruggs and Allan, 2006). Esping-Andersen has also been heavily criticised for not including a systematic discussion of the role of the family in welfare and the extent to which women are included in the labour market (Arts and Gelissen, 2002, p 147). In the EU context two major amendments have been proposed. The first is to have a separate category for the Mediterranean countries (alternatively classified as southern or Latin rim), which have less decommodification and are less corporatist than the conservative ideal type. Similarly, Leibfried (1992), in a paper speculating on moving towards a European welfare state, identifies four regime types within the EU, with a perspective somewhat different to Esping-Andersen's: Leibfried identifies Scandinavian, Bismarckian, Anglo-Saxon and Latin rim types, having modern, institutional, residual and rudimentary policy models, respectively. The first three map on to Esping-Andersen's typology and the Latin rim countries lack both an articulated social minimum and a right to welfare.

The second major amendment is the addition of a group of East and Central European (ECE) and Baltic ex-state socialist nations, which have recently acceded, or are in the process of acceding, to the EU. This addition is not so much a criticism of Esping-Andersen as a recognition that the world has moved on from the late 1980s when his book was being written. As early as 1992, Deacon speculatively predicted the emergence in these nations of liberal and social democratic features, along with a form of 'post-communist conservative corporatism' (Deacon, 1992, p 180). By 2000 he, again, tentatively identified most of the 'first wave' ex-communist EU accession states as 'developing into one or other variant of a West European welfare state, combining a mix of Bismarckian-style insurance and Scandinavian-style state financing' (Deacon, 2002, p 151). Manning (2004, p 219) identified first wave ex-communist accession countries as a distinct group and categorised them as the '*recovery group* in which economic growth has returned, governments have the capacity to tax and spend for social intervention, and social costs have been contained'. This is in comparison to the other ex-communist countries which Manning various classifies as *disintegrating, in conflict* or *struggling*. According to Deacon (2000), the two most recent accession states, Romania and Bulgaria, were still trying to conserve state and workplace benefits at the turn of the millennium, with potentially dire consequences for their welfare systems.[1]

Other commentators have suggested more modest refinements of Esping-Andersen's model. Most of these have reclassified the Netherlands and Belgium as 'conservative', often relabelled as 'continental', and Finland as social democratic, often relabelled as 'Scandinavian'[2] (Siaroff, 1994; Ferrera, 1996; Bonoli, 1997). These refinements are incorporated in the classification used here (see Table 3.1, p 46).

It would be relatively easy to devote a considerable amount of space to a discussion of the literature on fine-tuning these classifications, and, as seen above, the inclusion of extra dimensions of welfare can change the picture. For the purpose of this chapter, however, it is the broad picture that is most important. This can best be portrayed by five ideal types, each of which is approximated, to a greater or lesser degree, by virtually every one of the EU 27 countries: social democratic, conservative, liberal, southern rim and ECE/Baltic. Most, and especially the social democratic and the ECE countries, have strong cultural, geographical and historical ties with other members of their ideal type category, and nearly all can be relatively easily placed in just one category. There is some lack of clarity about a couple of countries – Finland and the Netherlands have already been mentioned, and Italy has a foot in both the conservative and southern rim camps. But the typology provides an effective, albeit broad-brush, classification of five contrasting models not only of welfare regimes but of values, each relating to a distinctive notion of what constitutes 'the good society'. It is the coming together in 'an ever closer union' of these models that provides the challenge addressed here.

Policy and welfare regimes: Bernard's 'democratic dialectic'

Bernard (1999) has developed a helpful conceptual approach for classifying 'the good society'. The framework he uses is based on a noble pedigree; the watchwords of the French Revolution, with one textual amendment – liberty, equality and now 'solidarity' in place of fraternity. Bernard represents these diagrammatically as a triangle, as seen in Figure 3.1. His thesis is that all three are necessary for democracy, and that their interaction and the tensions between them provide the space within which the 'democratic dialectic' takes place. Bernard identifies strengths and weaknesses, problems and distortions, both in relation to individual points on the triangle and to the three sets of pairings between them.

Figure 3.1: Amended version of Bernard's democratic dialectic

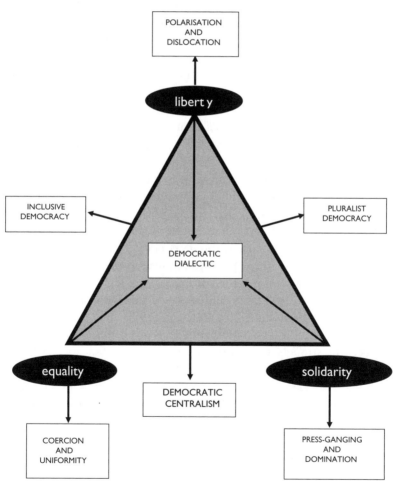

Reprinted and amended with permission from Bernard, P. (1999) *Social Cohesion: a Critique*, CPRN Discussion Paper #F09

In relation to the individual attributes, first, it is clear that a society without liberty is in danger of coercion, enslavement and servitude but that excessive freedom or libertarianism can lead to polarisation, dislocation and social fragmentation – and, ultimately, to a complete disregard of one's fellow citizens. Second, equality before the law, equality of access and equality of opportunity are – arguably – non-controversial in any democratic society, as are combating inequalities of condition so gross that serious material poverty would result. However, reducing disparities of wealth and income and striving for equality of outcome or condition can lead to enforced uniformity, as well as being in conflict with liberty. Solidarity, the essence of cohesion, is of course necessary for any group, community or society to survive. But a sense of togetherness and mutual obligation can result in reductions in freedom by 'press-ganging and domination' (Bernard, 1999, p 6). Thus, some highly solidaristic countries can also be totalitarian in nature, such as Nazi Germany or Stalin's Soviet Union.

Bernard argues that these three attributes cannot be optimised in isolation from each other. Liberty needs to be leavened by a sense of community and respect for the needs of other individuals. Any solidarity, which is essentially inegalitarian, is exploitative and solidarity without freedom, like equality without freedom, does not respect individual human rights. Finally, respect for equality that takes no account of solidarity, while utopian in an individualistic sense, provides an alienating vision of a land populated by 'atomised' individuals but with no *society* to speak of. Bernard did not make a direct connection with Esping-Andersen's typology but he did identify the three pairings of the individual elements of the democratic dialectic with different welfare regimes. All three pairings are indeed relevant to the above discussion of regimes, as is the combination of all three.

The pairing of solidarity and equality was originally labelled as 'participatory democracy' by Bernard (1999) but Phillips (2006) relabelled this as 'democratic centralism' given that it appropriately reflects the strongly solidaristic and egalitarian – but not libertarian – nature of the pre-1989 Soviet and Eastern European state-socialist nations. This classification gives a fair representation of the ethos previously paramount in the welfare regimes of the ECE EU members; in other words, of their starting points on the path to EU membership.

Bernard's second pairing relates squarely to the liberal, Anglo-Saxon regime epitomised by the UK and Ireland. Bernard labels the pairing of equality (or, more precisely, *social* equality) and liberty as 'inclusive democracy', echoing the spirit of Marshall's (1972) notion of 'hyphenated citizenship' (Leisering, 2003). Following on from his thesis of social citizenship depending upon legal, political and social rights providing a threshold of social equality – equality of status as citizens – which legitimates economic inequalities, Marshall developed the notion of democratic-welfare-capitalism where the political, the social and the economic interact. A person has political rights as a citizen and has social rights to welfare benefits to avoid poverty but has to make her or his own way in the economic system where unequal material outcomes are the rewards for ability, hard work and entrepreneurial skills. Thus Marshall envisaged a trade-off between, on the one hand, equality of status, along with social security and, on the other hand, personal liberty, along with economic inequality. Bernard identifies a 'fragile bipolar equilibrium' between liberty and equality here. Rather controversially – but with considerable insight – he claims that solidarity is missing from this model. Bernard defends this claim as follows:

> When the rich want unimpeded access to the medical care that their money allows them to purchase, how can one object except by saying that our common fate as mortals imposes on us all a compassion without exclusion? When they quit the public school system, what can we say except that they are weakening one of the most basic institutions of their own society? (Bernard, 1999, p 12)

Here the tension identified by Marshall and Bernard is clear: there *is* social equality of a sort, in that everyone has equal access to state-run health, welfare and education services, but the economic inequality fostered by individual liberty enables the rich to get 'better than equal' provision. And it is the call to solidarity that provides the moral resolution to this tension without falling prey to coercion – or at least without falling prey to *explicit* coercion. In order for this to happen, of course, the call to solidarity here has to be answered by the rich of their own free will.

The bipolar equilibrium is even more fragile in relation to the third pairing, labelled as 'pluralist democracy', which fits well with the conservative welfare regime. This is the interaction between liberty and solidarity, the dynamic of which 'is intended to soften the hardships brought about by the free play of the economy' (Bernard, 1999, p 13). His complaint here is that the state is enjoined to promote consensus on *values* (often familial) rather than to resolve conflicts of *interests*. Liberty and solidarity combined can, according to Bernard, certainly lead to an integrated society but it can also be a highly unequal one.

Bernard identifies one more model, where all three elements come together in the fully-fledged democratic dialectic, but before moving on to this it is worth exploring a diluted version of the pluralist democracy pairing, where the political and social institutions for softening economic hardships are not fully developed, and the state does not have enough political resources to effectively promote value consensus. This 'underdeveloped pluralist democracy' can be seen as adequately representing the Mediterranean or southern rim welfare regime. This classification is particularly apt given the debate about whether these nations comprise a separate classification or whether they should be seen as an 'underdeveloped' sub-category of the conservative regime (Leibfried, 1992; Ferrera, 1996; Katrougalos, 1996; Bonoli, 1997).

Bernard's final classification incorporates all three elements of liberty, equality and solidarity and epitomises the ideal of the democratic dialectic where belonging, participation, social justice, recognition, legitimacy and inclusion are all maximised. Bernard's rather pessimistic, but realistic, perspective is that no countries are yet approaching this situation. It is argued here, however, that an ideal type model of the Scandinavian welfare regime comprises, albeit in a rudimentary form, an embryonic version of the full democratic dialectic. This is because there is a trade-off, if not a full balance, between liberty, solidarity and equality. It is true that Bernard's pessimism is not entirely misplaced because the coercion required by the levying of high progressive rates of taxation in order to fund egalitarian state welfare can be see as potentially anti-libertarian unless it is fully supported by value consensus across all sectors of society. This critique is certainly a position taken by many neoliberal commentators, the most iconic of whom is Hayek (1944). Also the dilution of universalistic solidarity resulting from political pressure to reduce social protection in Scandinavian countries (Therborn and Therborn, 2005; Vuori and Gissler, 2005) adds weight to Bernard's critique here. As can be seen below, a strong case can be made for the democratic dialectic being a model for the implementation of a strong version of the European Social Model.

Welfare regimes and values in EU countries

Table 3.1 brings together all the above themes, along with a brief indication of historical and geographical commonalities, for all 27 EU nations. This has involved a little extrapolation, by including Malta and Cyprus in the southern rim countries. This is unproblematic, as are the refinements to Esping-Andersen's groupings noted above, but a difficulty remains with Italy whose membership is finely balanced between the conservative and southern rim countries. Esping-Andersen (1990), as noted, places it in the former group but it is undeniable that the culture of southern Italy is more akin to that of the latter grouping. Similarly, Ahonen et al. (2006), in their study of governance of European welfare states, identify it as an anomaly and omit it entirely from their classification. As a rather unsatisfactory compromise it has been included here, in italicised form, in both groups. Of course, once this precedent has been set it could be argued that several countries could be treated in the same way. This will not be done: Italy can be seen here as a token indicator that such classifications are at best oversimplifications of a complex reality.

The table is intended to provide a justification for narrowing down the values of 27 disparate nations into five more-or-less coherent groups, each sharing some aspects of geographical, historical, cultural, social, economic and political commonalities. In one sense it is the geographical propinquity and historical ties which most vividly link members of each group together. The most striking exemplar here is the British Isles, which comprises the liberal grouping in its entirety. But another politico-historical grouping (even including the italicisation of Italy) is that the conservative group comprises the original six EEC members.

Perhaps the weakest of these commonalities is among the southern rim countries. Even though they are undeniably Mediterranean (with the exception of Portugal in terms of physical geography) and all have a strong familial orientation, and were later economic developers than the social democratic, conservative and liberal nations, nevertheless their historical and political ties are rather tenuous. It is difficult, for example, to find a strong historical or political connection between Portugal and Greece. Their relative early stage in socioeconomic development – their 'rudimentary' status according to Leibfried (1992) – may be more of a distinguishing characteristic of them as a category than any positive bonding they may have with each other. Here a comparison between the southern rim and the ECE/Baltic group is salutary. The countries in the latter group straggle across Europe from north to south just as the southern rim countries straggle from west to east, but these ex-communist countries share the extremely strong politico-historical heritage of all being outposts of the Soviet bloc.

It is at this point that the enormity of the task of the EU in moving towards an ever closer union becomes clear. Moreover, the cultures within the different regimes might be even more disparate than their political histories. We have here five radically different types of society, with different conceptions of what 'the good society' might look like.

Table 3.1: Welfare regimes in the contemporary EU: commonalities and classifications

Regime	Countries	Historical and geographical links	Leibfried classification	Bernard's democratic dialectic	Esping-Andersen's elements	Women/the family
Social democrat	Denmark, Sweden, Finland [Norway – not in EU]	Yes – all Nordic with strong historical, cultural and geographical links	'Modern'	Full democratic dialectic: equality, solidarity, liberty in balance	High decommodification and universalism	High female employment, particularly in public sector. State substitution for family responsibilities
Conservative	France, Germany, Italy, Netherlands, Luxembourg, Belgium, Austria [Switzerland – not in EU]	Yes – all continental Europe: most border each other	'Institutional'	Pluralist democracy: solidarity and liberty	Modest decommodification along with subsidiarity and corporatism (and Catholicism in most countries)	Strong support for family and discouragement of women's labour

Table 3.1: Welfare regimes in the contemporary EU: commonalities and classifications contd .../

Regime	Countries	Historical and geographical links	Leibfried classification	Bernard's democratic dialectic	Esping-Andersen's elements	Women/the family
Liberal	UK, Ireland	Yes – same language: previously the same country	'Residual'	Inclusive democracy: (social) equality and liberty	Low decommodification along with individualism and self-reliance	Women encouraged to work, particularly in service sector. Child care provision encouraged
Southern rim	Spain, Portugal, Greece, Cyprus, Malta, Italy [Turkey – not in EU]	Only by default via proximity to Mediterranean (except for Spain and Portugal)	'Rudimentary'	Underdeveloped pluralist democracy: limited solidarity and liberty	Very limited decommodification and corporatism. Very high subsidiarity. (Strong Catholicism in most countries)	Family (and church) central pillar of social support. Women strongly discouraged from working

contd.../

Table 3.1: Welfare regimes in the contemporary EU: commonalities and classifications contd .../

Regime	Countries	Historical and geographical links	Leibfried classification	Bernard's democratic dialectic	Esping-Andersen's elements	Women/the family
ECE plus the Baltic States (Deacon: Bismarckian–Scandinavian mix. Manning: 'recovery' states)	Czech Republic, Poland, Slovakia, Slovenia, Estonia, Latvia, Lithuania [Romania, Bulgaria]	Yes: all were previously Soviet satellite states and all were on the East–West Border. Each state is a neighbour to at least one other state in this group	Not classified by Leibfried. Could be identified as 'ex-normative'	(Ex)Democratic centralism: equality and solidarity	History of high decommodification and universalism followed by rapid marketisation	Previous state provision of family services. Now necessary for as many family members as possible to work

A specific example might be useful here. The author is a member of a group of EU academics constructing indicators of 'social quality' across Europe. In our discussions the following question emerged: are high levels of state-funded residential provisions for frail elderly people a sign of high or low social quality? From a northern European, particularly Scandinavian, perspective this can be seen as an indicator of high social quality because it demonstrates high levels of collective solidarity, inclusion and socioeconomic security, ensuring that no one is forced to live on their own in poverty. From a more Mediterranean perspective, it can be seen as a sign of low social quality with the state being forced to intervene to replace the role of the family in caring for its own members as a result of a low level of family solidarity and a breakdown in informal social inclusion networks (van der Maesen et al., 2005). This particular example focuses on the role of women, the family and the extent to which the state should provide universal services. But a similar example could have been given of the role of state intervention in regulating wages or retirement ages.

Values and policy: the ubiquitous European Social Model

All this raises the question of the relationship, or relationships, between national and European values as the EU strives to construct policies leading towards the goal of a social Europe, moving away from the initial economic foundations of the old EEC, the European *Economic* Community, to the EU, the European *Union*. Noll (2002) reminds us that the goals of EU policies are formally documented in treaties and other documents including white papers, action programmes and communications:

> Some of them are formulated at a rather general level. The promotion of economic and social progress, the improvement of living and working conditions, the increase of the standard of living and the quality of life, the fight against social exclusion, the strengthening of economic and social cohesion, the promotion of equal opportunities, the commitment to the principle of sustainability are general goals which have been strongly emphasised. (Noll, 2002, p 64)

Absolutely central to this project is the ubiquitous and somewhat amorphous ESM, which, in principle, simultaneously promotes economic growth and social cohesion and inclusion via a marriage between economic, social and employment policy.

The amorphousness of the ESM soon becomes apparent when trying to pin it down to a definition. Jepsen and Pascual (2005, p 232) somewhat wryly comment that a clear definition of the term is lacking in most official documents, and that where there are definitions they often differ from each other. Indeed Jepsen and Pascual identify four different approaches to defining the ESM. In the most straightforward and highly normative definition, it is seen as an entity incorporating common aims: institutions, values and forms of regulation all particularly concerned with full employment, social inclusion, protection and equality. In other words, the ESM is seen here as a group of welfare regimes characterised by extensive social protection, labour market institutions and democratic resolution of social conflict. This broad definition has much in common with the social democratic welfare regime but is also compatible with the conservative regime, depending on the extent to which – and what sort of – equality is foregrounded in the definition.

The link with the more 'developed' welfare regimes in the augmented Esping-Andersen classification given above, is also clear in two other of Jepsen and Pascual's approaches to definition: the second as a Weberian ideal type to be aimed for; and the third as an ongoing, transnational, essentially European project which is distinctly non- (or even in one sense *anti*-)American – and anti-globalisation too. In this context, O'Connor (2005, p 346) states that the ESM is a 'work in progress' that reflects a tension between aspirations and statements of values expressed at EU level and the goal of subsidiarity, and it 'is not a reality in the way that we think of national welfare states, it is an overarching aspirational model incorporating the broad parameters to which European welfare states conform'.

According to Alber (2006, p 1), one of the clearest of the first kind of definitions came out of the Nice European Council meeting in 2000. Here the ESM is based on a common core of values and is characterised by three specific features: systems offering high levels of social protection; the importance of the 'social dialogue'; and services covering activities vital for social cohesion. Jepsen and Pascual (2005) report that the ESM was popularised by Jacques Delors in the 1980s but, according to Alber (2006), first defined in the early 1990s in terms of a set of common values: commitment to democracy, freedom, social dialogue, equal opportunities, social security and solidarity towards weaker members of society. Alber (2006, p 12), however, sees a fly in the ointment of this commonality of values central to all these definitions:

he maintains that the ESM cannot be grounded on a set of key features which all member states of the EU would have in common because there is just too much diversity among them. Korver and Oeij (2006) agree; they say that positive social policy has been hard to achieve since there is no consensus, particularly between north and south, on what this social policy might be.

Here then, is an explanation for the imprecision, and what can be seen as fudging, in approaches to defining the ESM, and this rationale can appropriately be framed within Jepsen and Pascual's (2005) fourth set of approaches to defining the ESM – as a *political* project. They see it as a loosely defined, hegemonic and normative construct comprising rhetorical resources intended to legitimise the politically constructed drive towards supranational government (Jepsen and Pascual, 2005, pp 232, 239). Guillen and Palier (2004) take a different line here. They identify the political project of the ESM as being far more contested than in Jepsen and Pascual's analysis and they claim that the view of the ESM emanating from the powerhouse of the EU in Brussels is ambiguous. Moreover, they contend that the ESM has recently changed and become closer to neoliberal ideas:

> at the present stage, there is no clear European social model promoted at the EU level, but rather a conflict between 'economically oriented actors' promoting market-type solutions, and 'socially oriented actors' trying to find new perspectives for a productive approach to social policy, linking them positively to employment and economic policies. (Guillen and Palier, 2004, p 206)

Other writers, such as O'Connor (2005) have identified this recent change as 'modernisation' of the ESM emanating from the deliberations of the 2000 Lisbon Council. The resulting Lisbon accord led to what could be seen as a dramatic shift away from the old social democratic or conservative visions of a European ideal type welfare regime to one more in accord with the liberal model (particularly in its US manifestation and perhaps even moving towards a globalised approach). The basis of the Lisbon accord was a commitment to bring about economic, social and environmental renewal in the EU. It set out a 10-year strategy to make the EU the world's most dynamic and competitive economy by 2010. The strategy includes:

- preparing the transition to a knowledge-based economy by enhanced informatics and research and development and by speeding up the process of structural reform for competition and innovation and by completing the internal market;

- applying a macro-economic policy to sustain favourable growth prospects and a healthy economic outlook;
- 'modernising' the ESM, investing in people and combating social exclusion (Korver and Oeij, 2006).

But there are immense tensions between the different sets of actors involved in the strategy and it seems increasingly unlikely that the goals will be met. One of the main tensions is between the economic drive behind the Lisbon strategy and the social drive behind the ESM. In this context, Juhasz (2006) and Korver and Oeij (2006) take a positive perspective on the achievements of the ESM so far. Juhasz praises the ESM for its achievements in promoting social solidarity and protecting pensioners, people in secure jobs and more generally promoting the economic and social welfare of women. Similarly, the ESM in its combination of employment, social and economic policy has been remarkably stable according to Korver and Oeij (2006), but they express concern about its sustainability in the face of demographic trends, fierce global competition from low-cost economies, and EU expansion.

Juhasz (2006) is particularly concerned about the potential impact on the ESM of the widening of EU membership. Following Ferge (2001), he notes that issues central to the continuation of the ESM have been sidelined by the more practically pressing issues of political, market and legal reforms necessary for membership. He claims, rather depressingly, that the World Bank played a more active role than the EU in shaping the social policies of East and Central Europe in the 1990s. Guillen and Palier (2004) go even further and claim that the World Bank has had more influence on the content of social policies in the accession countries than the EU. For further discussion of the international context surrounding these events, see Deacon, Chapter Seven, this volume. Before moving on to assess future implications for the ESM and the EU as a whole, it is necessary to address the thorny issue of the extent to which European values actually exist.

European values – convergence or divergence

Berting (2006) addresses the relationship between national and European values in the context of globalisation and he reminds us of the challenges in achieving commonality, given the different meanings that are inherent in values such as equality in different social settings, each with different value clusters. In other words, values always have a specific social, economic, political and cultural context and these are missing in most value discussions. An example of this issue came to light in the discussion of Bernard's 'inclusive democracy' classification in relation to the different nuances of the meaning and categorisation of equality in these contexts – equality of access, opportunity or outcome. These are problematic enough within individual nations with common languages and sets of cultural understandings; but these problems multiply exponentially in a European setting. Lendvai and Stubbs (see Chapter Ten) give examples of just such problems in the implementation of EU policies in the ECE post-accession countries.

On a more positive note Berting (2006) postulates the existence of, first, a modern European culture in the making and, second, an – admittedly weak – European identity incorporating consciousness of both what Europeans have in common and their cultural variety with associated pluralistic meanings. Berting's central themes here relate to the nature of national vis-à-vis European values. He reminds us of the long and complex history of the common values inherent in European democracies. He also postulates that this common heritage provides the basis for a fledgling European culture built on a sense of solidarity. The commonality of this heritage seems very thin when considering the diverse paths of the 27 independent nations but the five sets of welfare regimes, each with its own core of more or less shared history, do point the way to the identification of a small number of 'value arenas' each with their own common attributes which may eventually form the basis for negotiating a possible European frame of reference. In this context it is interesting to note that Alber (2006, p 12), in his review of contemporary research, says that there is no consistent evidence of ESM convergence except in employment levels: on the contrary, EU nations 'have become even more dissimilar with respect to public expenditure, public revenues and net social expenditure'. But this is not just a lack of ESM convergence – it means too that there is little evidence of globalisation convergence either. So much for the present, though; what of the prospects for the future?

EU expansion and the future

The bigger question than 'Is there convergence?' of course is 'Convergence to what?' There are two contenders. The first is towards the vision of a social Europe which is not only working towards European solidarity but also building common social rights throughout Europe, with southern, eastern and central Europe converging towards the continental, conservative, model and perhaps eventually to a more social democratic orientation: that is, towards the full implementation of Bernard's democratic dialectic. The second, international heavyweight, contender is the ubiquitous economically liberal model of globalisation within which the European ideals of social protection and social rights are seen as highly uncompetitive and thus redundant – here moving inexorably towards the apex of liberty, relegating solidarity to the sidelines and entirely banishing equality, all in the direction of the 'race to the bottom'. Such a perspective is taken by Zielonka and Mair (2002) who postulate the development of a dynamic convergence, fuelled more by globalisation than Europeanisation.

The EU has made a choice between an ever deeper union or a wider union. If it had gone for a deeper union of a restricted number of well-established EU member countries, then its membership would have been more cohesive and it would have retained its old label of a rich nations' club. In going for the wider union, embracing a pan-European membership, it has become a less cohesive club of nations, weaker in terms of shared values and with barriers to employment between old and new members being distinctly exclusionary. It is important, however, not to overplay the purported previous 'strength' of the common values of the earlier manifestations of the EU: even the original EEC six, although all from north-western Europe, had a centuries-long history of cultural difference, discord and war. And it can be argued that the EU enlargements taking in Scandinavian and Nordic, English-speaking and Mediterranean nations diluted its commonality even further. But the cultural differences within the EU 15 can be arguably counterbalanced by the notion of a 'Western European' cultural heritage stretching back to the Holy Roman Empire and the Crusades. The EU 27, again, can be seen both as having further diluted and weakened common values – particularly in relation to the additional languages and wide-ranging cultural and geographic diversity of the new members – but, yet again, perhaps also providing a more 'complete' and holistic European identity: in other words the jigsaw map of the EU now more closely approximates the geographical continent of Europe. Even if the rosy 'holistic' view of the EU 27 is taken, it cannot be denied that the social and economic diversity of the EU has increased and that convergence – in any of its manifestations, social, economic, cultural, linguistic – is now more challenging than previously. Furthermore, the potential inclusion of Turkey sometime in the not-too-distant future with its 70 million Muslims would both stretch and change the nature of the EU and of common conceptions of what is 'European'.

Perhaps, then, it is salutary to focus on what common European values there might be, even if they are seen only as a lowest common denominator. If this basic level of European values can be seen as a sense of European solidarity and 'togetherness' based on a common heritage, then it is evident that EU expansion has led to an increased tension between the two ESM policy goals of social cohesion and social inclusion. In the past, the EU had unequivocally taken an ideological, egalitarian perspective on social cohesion, with an emphasis on reducing regional disparities. But this all changed with the enlargement from 15 to 27 (Ferge, 2001; Juhasz, 2006). With the addition of several, much poorer, countries and thus increasing inequality across the EU, it became much harder to provide homogeneous, egalitarian-oriented cohesion. The dramatic increase in the number of its members has led to a change in the nature of EU cohesion with an associated dilution in its ideological, egalitarian content. This is certainly more compatible with the Lisbon accord than with older, more socially protectionist and egalitarian versions of the ESM, although only time will tell if the proposed abolition of employment restrictions and the creation of an EU-wide free labour market in 2011 will actually take place in any meaningful way and thus reinvigorate the inclusionary aspect of the ESM.

There is, of course, a close interrelationship between shared values and shared economic circumstances and societal institutions: the greater the economic inequality and disparity between institutions, the smaller the opportunity for shared values to thrive. Juhasz (2006) points out that while there has been a convergence in economic and fiscal policies in the post-accession countries this has not led to GDP convergence, even with EU subsidies. And paradoxically in relation to social policy, there is no longer any clear welfare model in the post-accession countries – or indeed in the EU generally – thus leading to divergence in social policy institutions. In contrast, the post-Maastricht representation of social protection as an economic burden, has led to some convergence in policies and levels of social expenditure (Zielonka and Mair, 2002). In this context Kovics's (2002) three models of accession, as interpreted by Manning (2004), are instructive. These are: 'leaping in the dark' towards a neoliberal approach; 'marking time' with little change from the previous statist system; and 'muddling through', allowing for growing varieties of both policies and social conditions. It is the last of these that Manning claims to have found.

Guillen and Palier's (2004) typology of four future scenarios is helpful in addressing the bigger question of whether EU values will coalesce either towards collective social values or individualistic economic values.

They remind us of the importance of institutional capabilities within the EU and how they might interact with both the liberal and the social model. Weak national institutional capabilities across the EU would have negative consequences for both the liberal and the social model: the former case, according to Guillen and Palier, leading to chaos and the latter to a race to the bottom. Strong institutional capabilities in conjunction with the liberal model lead to the privatisation of social policy (or perhaps more aptly to its *further* privatisation). The final case – and Guillen and Palier's preferred solution – of strong institutional capabilities combined with the social model leads to 'catch up', which necessitates increased social funds, particularly the redirection of funds from the Common Agricultural Policy to structural funds targeted to the accession countries. This scenario matches what happened after Spain, Portugal, Greece and Ireland joined the EU. Manning (2004, p 231) is relatively, albeit guardedly, optimistic that this final case might prevail: 'it would appear that the new CEE members are currently poised for a period of economic growth, and dynamic and flexible policy making, with an improving social base which may look quite positive after a further 10 years of EU membership'. This potential realignment is reminiscent of Clark Kerr's (1962) original convergence thesis based on the notion that industrial maturation would lead to increasing similarities in political and social institutions among nations.

But perhaps it is still necessary to return to the spectre of the race to the bottom. Guillen and Palier (2004) claim that even if the ESM eventually gains domination over the liberal model this might not preclude a race to the bottom if there are pervasive weak institutional capabilities among the newer members. Here old member states, while retaining nominal allegiance to the ESM and pretending to welcome the newcomers, might close their borders and reduce their social protection, both to keep out 'undesirables' and to retain competitiveness in the face of increased competition. Guillen and Palier (2004, p 208) conclude: 'If only lip service continues to be paid to the European social model but no concrete means are forwarded to support it, then a race to the bottom is possible.'

This possibility is explored in some depth by Kvist (2004) who demonstrates that all the EU 15 members had put policies in place to restrict either entry or entitlement to social benefits to migrants from the East and Central European accession countries, with only the UK, Finland and Ireland allowing relatively free entry. Even the UK which placed no restriction on the entry of workers, required migrants to register in order to access the NHS and to enable their children to attend schools, and it required them to work continuously for two years before gaining eligibility to social security benefits. Moreover, the British government is taking a much more restrictive line in relation to potential migrant workers from the newly acceding Bulgaria and Romania. Kvist (2004) charts increasing EU-wide concerns also about social tourism, social dumping and the more insidious 'social raiding'. Social tourism is where people migrate to get as many social benefits as possible and to contribute as little as possible. Social dumping is where wages are lowered to maintain competitiveness in the face of competition from lower wage economies in the EU. Social raids occur where migrants are provided with part-time jobs or, in effect, sinecures in the richer countries in order to enable them and their families to gain health and social benefits. Kvist expressed concern that fears of these eventualities might lead not only to restrictions in entry and to benefits for migrants, but also to social protection in general and thus to a self-perpetuating race to the bottom, as the EU 15 nations compete with each other to be less attractive to migrants from the post-accession countries.

Writing in 2004 he was relatively optimistic that this would not happen, on two grounds: first, predicting that there might not be much migration anyway; and, second, on the grounds of institutional resistance and the popularity of social policy programmes among indigenous national populations. Institutional resistance is certainly a formidable hurdle to across-the-board and wholesale retrenchment in social protection.

With hindsight it is clear that his first grounds for optimism have not been met. By mid-2006, for example, at least 400,000, and possibly 600,000, Poles had entered the UK to work. Also, the rise in xenophobia throughout Western Europe in the new millennium, and particularly in the wake of the 'war on terrorism', and the often hysterical reaction to economic migration since the inception of the EU 25, does not augur well for equitable and inclusive treatment of migrants at the end of the transition period in 2011. Here the extent to which, for example, a citizen of an accession country can become fully included within the EU depends on the extent to which the ESM and 'social Europe' can be seen to truly exist in the EU in the first decade of the twenty-first century. This leads back to the original questions about the EU goal of constructing an agreed set of values, through action towards a progressive convergence of policy objectives.

Conclusions

How far, then, can the EU move away from the distinct welfare regimes outlined earlier in this chapter, towards a common set of values? And in which direction will it move? Will it be towards Bernard's democratic dialectic ideal of optimising solidarity, equality and liberty in an idealised post-social democratic regime; will it coalesce around the conservative regime, representing the more traditional Central European heritage and values – either in its original strong version or in a more diluted version akin to the southern rim regimes; will it focus on the combination of social equality and liberty embedded in the traditional Anglo-Saxon model; or will it move towards a more full-blooded and single-mindedly libertarian, market-oriented and globalised approach?

Even the most optimistically minded supporter of the ESM would probably not anticipate the full democratic dialectic coming to fruition in the near future. However, in 10 years' time there may be a move towards sustained reduction in disparities between the GDPs of EU nations, as happened in the decade after Spain, Portugal and Greece joined the EU. If that does occur then, in the longer term, a weak version of the full democratic dialectic might become a possibility. But this is not the only option accruing from decreased inequality and the potential for increased solidarity – perhaps, alternatively, the conservative, corporatist model may thrive if the East and Central European EU members rekindle their historic cultural links with their western neighbours.

Both of these potential scenarios depend on the prospects for solidarity. For solidarity to prosper it will be necessary for the faint stirrings of a proto-European identity, based on values emanating from a shared heritage, to be nurtured so that Berting's vision of a fledgling European culture can become reality. Here Manning's (2004) 'muddling through' and Guillen and Palier's (2004) 'catch-up' scenarios offer at least hope that some form of social as well as economic convergence, as a prelude to potential solidarity, might take place.

Is such an increase in solidarity too much to hope for and will limited (social) equality and liberty, as in the Anglo-Saxon liberal model, thrive instead? Or will the threats of social tourism, dumping or raiding be too worrisome for the rich countries to promote this aspect of the ESM vision? And if this is the case, will another form of convergence, this time leading to untrammelled liberty and a race to the bottom take place, as predicted by Zielonka and Mair (2002)? If we accept that there is no predetermined outcome then we will have to accept that whatever happens will depend upon the politics of policies leading towards either social Europe or a globalised race to the bottom. This will take place in individual European nations and both within and outside the EU.

Notes

[1] Consequently these have been parenthesised in square brackets in Table 3.1 to distinguish them from the other, more cohesive group.

[2] Although it should be called 'Nordic' because geographically Finland is not part of Scandinavia.

FOUR

Categorising and policy making

Joanne Britton

Introduction

The task of reconsidering policy requires that we take a closer look at processes of categorisation in policy making. Categorising is integral to the dynamics of the policy-making process so playing a key part in the conception, design and implementation of policies. It demonstrates very clearly how policy is above all a meaning-making process in which categories are symbolically constructed according to the policy-making context (Innes, 2002). Theorising policy entails considering both how and why categorising occurs. This involves examining the reasons why categories are required in policy making, the ideas that inform the adoption of particular categories and the impact of the adopted categories on policy development. This highlights the fact that the categories used by policy makers cannot be taken for granted or ignored but should always be questioned as an important part of problematising policy overall. In common with Chapters Two and Ten by Jenkins and Lendvai and Stubbs in this volume, this chapter begins from the understanding that theorising policy involves defamiliarising the familiar.

This chapter contributes to the overall aims of the book in three main ways. First, it shows that categorising is part of the meaning and language of policy as policy making inevitably involves putting people into categories. The terms used to categorise people, and the meanings associated with them, are chosen in a specific social, cultural and political context. Acknowledging this is a good starting point for casting a critical eye over the political process of categorising in policy making because it reveals categorising as a crucial site for challenging the aims and objectives of policies. Second, it explains how categorising is part of the practical framework for the expression of political messages and achievement of social goals. Like policy itself, it is inherently political and so never politically neutral. As this book consistently demonstrates, policy is always a contested domain with competing interests. Likewise, the way that people are categorised, or indeed if they are categorised at all, is the outcome of a political process in which categories are negotiated, and thus always open to challenge. Finally, this chapter reveals how a critical look at categorisation contributes to a better understanding of the practice of policy, as it contributes to our awareness of the extent to which policies can attain their stated goals. This is important given that categorising can risk reinforcing wider social classifications that should be challenged and resisted.

What is categorising and why does it occur?

In order to begin critically assessing the meaning and role of categorising in policy making, a working definition of categorisation is first required. Categorisation is the process of placing people into collectivities or sub-populations based on any given criteria. People are frequently categorised according to sociodemographic characteristics such as age, ethnicity, race, social class, gender, sexuality and disability. These kinds of category are indeed negotiable and open to change but other forms of category used by policy makers are more likely to be seen as a matter of choice, ideology and the outcome of the agency of those involved in making policy. Examples include the categories of 'youth', 'juvenile' and 'elderly' in policies aimed at specific age groups and the categories of 'deserving' and 'undeserving' in welfare policy. Categories such as these are more readily understood to include a value judgement about the people they include. Importantly, it is the categoriser, in this instance the policy maker, who decides on the definition and composition of the category and not those being categorised. This means that there is not necessarily any perceived mutual recognition on the part of the members of a category (Jenkins, 1996, p 82) and the categories may not be meaningful to those placed in them. It does not, however, mean that those being categorised automatically have no say in either the categories created or where they are placed in any system of categorisation. It simply emphasises that both the definition and composition of any category are recognised and legitimated primarily by those doing the categorising. In addition, it is also worth drawing attention to the fact that categorising plays a crucial part from the earliest stages of the policy process because policies cannot be designed and implemented until policy makers have decided on the categories to be used.

It is useful to begin by considering the purpose of categorisation. Why does categorising occur and why is it integral to the work of policy makers? First and foremost, categorising is a way of creating order so that the business of policy making can begin. Extremely heterogeneous and diverse groups of people are organised into discrete collectivities that can be operationalised to form the basis of any policy. Without categorising, policy making would be unavoidably imprecise and incoherent. Second, categorising enables the measuring and monitoring of a population by, for example, making possible the collection of statistics that inform the development of policies. Finally, categorising occurs so that finite resources can be allocated in the most effective way. In principle, it helps to ensure that policies are targeted at those who can make best use of, and benefit the most from, the resources allocated or, alternatively, that social sanctions are applied appropriately. Categorising therefore plays a crucial part in the development of a range of policies from those that aim to improve life chances, quality of life and well-being to those that aim to modify, restrict or penalise certain behaviour.

As the largest source of data collected at national level, the census is a good example of how and why categorising occurs. The census provides a comprehensive snapshot of the national population by operationalising categories based on various sociodemographic characteristics such as age, gender and ethnicity. It provides a key basis for policy making by organising the national population into discrete collectivities and providing a means of measuring and monitoring it to a range of potential users from all levels of government to commerce and industry. This then underpins the development of policies aimed at meeting the goals of the user. For government in particular, it is a crucial source of information influencing resource allocation, such as state support for childcare or pensions. For users in commerce and industry, it informs advertising and marketing policies by enabling them to learn more about whom and where their consumers are, and thus target their resources most effectively (Diamond, 1999).

All other sources of data collected nationally are based on sample surveys. One such example is the Labour Force Survey, a quarterly sample survey of households and individuals that provides information on the labour market. This information is used to develop and evaluate the government's labour market policies. The key census variables used (which include age, gender and ethnic and socioeconomic group) enable the comparison of labour market activity between different sociodemographic groups. For example, an analysis of ethnic differences in demographic characteristics and economic activity using Labour Force Survey data over a 10-year period revealed significant differences between women (Dale et al., 2004). This information helps policy makers to decide how to target resources most effectively in developing policies aimed at increasing labour market participation rates.

Examining the process of categorising

Policy makers charged with devising policies to achieve a given end unavoidably operate within specific political constraints, and it is reasonable to assume that there are limits to critical reflection when faced with the pressures of delivering measurable outcomes within a specific time period. However, the current direction of policy making towards a reliance on evidence-based practice encourages more attention to be paid to categorising because strong evidence requires rigorous conceptualisation and utilisation of categories. We cannot therefore consider the position of policy makers without paying close attention to the research–policy interface, as researchers too have an important part to play in the selection and implementation of categories. Above all, researchers must ensure that the categories adopted fit the purpose of the research so they must never be complacent about the categories they choose (Aspinall, 2001, p 853). Researchers need to critically reflect on the process of categorising in order to do a good job. The emphasis on evidence-based practice means that the decisions of policy makers are crucially dependent on the quality of the evidence produced so there are significant negative consequences for the development of policy if categories do not fit the purpose of the research. This is important because it is both researchers, including the academic community, and the policy makers themselves who possess the so-called 'expert knowledge' that informs the development of policy, and who also have the legitimate authority to make the political decisions around *whom* to categorise and *how* (Giddens, 1990; Colebatch, 2002). Examining the process of categorising therefore involves paying attention to the contribution of both groups.

This reinforces the case that policy makers and researchers are engaged in a political process when they decide on *whom* to categorise and *how*, because their decisions are always open to question and revision so inevitably involve an element of risk (Hill, 1997). It is essential not to overlook their legitimate authority as categorisers because this raises the question: in whose interests are the categories chosen? The politics of categorising ensures that categories are chosen as much for political reasons as for reasons of analytical and conceptual clarity. Chosen categories can reflect the interests of powerful groups and the expert knowledge of those responsible for categorising can serve to disguise any political motivation (Giddens, 1990, pp 83–92). There are other reasons influencing the choice of category that have nothing to do with being analytically and conceptually precise. Categories can be chosen because of historical precedence, raising the probability that many categories are adopted as a matter of convenience. Even in a dominant policy context of reliance on evidence-based practice, it cannot be assumed that policy makers devote a great deal of time to thinking about their choice of categories. It is possible that they are unaware of the limitations of the categories chosen or are unable or unwilling to invest the required time and effort in seeking better alternatives. Exploring the politics of categorisation is therefore a vital part of understanding the process of categorising overall.

The many ways in which people are categorised and the various contexts in which categorisation occurs give the impression that categories have little, or nothing, in common. There are, however, a number of important commonalities that demand our attention in order to adequately explain the process of categorising. First, it is clear that policy makers charged with devising policies to achieve a given end are involved in a complex process of categorising, the outcome of which provides the appearance of overall order and consensus (Hill, 1997). This is important, as the work of policy makers would not be able to begin without a basic agreement on the general acceptability of the categories decided upon. The appearance of order and consensus is, however, a necessary fiction that enables policy making to proceed. In order to fully understand the policies themselves, we need to look beyond the appearance to investigate how and why categories are chosen.

Second, all categories are socially and politically constructed, are never fixed or permanent, despite the appearance of being so, and are always open to contestation and/or negotiation. It therefore makes sense to refer to categorising as a meaning-making process because it is inherently a course of action that is never complete and always open to further development and amendment. Again, we must look beyond the appearance of fixedness and permanence in order to understand how and why categories are chosen. Third, the categories chosen by policy makers require scrutiny because they, at best, overemphasise unity, and, at worst, imply unity among people when there is little, if any. By placing people into single categories, the process of categorisation can disguise heterogeneity and diversity. In so doing, it maintains the illusion that people can be placed straightforwardly into a single category. This provides a further reminder of the contingent nature of categories, involving strategic positioning as collective identity claims are made according to the political context. In other words, the categories chosen by policy makers are influenced by the allegiances formed by different groups of people at a particular time and place. Again, this reinforces the argument that categorising is essentially a political process in which boundaries shift according to the social and political context and the associated perceived value of different alliances. It also suggests that the legitimate authority of policy makers and researchers to categorise by no means renders the identity claims of those being categorised irrelevant.

Fourth, for the purposes of allocation, policies require the operationalisation of categories that can be quantified, as policy makers need to put people into categories that can, in some way, be counted or measured. The socially and politically constructed basis of any category means that this task is inherently conditional because it involves quantifying what is ultimately unquantifiable. For policy makers, whose job it is to prioritise the practicalities of policy making, this charge is difficult to address but it is crucial to our understanding of how and why policies are adopted. Taking a critical look at categorising in policy making involves considering how and why the unquantifiable is quantified.

Finally, the categories chosen by policy makers are inevitably open to the criticism of essentialism because they are utilised in a way that suggests they represent an absolute truth. The common-sense understanding that there is an inescapable essence to being, for example, a 'man' or 'woman' or 'black' or 'white', disguises the inherently provisional nature of categories. Above all, this criticism draws our attention to the way in which particularly commonly-used categories are adopted in a taken-for-granted, uncritical way. The charge of essentialism is also difficult for policy makers to avoid but it is nonetheless an important consideration for our critical understanding of the meaning and role of categorising because these essentialist categories inevitably have a direct impact on the reach and scope of the policy implemented.

This section has presented an overview of the process of categorising and, in so doing, it has provided a summary of the key points that require examination in any critical analysis of categorising in policy making. The following section takes a closer look at categorisation in order to explore further how and why it occurs.

Categorisation and its consequences

The ways in which people are categorised by policy makers has attracted a significant amount of critical attention in recent years (for example,

Ahmad, 1999; Nazroo, 1999; Aspinall, 2001, 2003). There is cumulative evidence that categories based on 'race' and ethnicity are problematic and are more likely to be the subject of dispute and amendment than are categories based on other sociodemographic characteristics. As a consequence, they provide a useful focus in exploring critically the process of categorising in policy making.

Before examining how and why groups of people have been categorised according to 'race' and ethnicity, it is important to note that the status of 'race' and ethnicity per se as social and analytical concepts has attracted much theoretical and political debate. For example, the use of the term 'race' is hotly disputed in academic circles because although it indicates the existence of racism (which is itself another disputed term) it also arguably perpetuates the notion that people can be divided into distinct racial groups (Miles and Brown, 2003, pp 1–10). The terms 'race' and ethnicity are sometimes used interchangeably but are usually distinguished on the basis of physical markers, such as skin pigmentation for 'race', and cultural markers, such as religion, for ethnicity. In fact, the meanings attached to 'race' and ethnicity vary considerably according to who is using the terms and so it is not always clear that people are referring to the same thing. For example, it is possible that the definitions and understandings of policy makers differ from those of researchers working in this area. This is significant because policy makers and researchers must agree on what they mean when they use the terms 'race' and ethnicity if they are to develop the most appropriate ways of categorising people accordingly.

In Chapter Three, David Phillips discusses different visions of 'the good society' expressed at national level. The political impetus to categorise and develop policies according to 'race' and ethnicity arguably reflects notions of the good society as one that pursues social equality for its members by seeking to address all forms of disadvantage and discrimination. Persistent evidence of substantial inequalities arising from racialised disadvantage and ethnic diversity has therefore ensured that categorising on the basis of 'race' and ethnicity is of key importance to policy makers. The social reality of disadvantage and discrimination on the basis of 'race' and ethnicity means that policy makers are compelled to adopt such categorisations in order to both express the political message that reducing disadvantage and discrimination is desirable and to pursue it as an important social goal. As a result, there is an increasing array of policies aimed at tackling evident cumulative disadvantage and discrimination in various areas of social life such as education, employment, health services and housing. Over the years, policy makers have used a variety of different ways to categorise people according to 'race' and ethnicity. There is plenty of evidence that all have had their limitations and have been subject to challenges from those being categorised.

First and foremost, categorising in this way is inevitably contradictory and imprecise because it risks reinforcing the notion that racial and ethnic differences are natural or fixed and can be reduced to either biology or culture. Moreover, resulting policies risk overstating the significance of 'race' and ethnicity as key explanatory variables in accounting for forms of disadvantage and discrimination. This clearly illustrates a significant problem in categorising in policy per se, that the categories adopted can reinforce the ideas underpinning the disadvantage and discrimination they are aimed at addressing and potentially contribute to the associated social problems.

For example, policies aimed at raising the educational achievement of young people from minority ethnic groups have required the collection of statistics that reveal substantial differences in attainment according to ethnicity. Particular attention has been paid to the high educational attainment of young people of Chinese and Indian ethnicity, in contrast with the apparent underachievement of young people from Caribbean, Bangladeshi and Pakistani backgrounds. The statistics and policies that result have been widely criticised because they arguably use ethnicity as a signifier for 'race'. This means that they overemphasise the relevance of ethnicity in explaining the attainment levels of young people and, in so doing, reinforce essentialist notions about the abilities and propensities of different groups. They, therefore, contribute to the perpetuation of stereotypes, such as the view that black young people are not 'academic' and Asians are 'docile' and 'hard-working' (Mirza, 2006, pp 150–1). They also serve to place the blame with the young people and their culture, and detract attention away from the discrimination they encounter. There is, however, statistical evidence that reveals radical diversity not only between but also within ethnic groups (Modood, 1997, p 80). This indicates that focusing mainly on ethnicity provides a limited explanation as to why some young people do well at school and others do not and suggests that resulting policies are likely to have only some degree of success in raising educational achievement.

Similar problems beset categorisation according to ethnicity in health policy. Policies aimed at improving the health of different ethnic groups have relied on the collection of statistics that reveal significant health inequalities. For example, African-Caribbeans, Bangladeshis, Pakistanis and Irish people have higher than average mortality rates from stroke than other ethnic groups (Balarajan and Raleigh, 1995). However, the categories used have been criticised for merging the concepts of 'race' and ethnicity and for identifying ethnic groups in an untheorised way (Nazroo, 1999, pp 215–17). Consequently, there has been a tendency to link health disadvantage with cultural and genetic weaknesses, again placing the blame with the ethnic groups that disproportionately experience these disadvantages, and underplaying the role of other factors, such as discrimination. Categorising according to ethnicity in health policy has therefore led to an overemphasis on ethnicity as a key explanatory variable and it is to be expected that resulting policies can only achieve partial success in addressing health inequalities.

Categorisation in legislation further highlights the problems inherent in categorising according to ethnicity. For example, the third Race Relations Act (1976) was based on the premise of equality of treatment for all and was extended to cover indirect, organisational forms of discrimination. Interpretation of the law by the judiciary has involved establishing which groups are distinctly 'racial'. In 1982, a Sikh parent instituted legal proceedings on the grounds of racial discrimination, against a school that had refused to admit his son. The Court of Appeal overturned the initial ruling that it is lawful to discriminate against Sikhs because they are not a racial group and, consequently, the Race Relations Act covers Sikhs. The final ruling indicated that 'ethnic' should be interpreted widely and that cultural traditions should be considered in defining a group as racial (Jones and Gnanapala, 2000, pp 35–41).

In contrast, Muslims are not covered by the Act because it is argued that they do not have a common culture and their shared religious practices are not enough to establish them as a separate racial or ethnic group (Jones and Gnanapala, 2000, pp 53–5). The meanings applied to the categories 'Sikh' and 'Muslim' reveal that legislating on the basis of racial or ethnic categorisation is problematic because it serves to reinforce the notion that racial and ethnic differences are natural or fixed and can be reduced to either biology or culture. Moreover, the argument that the exclusion of Muslims is discriminatory draws attention to the contested nature of the categories created and their potential limitations in facilitating the equitable application of the law.

Having taken a general look at categorising according to 'race' and ethnicity, the following section examines two commonly used categories in order to further our critical analysis of categorising in policy making.

The use of the categories 'black' and 'white'

The categories 'black' and 'white' both appear perfectly reasonable, straightforward categories to use from a common-sense, everyday point of view. However, this section considers them in some depth in order to show how they prove to be extremely problematic on closer inspection. Together they are a good example of the problems of categorising per se, and not simply when minority groups are being categorised. It is important to note first that 'black' and 'white' are socially and politically constructed categories that are inherently and permanently open to negotiation. Who is categorised as 'black' or 'white' is never fixed, in spite of our usual assumptions to the contrary. More seriously, using these categories points towards the apparent inevitability of a racialised social world and so reinforces the racialised status quo. By adopting these categories, policy makers unavoidably limit the extent to which they can pursue equality of treatment and opportunity, and address related forms of disadvantage and discrimination. Ultimately, it is only by comprehensively challenging these categories that disadvantage and discrimination can be eliminated. If a post-racial world is part of what ultimately constitutes a good society, using the categories 'black' and 'white' will only inhibit its creation. This section refers to 'black' and 'white' in inverted commas to draw attention to the little acknowledged fact that their use under any circumstances is contentious. We now take a closer look at the two categories.

The category 'black' has arguably been a major focus of ideological struggle and political action over the years, and so it is a useful example to highlight the problem of categorising. Policies that have adopted this category cannot be fully understood without examining the meaning-making processes through which it has come to be chosen. The use of 'black' to order, and imply consensus among, disparate groups of people has inevitably had its limitations. Since the period of large-scale post-war immigration to Britain, 'black' has been used primarily to refer exclusively to people of African origin, or, more broadly, to all people defined as 'non-white'. These different uses of the category highlight that it is socially and politically constructed and the ensuing debates surrounding its various uses emphasise its negotiated, contingent nature. For example, the broader use has been extensively criticised because it is seen as detrimental to the identity of British Asians and arguably subordinates their interests to those of people of African origin (for example, Modood, 1990). On the other hand, it can be argued that the interests of people of African origin are similarly demeaned by a category that disguises their cultural heritage and the specificity of their experiences of racism. From this perspective, policies that adopt the umbrella category 'black' disguise heterogeneity and diversity to their detriment. They cannot possibly address the diverse needs and interests of the various groups subsumed under the category so are destined to be ineffectual.

Regardless of which of the two meanings is preferred, the category 'black' is arguably essentialist. It implies that 'blackness' can be reduced to a single essence or truth that only 'black' people can know. This position has been extremely influential in the development of social work policy from an anti-racist perspective, particularly in supporting opposition to both transracial adoption and the placing of children categorised as 'black' with 'white' foster parents. It has, therefore, been common social work practice to assume that children categorised as 'mixed race' (children understood to have one 'black' and one 'white' parent) are better served being placed with 'black' families. From this perspective, only 'black' families can adequately relate to the child's racialised sense of self and experiences of growing up in a racialised society. This categorisation is open to question precisely because it essentialises 'black' identity, while seriously oversimplifying the complex identities of people categorised as 'mixed'.

Jenkins (see Chapter Two) observes that being seen to do something, whilst doing something else or nothing at all, is a device of policy in general. This calls to mind a wider criticism that the broader use of the category 'black' to mean 'non-white', has been a convenient ruse used by Britain's 'race relations establishment' in order to give the appearance of being committed to tackling disadvantage and discrimination whilst actually doing very little. This argument reflects the understanding that developing policies based on an all-encompassing 'black' category is notably less complex, expensive and successful than developing policies specifically tailored towards very diverse minority ethnic groups. Although the criticism does carry weight, it is important to note that 'black' was adopted by an anti-racist movement keen to draw attention to and tackle what was increasingly being referred to as institutional racism. The use of the category 'black' is investigated further in the case study below but it is important to emphasise here that where the boundaries are fixed in terms of who is included in, and excluded from, the definition is a political decision. Identity claims are staked in the political context of the time and place, as collective allegiances are sought according to the perceived costs and benefits to all the parties involved.

By the 1990s, the inclusive use of the category 'black' fell out of favour because wider social and political changes ensured that its use in policy circles was comprehensively challenged. For example, the limitations of an anti-racist movement that prioritised the identification of racism as purely a matter of 'black' versus 'white' were increasingly recognised. The political coming to voice of British Asians was another influential factor. This group of post-war migrants immigrated slightly later than their African-Caribbean counterparts and faced additional barriers to political inclusion, such as language differences. However, due to the fluidity of collective allegiances, it is possible that in certain circumstances the benefits of using 'black' inclusively may still outweigh the costs. Once more, this highlights that categories are always contingent and involve strategic political positioning.

Finally, both of these uses of the category 'black' are clear examples of how any category inevitably overemphasises unity. Even using the term to refer exclusively to people of African origin masks significant diversity among people arising from ethnic and national differences. It begs the question of how it is possible or desirable to group together people from the entire continent of Africa and the diverse islands of the Caribbean. In order to answer this, we must again remember that shared experiences of disadvantage and discrimination are a source of mutual recognition among groups that would otherwise have very little in common and, as a result, it can be seen as politically beneficial to those being categorised to overemphasise unity. In certain circumstances, the legitimate authority of policy makers to adopt the category 'black' is therefore defensible, not least by those being categorised as such. This is clearly an example of how policy processes contribute to the imagining of collectivities.

The category 'white' has not been a focus of ideological struggle and political action in the same way as the category 'black', but it is nevertheless an important, and complementary, category to consider in highlighting the problems of categorising. In recent years, the development of critical white studies has drawn attention to the importance of examining how and why people are categorised as 'white' (for example, Roediger, 1994; Dyer, 1997; Knowles, 2005). In terms of the critical assessment of categorising in policy making, this involves asking why the category 'white' is more likely than most other categories to be adopted in an uncritical way. The answer lies first and foremost in the social and cultural construction of whiteness as normative. 'White', it is argued, is an empty category, a non-colour that has an 'everything and nothing' quality about it (Dyer, 1997). This means that 'white' people do not usually see their whiteness and are unaware of how it structures social reality, providing significant social privileges. Thus, the category 'white' is usually viewed from an everyday, common-sense perspective as especially unproblematic. In terms of policy making, there is always the risk that it can result in the development of so-called 'colour-blind' policies that obscure the privileges that a white identity provides. A veneer of race neutrality disguises how disadvantage and discrimination on the basis of 'race' and ethnicity are sustained by various institutional and cultural practices. This risk is much reduced given that questions about 'race' and ethnicity are now an established part of the political and policy-making scene.

Even when policies are not colour-blind, the use of the category 'white' is inevitably open to question because who is included in and excluded from the category 'white' is context-specific and inherently changeable. Like the category 'black', the category 'white' is essentialised so that its dynamic nature is overlooked and it is not usually perceived to be open to negotiation. There are many ethnic groups that, although commonly categorised as 'white', experience forms of disadvantage and discrimination. Historically, people of Irish and Jewish heritage are two such groups that are commonly perceived to have crossed the borders of whiteness, having been 'probationary' whites during the nineteenth and well into the twentieth century (Jacobson, 2000, p 239). In contemporary society, migrants from the newer member states of the European Union, such as Poland, are arguably racialised in a way that positions them as being at the margins of who is appropriately categorised as 'white'.

The category 'white' is, therefore, extremely heterogeneous and diverse and the argument that whiteness necessarily equates to privilege requires critical thought because not all 'white' people are privileged in the same ways or all of the time. With regard to the use of the category by policy makers, we need to ask which 'white' people are being included in the category and why. To recall two examples that have already been discussed in this chapter, significant health differences and differences in educational attainment among people categorised as 'white' may be overlooked if the category is used in an all-encompassing way. This then inhibits pursuing the social goal of equality of treatment and opportunity and addressing disadvantage and discrimination.

This section has taken a critical look at two important categories from the study of 'race' and ethnicity in order to illustrate, first, how categorising is an important part of the meaning and language of policy and, second, how it is an integral part of the practical framework for expressing political messages and achieving social goals. In Chapter Ten, Lendvai and Stubbs argue that short vignettes or case studies based on ethnographic research are useful because they help us to understand how social actors involved in the site of study construct meaning.

Through the presentation of a case study, the following section does exactly this by presenting fragments of research based on interviews and detailed participant observation. This vignette allows a closer look at the use of the category 'black' in order to examine how categorising helps us to gain a better understanding of the practice of policy.

Categorising and policy: a vignette

'The project' was a small voluntary organisation that explicitly identified itself as being formed, managed and run by 'black' people for the local 'black' population. The overall stated aim of the project was to pursue justice for 'black' people, principally through addressing discrimination in the criminal justice system, and it developed a range of policies designed to meet this aim (Britton, 2000). In order to assess critically the way that the project used the category 'black', it is first important to understand the wider social and political context in which it came into being. Following the urban disturbances of the early 1980s, it became politically expedient to consider the specific needs and interests of minority ethnic groups. In terms of the policy response, increased attention was paid to finding viable ways to implement an apparent commitment to reform and redistribution by the institutions of both the local and central state (Benyon and Solomos, 1987). Issues of minority ethnic participation and representation were given more attention at both central and local government level and one consequence of this was that community activists began to work more closely within the institutions of the local state (Solomos and Back, 1995). This together with the new impetus towards racial and ethnic equality resulted in the increased funding of initiatives aimed specifically at minority ethnic groups.

However, by the 1990s, concerns over the effectiveness of public sector organisations and their financial management meant that many local authority initiatives aimed at tackling racial and ethnic inequality were cut back or ended. It is interesting and, on the face of it, paradoxical that it was in this climate that the project first received its statutory funding, initially from the Home Office and then from the regional probation service.

In order to understand why the project was supported, we need to consider that its institutional origins arose from a process of legitimacy through which its aims and objectives reflected the broader policy context. This meant that processes of categorising occurred within the institutionalised micro-space of the voluntary organisation but were heavily influenced by the macro-institutionalised space of statutory agencies. The idea and initial impetus for the project came from three of its management committee members whose dual positions as community activists and paid employees within relevant institutions of the local state enabled them to create a project that pursued minority ethnic interests in a way that proved attractive to those allocating funding at statutory level. Generally, by offering services previously provided by the public sector, the project explicitly positioned itself within a growing mixed economy of welfare that sought an increased role for the voluntary sector. In terms of illustrating the problem of categorising, the project was attractive to potential funding bodies specifically because it used the category 'black' inclusively. In a climate of reduced funding for racial equality initiatives, the project maximised its potential to be funded by claiming to provide services for a range of minority ethnic groups.

The project's use of the category 'black' was, therefore, a strategic staking of identity claims in a specific political context, which was convenient in terms of securing statutory support but problematic in terms of the extent to which it could meet its objectives (see Ray, 2003 for a comparable analysis of the collectivity, 'Asian women'). By adopting the category 'black' inclusively, the project enabled competing interest groups to form an anti-racist alliance, ensuring that the boundaries of who was included in the project appeared fixed in order to legitimise its claim for funding. Politically expedient assumptions of homogeneity and unity did, however, prove to be shaky in the day-to-day running of the project. Stuart Hall's 'politics of the contingent' draws attention to the fact that all identifications, and the categories that are created as a consequence of them, are inevitably fluid throughout any process of alliance building (Hall, 1991). Among the project's volunteers, there was an understanding that the resources and services they provided disproportionately benefited the local Caribbean population, and the Pakistani population to a lesser extent. Many of the volunteers also challenged the understated inclusion of 'white' minority ethnic groups, such as Irish people, within the project's remit. Thus, the day-to-day running of the project involved negotiating competing claims to belonging and, by implication, competing claims to the resources and services it provided.

Above all, this vignette shows how the practice of policy highlights the problem of categorising per se. By undergoing a process of legitimacy that involved adopting a politically expedient categorisation of 'black', the project successfully secured the funding and support of statutory agencies. However, the category did not straightforwardly provide unity, nor did it ensure the project's success in practical terms.

Conclusions

This chapter has shown that categorisation is very much part of the language of policy and, as such, is about the production and reproduction of meaning. By taking a closer look at the meaning-making process involved in deciding whom to categorise and how, the discussion has highlighted that, as linguistic representations, categories are specific to the cultural, political and social context and are thus always open to challenge and change. Defamiliarising common-sense, taken-for-granted categories, such as 'black' and 'white', helps to reveal the context-specific, negotiable nature of all categories, and reminds us that decisions about whom to categorise and how are inherently political. Although this chapter has focused on examples from the study of 'race' and ethnicity, the arguments advanced are applicable to all kinds of category. A critical understanding of policy processes requires that close attention be paid to how and why categories, in general, are chosen.

The chapter has also shown that, from a practical perspective, categorising is tied up with both the expression of political messages and achievement of social goals. Acknowledging this is important because it draws our attention to how the categories chosen impact on the reach and scope of any policy. The extent to which any policy is able to reach its target population and stated goals crucially depends on the appropriateness of the categories chosen. Despite this, the political process of categorising ensures that theoretical and conceptual clarity are by no means central to the decisions made. It is also worth reiterating that expressing political messages and achieving social goals are not necessarily two sides of the same coin. The examples discussed here reveal that chosen categories can help to express a socially desirable political message about the value of pursuing an important social goal, whilst at the same time limiting the success of the policy in question. This helps to explain why examining categorising provides us with a better understanding of the practice of policy.

Critical understanding of the role of categorising in policy making would be further improved by micro-level ethnographic study of the decision-making processes of those who have the legitimate authority to categorise. In order to capture the complexity of this process, it would need to include an examination of the ways in which the strategic staking of identity claims by various interest groups influences the decisions made. Categorising is an inescapable part of policy making, and thus modern governance, and so deserves more detailed attention in our efforts to reconsider policy.

Part Two
Politics

Introduction

The chapters in Part I share an interest in the exploration of meanings generated within and by 'policy': as a concept; as a means to draw social and economic boundaries; and as the more tangible expression of abstract values. What they also have in common, however, is recognition that policy is essentially political. As Richard Jenkins points out, in many languages 'policy' and 'politics' are described by the same word. David Phillips and Jo Britton make clear the connection between policy as values, policy as categorisation and the operative role played by politics in drawing down values and categories from the abstract to the concrete. Traditionally, policy's inherently political nature has informed the dominant structure of research and theorising in policy studies. Politics has been the mainstay of policy analysis and policy analysis has developed within the boundaries of political science. This is clear in the core texts, classic studies, theories and models widely associated with the study of policy (for example, Hogwood and Gunn, 1984; Dahl, 1961; Lukes, 1974; Lindblom, 1959, respectively). In view of this, it would be impossible to reconsider policy without reconsidering politics at the same time. Having examined policy at the conceptual level, Part Two is, therefore, intended to return readers to issues of power and process.

The chapters in Part Two represent a reappraisal of some of the boundaries and assumptions, which have hitherto underpinned traditional analyses of the policy process: first, that the language used to present and describe policy is neutral or permanent; second, that the analytical 'rediscovery' of the state and interest in the workings of policy communities and networks has tended to eclipse investigation of the role of capital; and, third, that the policy process is principally of interest at the national and/or local level. The need to question these features of the policy process literature arises because they correspond to three critical aspects of change in the policy arena in the twenty-first century.

First, the expansion of the technological routes by which the communication of ideas can take place means that we find ourselves in an age of significant media reliance as far as policy is concerned.

The kinds of values discussed by David Phillips in Chapter Three are symbolised in the concepts and ideas cascaded down from policy 'thinkers' to policy 'subjects' in the sound bites and announcements that litter our everyday lives. Policy, then, is increasingly about messages and subtext, and in response to this, Marilyn Gregory (Chapter Five) examines the evolution of values and their impact on practice. She explores how and why values alter according to the politics of policy and professions, and in so doing highlights a different form of implementation gap. The example of the policy process within the probation service captures the flow of ideas, the ways in which they are channelled and how they determine the supply of policy. Examination of the probation service, as an example, highlights the importance of language in relation to what gets said and what gets done: the message and the action. However, the discussion could equally describe what goes on in relation to other welfare services such as health or education, as well as the environment, immigration or any other area of policy development.

Second, the shape and spheres of influence of policy actors has changed as the power of organised labour has declined. The role of business within processes and practices of policy is not commonly appreciated, and, notwithstanding the neo-pluralists (such as Lindblom), neither is it often subject to analytical scrutiny. Yet, as Kevin Farnsworth argues in Chapter Six, business plays a pivotal, and increasingly visible, part in contemporary social policy making. With capital in the ascendant, he invites us to rethink the potency of business in the policy process while cautioning against any assumption of homogeneity with regard to 'business' interests. He provides a contemporary analysis of the UK policy context under New Labour, but one that also contains a historical perspective, drawing on traditional theory while highlighting its limitations in terms of empirical reality.

For the purpose of the argument presented here, Farnsworth's discussion is located at the national level since this remains significant as a point of mediation between the local and the global. However, as a category, the 'national' is becoming increasingly problematic given the globalising contexts of the business world and related shifts in policy. Bob Deacon, in Chapter Seven, thus explores a third dimension of the changing politics of policy development, which also focuses on the input of actors but seeks to situate these within a framework that accounts for both the 'international' and matters of scale in policy making. The meaning, politics and impact of globalisation are subjects that continue to vex the imaginations of social scientists in every discipline and school of thought. Deacon's analysis uses insights and concepts from a range of disciplines and schools to demonstrate that both abstract and applied theory and knowledge are necessary to better understand the complexities of policy making in the modern world. From a realist standpoint, he argues that discourses are one of many tools in struggles and disputes, which continue to reflect traditional cleavages of class, gender and ethnicity. What the study of policy now needs to account for is the lack of solid boundaries between levels of policy making and the changing shape of policy-making bodies. With important implications for policy practices, Deacon's work shows that much of the politics of policy now happens outside the formal institutions, among actors whose policy identity and 'business model' (the way they present themselves and engage in the process) is fluid and amorphous depending on the who, where, what and how of their involvement.

Taken together, then, the reconsideration of policy found in the following three chapters encourages us to (re-)acquaint ourselves with traditional approaches to policy analysis rather than to discard them. The challenges which do become apparent, however, are related to questions of linearity, simplicity or political neatness in the contemporary policy arena; the problems of static explanations where a longitudinal perspective would better accommodate transformations of scenery and actors, and attention to the genealogy of concepts and ideas.

FIVE

Language, politics and values

Marilyn Gregory

This chapter discusses a specific example of the politicisation of social policy. I contend that shifts in language that have taken place across different policy sectors, at different rates, over the past three decades, give us access to transformations in the underpinning values of policy work. Thus I consider the nature of the language, the knowledge and the values of policy – using the probation service as a case example – to analyse 'policy politics'. This chapter links the specific case with wider developments in crime control policies. Faced with the distinctive socioeconomic features of late modernity, including the penal crisis that has developed since the 1970s, governments in Britain and the US have engaged in two strategies: an *adaptive strategy* focusing upon 'preventive partnership' and a *sovereign state strategy* involving 'punitive segregation'. The first is a way of spreading the responsibility for crime control to the wider society, to the 'responsible citizens', the shopkeepers, business people and community members, engaging them in partnerships to take preventive action against crime; redefining the roles of criminal justice agencies such as the police and the probation service (Garland, 2000, p 348). It is an approach that focuses less on crime causation and more upon the management and processing of offenders. The second is a politically driven 'tough on crime' stance that involves harsher penalties, fewer opportunities for early release, harder prison conditions and a move away from treating young offenders as children and towards treating them as criminals (Gregory, 2006).

This chapter traces probation policy language from the late 1970s to date, and shows how language supports particular versions of values and practice. The chapter is not intended as a detailed discourse analysis of policy documents, rather the aim is to demonstrate how attention to language enables us to access some of the conceptual matters that underpin policy intent. At a macro-level, a discourse both shapes and is shaped by the prevailing socioeconomic context. At the micro-level, language choice preferences certain concepts and values above others; from the designations used to describe policy actors, to the characterisation of what is done, to the terms used to refer to recipients of policy services (Gregory and Holloway, 2006). Thus language serves as a way in which to explore changing contexts of policy making, underpinning values and the relations between policy, politics and values. The case explored here, criminal justice and probation, forms an interesting lens as one key difference between this and other parts of the public sector is that 'service users' cannot become 'customers'; offenders cannot be seen as freely choosing a service from the courts, police, prisons or probation service.

Discourse refers to the ways in which people make sense of the social world through the spoken word and numerous other forms of communication (Purvis and Hunt, 1993); it is a framework of meanings which are historically produced in a particular culture at a particular time (Watson, 2000). Language is a critical component of discourse because the specific words we choose to describe a person, situation or event inevitably affect its meaning or importance to ourselves and to those with whom we are communicating. The labels we give to phenomena determine what is important, what is told, what is untold (Fook, 2002; Britton, Chapter Four, this volume). Language in this formulation is not neutral: it indicates the value system of the speaker or writer. At the same time, the prioritising of some language/values means that individual or critical voices may become marginalised or silenced (Fook, 2002). As Phillips notes in Chapter Three, policy is imbued with values, and language is one way in which values are manifest. This chapter seeks to demonstrate the power of language in the transformation of probation policy and practice, in particular, how changes in policy language become a vehicle for changing the way that practitioners operate.

The chapter begins with an overview of early social work/probation values and how this language of values became contested over time, as the criminal justice policy agenda changed. It then charts how the policy discourse that frames practice has shifted over more recent decades, away from 'advise, assist and befriend', towards 'manage, control and punish'. It will be argued that this latter form of language, that I term 'punitive managerialism', leads to differing forms of practice and certain consequences for service users. The chapter concludes by considering ways forward in potential underpinning values and the possibility for alternative policy discourse.

Probation values and the criminal justice context

Probation practice shares, more broadly, with social work a strong emphasis on language as the vehicle for practice. Talk, conversation and narrative are the very stuff of day-to-day practice. It was commented upon as long ago as 1968 that it was surprising how little theoretical interest the social work profession took in the concept of language (Timms, 1968). This has been rectified more recently by a number of commentators who have sought to develop critical and social constructionist accounts of social work in general and probation practice in particular (Healey, 2000; Gorman et al., 2006). While the research field may have neglected language in the past, it has always been self-conscious about the values with which its practice is imbued. It is not surprising, therefore, that successive governments' determination to move probation practice away from social work may be traced in the contours of the debate over what constitutes appropriate 'probation values' and how these are articulated.

From 1971, probation officers underwent shared training with social workers under the auspices of the Central Council for the Education and Training of Social Workers (CCETSW). In 1997, following a review that took place under the previous Conservative administration, the Labour government announced that probation officers would no longer train as social workers. Training is a crucial conduit of professional values to members of a profession, thus the decision was resisted by many. This struggle over training reinvigorated a debate that had existed since the inception of joint training in 1971. The essence of the debate is: what sort of values should a probation practitioner hold, and are generic social work values suitable for a probation practitioner given the context in which they work?

Probably the most abiding influences on generic social work values, and the codes of practice drawn up by social work organisations, have been the principles put forward by Biestek (1961):

1. individualisation
2. purposeful expression of feelings
3. controlled emotional involvement
4. acceptance
5. non-judgemental attitude
6. user self-determination
7. confidentiality.

These principles may be traced in the codes of practice drawn up by a variety of UK and other European social work agencies over a number of years (Banks, 2001). The emphasis on *individualised* values has been challenged by some practitioners who have pointed out that its basis in Kantian philosophy implies a masculine and rationalist essence (Belenky et al., 1997). The lack of recognition of structural disadvantage faced by oppressed groups, for example, black people and the disabled, has also been highlighted (Dominelli, 1988; Worrall, 1992). From a criminal justice perspective, there was also a criticism that individualised social work values failed to take account of the particular context in which probation staff had to work. In response to this, values for social work were put forward that attempted to encapsulate principles emanating from probation practice itself, for example, anti-oppressive practice. Anti-oppressive practice encompasses a much more relational approach to values in which the service user is seen within their full social context. It is a practice-oriented approach which demonstrates how to empower clients (Dominelli, 2002). A key document in this regard was a CCETSW paper (1991), which stated, in the section on 'values in context' for probation practice, that qualifying officers must be able to:

- demonstrate knowledge and understanding of ethical issues and dilemmas, including the potential for conflict between organisational, professional and individual values;
- recognise the need for and seek to promote policies and demonstrate practices which are non-discriminatory and anti-oppressive;
- demonstrate the capacity to manage the tension between the court, the offender, the probation service, the family and the wider community. (CCETSW, 1991, p 39)

Individualised values were not completely abandoned; rather they were stated alongside relational values so that a practitioner had to take account of the full social context of the person they were working with (Worrall, 1992). From other directions, leading probation practitioner-academics pledged a commitment to values such as:

- opposition to custody;
- opposition to oppression and commitment to justice for offenders;
- clients' right to confidentiality – and to openness;
- valuing clients as unique and self-determined individuals;
- victims and potential victims of crime to be protected;
- purposeful professional relationships can facilitate change in clients (Williams, B., 1992).

In what may be seen as an example of one of Foucault's rules of discourse, which make it possible for 'the rules (practices, technologies) which make a certain statement possible to occur and others not at particular times, places and institutional locations' (Foucault, 1989, p 21), Nellis (2001b) advocated that probation sever its link with traditional social work values because changes in management practices, and the demands upon the probation service, made it harder to express probation values. He argued that 'a straightforward reaffirmation of the old values is not a serious option' (ibid, p 34). The debate over the articulation of values for practice became shaped by the view that social work values were simply old hat. In place of social work values, Nellis proposed three key values which he felt were more relevant to post-1991 probation practice:

- anti-custodialism
- restorative justice
- community safety.

Anti-custodialism concerns the diversion of offenders away from custody and has traditionally been one of the aims of probation practice (Williams, B., 1992; Nellis, 1995). Restorative justice is expressed by Nellis as being concerned with victim–offender mediation and neighbourhood dispute settlement schemes (Nellis, 1995). Community safety takes the needs of victims further and addresses the high levels of anxiety community members now experience about crime. This latter value clearly reflects the valorisation of victims that has taken place within the criminal justice system in recent years (Garland, 2001; Tonry, 2004).

Alongside professional institutional and leading commentators, the government also put forward statements intended to contextualise how the probation service should work. Government publications such as the 2001 National Probation Service Vision and Ethical Framework deployed language such as:

- Victim awareness and empathy are central.
- Public protection is paramount, particularly where there are specific known victims of violent and sexually violent crimes.
- Offenders are to be rehabilitated, working positively to achieve their restoration.

Organisational aims were also set out in the document, for example:

- law enforcement, taking positive steps to ensure compliance but where this fails, acting swiftly to instigate breach or recall proceedings; and
- better quality services so that the public receive effective services at the best price. (National Probation Service, 2001, p 8)

In many ways then, professional commentators and the government used similar language and articulated similar values, creating an overarching ethos for practice and illustrating the links between practitioners, policy and politics.

These dominant values did have critics – for example, some argued that anti-custodialism is an aim rather than a value. While it is an aim that is accepted by most practitioners, it still needs to be underpinned by values (Spencer, 1995). Spencer suggested that probation values were 'Rehabilitation, reformation, hope for the individual, care for the person and an understanding that people have the capacity for change and growth' (ibid, pp 344–5). He further argued that despite the success of the probation service in offender mediation schemes, the role of the probation service in administering community sentences did not allow a restorative approach to the task as a whole, making restorative justice unrealistic as a value for the service. Finally, he took issue with community safety as a value for probation, suggesting that it was more appropriately viewed as an organisational strategy, which is properly the role of the police.

This debate around values, aims and language takes place within the clear confines of what is now a managerialised policy framework. On the one hand, while the feasibility of Nellis's value framework could be questioned, the discussion is simultaneously constrained by its implicit acceptance of the changed political climate. The language of anti-oppressive practice, for example, which had attempted to incorporate the claims of oppressed groups, disappeared. In the following section, the evolving climate, and concurrent rise of the discourse of 'punitive managerialism', is be discussed and its impact upon probation practice explored.

The arrival of managerialisation and marketisation language

On gaining power in 1979, the Conservative Party set out to restructure public services based upon its populist ideas of freedom, choice, self-reliance, enterprise, morality and responsibility. It did not turn its attention immediately to the criminal justice system, because another important element in its election victory had been crime and punishment; specifically a 'return to law and order'. Indeed, criminal justice services underwent a period of almost unprecedented growth in the early years of the Conservative administration (McLaughlin and Muncie, 2000). The managerialising and marketising principles the new government used in its radical restructuring of all public services would, in due course, be applied to the probation service. Thus, some of the key ideas are summarised here.

The principles and processes of the market are underpinned by an ideology which is at once anti-statist (the state should have a minimal role in people's lives and in the management of the economy) and anti-welfarist (welfare spending drains resources from the 'real' economy, that is, the private sector, and should therefore be curbed). Marketisation is achieved by treating the public sector as though it is a private sector business. In the early 1980s this was carried out in a number of ways: privatisation of public services; creating purchaser–provider splits in the provision of services; creating competition between public sector providers; promoting 'consumer' choice among public sector service users; and the development of the quasi-governmental organisation which became a conduit for the spending of public money. A transformation in language was one way in which these principles were disseminated and transfused to all parties in the process.

Change in language use is evident across all aspects of former public sector provision, in terms of the users of the services, the providers of the services, and the nature of the service provided. Thus, rail and bus passengers became 'customers'; social services clients became 'service users'; social workers became 'care managers'; and the part of local authorities that provided services directly in competition with the private sector became 'direct service organisations'. 'Pathfinder programmes', 'flagship schemes', 'pilots' and 'projects' all emerged over time.

Managerialisation is the concomitant of marketisation; if a public body is to behave like a private company, then the logic is that it must be managed like one. Managerialisation is the process by which management practices derived from the private sector are applied to the public sector in order to achieve the same objectives at lower cost. Managerialism embodies the knowledge, skills and values of the market. The focus is upon outputs rather than inputs and there exists a strong belief in competition and consumer choice (Dunleavy and Hood, 1994). Within the caring professions, managerialisation is demonstrated in the move away from *personal* casework supervision, characteristic of social work and probation, towards a more corporate style of management concerned with the organisation's external performance.

For most of the twentieth century, crime had not been a topic of general election campaigning by political parties. However, by the late 1980s, the party-political consensus on law and order that existed until the 1979 election campaign had completely evaporated, and crime was a party-political issue, with attendant tendencies towards popularisation and sound-bite politics (Downes and Morgan, 1994). Now, pressure was mounting on government to do something about crime because, despite expansion in all the relevant agencies, and tough talk by the government, crime continued to rise. Official statistics showed increases in almost all categories of crime, and public fear of crime was fuelled by sensationalist media coverage (Young, 1999; McLaughlin and Muncie, 2000). The government needed to turn its attention to criminal justice in order to demonstrate that it could produce criminal justice policy that was both tough and effective.

The *Statement of National Objectives and Priorities* (SNOP) (Home Office, 1984) signalled that it was the turn of the probation service to be exposed to marketising and managerialising principles. There would be a change in the underpinning ethos of practice, away from the needs of clients for a social work service, towards the provision of an effective and efficient service to the courts, which were now seen as the probation service's main users. At the same time there was a move towards a conception of probation as a matter of risk assessment, risk management and effective punishment in the community. Thus risk control and punishment would form the twin axes of a 'punitive managerialism' that would come to characterise probation practice.

A range of policy documents followed SNOP as policy actors and key participants responded to the policy changes. Initially, the Association of Chief Officers of Probation (ACOP), the Central Council of Probation Committees (that is, the employers' organisation, CCPC) and the National Association of Probation Officers (NAPO) tried to reassert some of the traditional aims and values of practice in their shared document *Probation: The Next Five Years* (ACOP et al., 1987). Quickly, however, ACOP produced another paper, *More Demanding than Custody* (ACOP, 1988), which was seen to be vying with the Home Office in the use of more punitive terminology than was used in the government's Green Paper, *Punishment, Custody and the Community* (Home Office, 1988). From the late 1980s on, probation policy eschewed language associated with 'care' and social work values and embraced a discourse associated with the 'logic of justice'. Thus, 'client' became 'offender';

'care' became 'punishment'; 'practitioners' became 'staff'; and the key objective of 'advise, assist and befriend' was marginalised in favour of an approach to probation practice that prioritised 'protection of the public'. This discourse shaped an approach to practice that emphasised process over content and marginalised the relationship between practitioner and client. As noted at the beginning of this chapter, users of the justice system are not easily conceptualised as 'customers'. Hence this rise in use of consumerist language within criminal justice policy can be seen as a *punitive* managerialist discourse.

Punitivism as a new value

The 1991 Criminal Justice Act signalled the government's stated intention to bring the probation service further to centre stage within the criminal justice system as part of the effort to reduce the prison population (Mair, 1997). Only those defendants whose offences were so serious that they required imprisonment would be sent to custody, while others would be dealt with in a series of tough community penalties. A probation order now became a sentence in its own right, rather than being a form of recognisance which replaced a sentence, as previously. The loss of this meaning of 'probation' itself is crucial. In its dictionary definition probation embeds a notion of testing the character or abilities of a person in a certain role. In turn this implies a timescale, a temporary period, and a goal to strive towards; a dynamic system in which someone is moving forward and changing for the better. It is predicated on voluntarism and it infers that an individual has some capacity and commitment to change.

Following the 1991 Act, National Standards were produced that for the first time structured probation practice within a framework that stipulated how often an offender was to be seen and on what basis they should be brought back to court for non-compliance, known as 'breach' (Home Office, 1992). The process of 'breach' was something probation officers had hitherto avoided, as it was seen as an unsuccessful outcome. Although this first set of National Standards defined the nature of probation practice much more closely than the previous injunction to practitioners to 'advise, assist and befriend' the offender, it nevertheless explicitly left room for practitioner discretion:

> The framework of the standards leaves, as it should, much of the application of probation and social services work with offenders to the exercise of skill, imagination, discretion and judgement on the part of individual practitioners and

services; it also provides a consistent basis for developing and promulgating good practice. (Home Office, 1992, p 4)

By 1993, however, a revised criminal justice act repealed some of the more progressive provisions of the 1991 Act, for example, unit fines. These were fines commensurate with the offender's ability to pay as well as the nature of the offence. The professional discretion given to probation officers disappeared bit by bit between the 1992 and 1995 versions of National Standards. Subsequent revisions in 2000, 2002 and 2005 were even more stringent in their requirements and in the language in which it was conveyed. For example, in the preface to the 2000 National Standards, Paul Boateng, then Home Office Minister for Probation, tells practitioners: 'We are a criminal justice agency, it's what we are, it's what we do' (Home Office, 2000, p 1).

One example of the translation of the policy imperative into the shaping of practice is the prominence given to the notion of 'enforcement'. The enforcement of community sentences soon became a key performance indicator for the probation service. In an effort to meet this, service managers curtailed practitioners' discretion further by requiring them to consult their line manager about the acceptability or otherwise of an offender's reason for failure to attend meetings. This 'enforcement of enforcement' serves as a useful metaphor for the punitive-managerialist mode of practice because it is punitive in both intent and in effect; increasing numbers of offenders are sent to prison for failure to comply with community sentences (Solomon, 2005). That is, more and more people become imprisoned due to non-compliance with the managerial regime, rather than due to the committing of offences. 'Enforcement of enforcement' can also be conceived as demonstrative of the *masculinisation* of service provision because it is a rational rather than relational approach to individuals.

Punitive managerialism into the new millenium

The 1998 Disorder Act was proposed as 'the most co-ordinated and coherent attack on crime in a generation' (Straw, 1999). The cornerstone of Labour government criminal justice policy demonstrated its commitment to the continuation of, rather than departure from, the processes of punitive managerialism. Key aspects included:

• consistent and mutually reinforcing aims and objectives;
• enhanced use of existing resources ('best value');

- evidence-based approach to crime reduction which embed a 'what works' occupational/professional culture;
- modernisation of the structure and operation of criminal justice agencies;
- improved performance management. (McLaughlin and Muncie, 2000, p 174)

In the face of overwhelming crime figures, official research has turned away from the social or psychological causes of crime, and towards research about crime prevention, limiting situations and opportunities in which crimes can occur. The underpinning assumption here is that crime is a normal social fact and that people will tend to commit crimes unless prevented from doing so. A 'new penology' has developed whose task is managerial not transformative. It incorporates ideas from environmental criminology – limiting the opportunity for crime, and from what has been called 'actuarial criminology', which is about the identification and management of risky populations (Feeley and Simon, 1992). Within this formulation, the probation practitioner's job is to focus upon the assessment of risk, the enforcement of legal sanctions, the challenging of offending behaviour, and case management (Goodman, 2003). Kemshall suggests that the assessment of risk is now the core business of the probation service 'supplanting ideologies of need, welfare or indeed rehabilitation' (Kemshall, 1998, p 1). Information gathering is carried out using increasingly structured and prescribed tools and pro formas, and the influence of professional judgement is restricted. 'Enforcement' has become a goal in its own right. Failures of probation or parole ironically become a kind of success, in that they indicate system efficiency (Feeley and Simon, 1992).

How did a profession that had a tradition of creating innovative ways of working and campaigning for support for the oppressed groups they worked with, come to be turned into a group of punitive case managers? The answer to this is complex. Garland (2000) suggests that appreciating the global and national political context helps us to understand why penal-welfare professionals have failed to protest strongly against the harsher regimes that they now help to administer. Their status as baby boomers – the first generation to enjoy the benefits of the welfare state – their middle-class education with its liberal, rehabilitationist stance towards crime, and their ability to live in relatively crime-free neighbourhoods, enabled them to distance themselves from crime and criminals and thereby adopt a 'civilised' approach to it. Garland provides us with the wider policy context, but attention to language use shows that more active steps have been taken by the government in its transformation of probation practice. It is not only the legislative context and the structure of the work that has changed, but the underpinning values and their explicit articulation in market language. In the process of managerialisation, *active* control is exerted over the acceptable knowledge base for practice, the training of practitioners, and the values that are deemed acceptable for practice. All of this is encompassed within a political discourse that renders opposing ideas as outdated and irrelevant.

The rise of cognitive behavioural methodology

As indicated above, concurrent with political/policy changes is a shift in the forms of knowledge that are valued as informing practice. Lupton (1992) noted how managerialisation led to a requirement for policy-focused knowledge that is then used to justify policy objectives. This approach prioritises rationalist perspectives to knowledge production and research evaluation, in opposition to the relational approaches favoured by many researchers, in particular, those who support bottom-up research involving service users and those who occupy an explicitly political stance, such as feminists (ibid). The narrowing of interest to quantitative and empiricist forms of evidence has led to an implicit value base which embodies a technical-rationalist approach to practice in which scientifically tested forms of intervention can be applied in a 'value free' way to systematically identified service users. In this way, only certain forms of practice are considered legitimate, and in the probation service this is an adherence to an overwhelmingly cognitive behavioural model of intervention. The move in probation practice from 'what works?' as a genuine question about what actually helps someone to move away from offending, towards 'what works' as a shorthand term for a prescribed mode of practice, is a case in point (Webb, 2001).

Martinson's (1974) challenge to the rehabilitative ideal in community corrections, though attributed with the view that nothing works, did not literally suggest that *nothing* works, rather that some things work less well than others, and that some things work better with certain groups of participants. However, the nothing works view that Martinson's article seemed to generate did undermine confidence in probation practice. In response to Martinson's challenge, the research community began the search for correctional programmes that could be shown to work. Mair (2004) documents the development, in Canada, of cognitive behavioural treatment programmes, coupled with evaluative research that claimed to demonstrate their effectiveness in reducing reoffending. A concomitant development was the use of meta–analysis as a research technique; comparing data from large collections of previous studies to establish a statistically significant claim that one kind of treatment was more effective than others. This, it was confidently asserted, was cognitive behavioural treatment (McGuire and Priestly, 1995). Cognitive behavioural packages were then marketed with an entrepreneurial zeal never previously witnessed within UK criminal justice. Bearing in mind that most practitioners were provided with this information via uncritical 'effectiveness' training events, conferences or workshops prior to being asked to implement a particular programme already purchased by their service, it is unsurprising that many accepted the idea of a 'proven' effective treatment package. 'What works' was no longer a question, but, as Mair notes, had become more akin to an orthodoxy (Mair, 2004).

Hard evidence of the efficacy of accredited programmes instituted on the basis of these claims remains elusive, and ambitious targets for putting offenders through cognitive behavioural schemes have been halved (Gorman, 2001; Gorman et al., 2006). However, probation practice now overwhelmingly employs cognitive behavioural programmes that have been centrally accredited as meeting the effectiveness criteria laid down by the Home Office.

The wholesale adoption of cognitive behavioural methodology has had a number of effects. It gives management firm control over practitioners and, in what is already a highly structured environment, acts to limit discretion still further. It has also ruled out many of the practitioner-led programmes developed in the 1980s that were influenced by critical practice. This seems in direct contradiction to the rise of the 'user involvement' paradigm discussed in Chapter Nine.

Perhaps of most concern, it has meant that probation practice is now informed by research using meta-analysis of studies of correctional populations of young white males, and not necessarily based in the UK. The authors reporting on this work frequently omit to discuss, or identify, the gender of their subjects. Difficulties of applying white male-oriented programmes to women and ethnic minorities have been seen as resolvable by making minor adjustments to the programme content (Gorman, 2001). This appears to be a backward step for probation practice which had hitherto been influenced by critical research about race and gender (Shaw and Hannah-Moffatt, 2004). In this way, we again see how politics and practice are interwoven in ways that are not often exposed by policy analysis.

Political futures

In 1998 the document, *Joining Forces to Protect the Public: Prisons–Probation* (Home Office, 1998) set out the then government's intention to move the probation service further towards a punishing rather than a rehabilitative agency. Direct reference to the change in language that was needed to accomplish this objective was clear:

> It is important that the names, language and terminology used by the services should give accurate and accessible messages about the nature and aims of their work. Some of the terms used have been criticised, for example because:
>
> • they are associated with tolerance of crime (e.g. 'probation' which can be seen as a conditional reprieve), or
> • they can be misunderstood (e.g. 'community service' which sounds like voluntary activity), or
> • they are too esoteric to be understood outside the two services (e.g. 'throughcare' which sounds more associated with the 'caring' services). (Home Office, 1998, para 2.12)

The same paper went on to consider renaming the whole service. It narrowly missed being renamed the 'Community Punishment and Rehabilitation Service' (which was soon colloquially known by the corrupted acronym 'CRAPS' among probation personnel) and became instead the 'National Probation Service' (NPS) in 2001. The renaming was then followed by restructuring, with the creation of the National Offender Management Service (NOMS) in 2004. This brought the NPS and the Prison Service into one regime. NOMS is thus intended to give 'end-to-end offender management' whether the offender is in custody or in the community.

Value futures

It has been argued that probation work is taking place in an increasingly punitive environment, and yet it remains fundamentally a practice that takes place through a relationship between one human being and another. It involves people meeting up, talking, identifying and dealing with the issues and problems in offenders' lives that contribute to their offending. The issue of values – how any professional worker should treat those with whom they work – remains pertinent and wider discussion on this matter continues. How these values become expressed in language also requires ongoing analysis. For example, the advent of a 'rights discourse' and the idea of 'constructive practice' could provide alternate languages within which probation and other policy services could articulate their values and subsequently operate. There is always the possibility that languages developed outside institutional political circles can influence the policy world (see Hodgson and Irving, Chapter Eleven, this volume).

The 1998 Human Rights Act has been put forward by several commentators as the basis of a positive approach to the kind of values that could underpin a humane and just form of probation practice within current society. It brings a different kind of politics into play. Hudson (2001, p 111) links this firmly to offenders' rights and responsibilities as citizens and suggests that probation is 'crucially and definitially involved with offenders' rights'. However, she also notes the effect of the Human Rights Act on probation practice with regard to members of the community who might seek redress against the service for wrongs they feel they have suffered from offenders and that the service has not protected them from. This highlights a tension inherent in a legislative approach to rights, as competing rights have to be managed. Hudson goes on to point out that this can lead to a zero-sum approach: when asked about young people's right not to be filmed by CCTV cameras as they go about their daily lives, the answer is returned that the right of law-abiding citizens to be free of the fear of crime takes priority. This she feels is a rights conflict that punishment and crime prevention cannot escape. Other commentators have acknowledged that the Human Rights Act is not in itself sufficient to infuse the kind of value base into professional practice that ensures every individual is treated with respect (Nellis and Gelsthorpe, 2003). Ignatieff summarises this by suggesting that human rights are something 'on the outermost arc of our obligations', but are only 'as strong as our innermost commitments' (2000, p 40). However, the rights approach continues to position service practice within a punitive-managerialist framework, rather than as a form of social work practice.

In 2005, Nellis reaffirmed his commitment to the three values he put forward in 1995, anti-custodialism, community safety and restorative justice. He suggested to his audience that they had to consider that in defending their value base, they needed to recognise the modernisation of the service and the mood of contemporary Britain. They should be prepared to '*change their vocabulary* so that it is attuned to public moods and intellectual currents, and *develop a language* that allows you to participate – never sound willfully or inadvertently old-fashioned or nostalgic' (Nellis, 2005, p 5). Yet just a few months earlier, the Probation Boards Association published findings from a survey of public bodies of whom they had asked: 'What values should be at the heart of a service that deals with offenders in today's society?' The key words put forward by thirty-two of the organisations surveyed included many of the traditional social work values, as the following list demonstrates: belief, care, citizenship, confidence, fairness, empowerment, anti-discriminatory practice, openness, dignity, humanity, inclusion, integrity, understanding, justice, accountability, optimism, proportionality, reform, respect, self-worth, decency, tolerance, sympathy, trust and empathy. It would appear that 'traditional' values continue to have currency and that there is incongruence between these and the punitive managerialism that characterises the government's contemporary approach to criminal justice.

It has been suggested that 'constructive practice' is a further way forward that draws on the UK government's wider citizenship agenda (Gorman et al., 2006). The meaning of 'constructive practice' would encompass its link to the theoretical perspectives of social construction as well as the common understanding of construction as in building, or putting together. In so doing, it acknowledges the findings of Barry (2000, 2006) and Howe (1993) that recipients of social work service interventions value the dialogue that takes place between themselves and their social worker, especially when they feel they have genuinely been heard. A constructive approach would also seek to help them towards a position where they can take part in the rebuilding of their communities, as active citizens. The literature on citizenship widely acknowledges that citizenship implies equality, and active citizenship requires social inclusion; therefore the basis of that rebuilding has to be access to the social capital needed to achieve social inclusion (Dwyer, 2004; Faulkner, D., 2004). Constructive practice recognises how a dominant discourse creates the 'othering' of offenders, and seeks to work in ways which challenge and resist these processes (Dominelli, 2006). It prioritises the value of the relationship as the basis of the work between the helper and the person being helped, and recognises that between them, in conversation, they construct the meaning of the encounter. Therefore, the solution to a person's difficulties are always with them, and the worker's task is to help the person to uncover those solutions (Parton and O'Byrne, 2000). This language of construction could be developed to provide an approach to policy and practice that encompasses both the needs and rights of offender and victim.

Aristotle provides us with two concepts that would aid this development. He used the concept of *eudaimonia* – translated as 'flourishing' – which relates to the ability of individuals to behave well in a social situation and enjoy a fully rounded humanity. In order to understand whether an individual had achieved *eudaimonia*, Aristotle believed that they had to be considered in relation to others, in keeping with the social work values, and not in the rational and abstract manner favoured by the punitive-managerialist approach (Pakaluk, 2005). Aristotle's concept of *phronesis* may also be relevant. He was against moral knowledge being codified into abstract rules that could be applied to any given situation. *Phronesis* is the term he used for the practical wisdom he felt was needed for individuals to act well, because in so doing they were required to reconcile what was deemed to be good behaviour with the particular context in which they were acting. This concern for the reconciliation of particular needs with particular situations is shared by the more relational, anti-oppressive social work values and, in a more general way, by social work practitioners from all the different strands of practice as well as probation workers. More broadly, it provides valuable lessons when reconsidering the links between politics and policy.

Probation practice (whether it is called social work or corrections) is a practice that continues to straddle the space between punishment and care. How we care and how we punish are both practices that have a great deal to say about society (Hudson, 1987; Tronto, 1993). In turn, the debate about probation values and the underpinning politics presented here, demonstrates how language is central in shaping 'policy politics' and in influencing practice.

SIX

Business, power, policy and politics

Kevin Farnsworth

This chapter examines the relationship between business and policy making. It outlines and explores, theoretically and empirically, the mechanisms of business power and influence over policy making. Here the term *business* refers to private profit-making institutions (firms) and the class of people that own or manage those institutions. The first half of the chapter theorises business power and influence. It argues that both are variable forces in politics. The second half examines changing business engagement, power and influence in the context of British policy making since the 1980s. This period has witnessed a great many policy transformations – a clouding of the boundaries between the public and private sectors, changing business–government relations, fluctuating economic fortunes and economic restructuring. These transformations, the chapter concludes, fail to make sense unless we consider the role of business in British politics over this period.

Business power and the policy process: from plural to privileged interests

The issue of the importance of business power to policy outcomes has divided the main theoretical traditions in policy analysis; most markedly classical pluralism – which suggests that power is diffuse and that political actors operate on equal, or potentially equal, terms – and elite and Marxist writings – which maintain that business is a privileged interest capable of accessing policy making and exercising power in ways not open to other groups. These divisions gave way to a loose consensus from the 1970s, however (see Dunleavy and O'Leary, 1987, ch 7; Marsh, 1995), as even the high priests of classical pluralism, Robert Dahl and Charles Lindblom, came to argue, business is a privileged interest in capitalist democracies:

> In our discussion of pluralism we made [an] error – and it is a continuing error in social science – in regarding businessmen and business groups as playing the same interest-group role as other groups ... [C]ommon interpretations that depict the American or any other market-orientated system as a competition among interest groups are seriously in error for their failure to take account of the distinctive privileged position of businessmen in politics. (Dahl and Lindblom, 1976, p xxxvi)

The biggest shift made by pluralists, in accepting the privileged interest thesis, was their recognition of the importance of structural power to business influence on policy outcomes. Structural power (the power to influence without taking direct action) is derived from the ownership and control of capital and the uneven dependence of states and employees on capitalists. Agency power, upon which most analysis of business power tends to focus, is exercised through the actions of individual business people, firms or business associations (which themselves organise at different levels). The problem with focusing purely on agency, as classical pluralists found, is that it underplays the importance of political and economic structures, which favour some interests above others, determine the nature and extent of agency engagement and shape the expressed views and opinions of actors. The mechanisms through which structure and agency are realised by business are discussed below.

The structural power of business

Structural theory is concerned with indirect influence – the ability of business to shape policy without having to place direct pressure on the state through agency. Rather, political and economic structures restrict the policy options available to governments to those that are favourable to business in one way or another. The following sections distinguish between two forms of structural power: investment-related power and ideological power.

The primary source of business' structural power is its monopoly control over existing and future private investments. Its investment decisions have long-lasting and far-reaching consequences, impacting on future production, employment and consumption. Governments are dependent, for their own revenues, on taxes levied on business activities and employees ordinarily depend for their own survival on their wages. However, as Przeworski and Wallerstein (1988, p 12) and

Lindblom (1977) explain, a firm's investment decisions are privately made in the interests of future profitability. Governments and employees can try to induce companies to invest, but they cannot compel them. And it is because of this dependence on future private investment and profitability, over which they have no control, that governments and employees ultimately have to prioritise the wishes and demands of private firms. The pursuit of any personal or 'national' gain must therefore take into account the impact that such pursuits have on the future investments and profitability of firms. Thus, whatever the complexion and programme of the government in power it cannot pursue policies that threaten capital accumulation (Offe and Ronge, 1982, p 137). To do so would risk undermining both the revenues of the state and the household sector and even the future electoral success of the party in power (Lindblom, 1977). For their part, employees must ensure that the pursuit of their interests does not undermine the continued profitability and accumulation of capital, and ultimately the effective and efficient exploitation of labour, by their employers. Thus, business interests are often considered to be synonymous with national interests (Offe and Wiesenthal, 1980, p 180; Korpi, 1983) and whether it chooses to act or not, business has a real impact on the behaviour and decisions of policy makers and trade unionists.

The other form of structural power lies in the ideological domain. A group may exercise ideological hegemony if its interests can be legitimised as the 'common interest'. Because of the foregoing arguments, this is precisely the position that business is in. The dependence of society and state on capital profitability and accumulation acts as a gravitational tug on the 'volitions' of the population, according to both Lindblom (1977) and the dominant ideology thesis within Marxist theory. The dominant *hegemon* reinforces the notion that most social and economic activities depend on the freedom of private enterprises to pursue and maximise profits. The state, for those reasons outlined above, plays a key role in reinforcing a pro-business ideology, which serves to further increase the power of business by preventing or neutralising opposition to it (a discussion of this process can be found in Miliband, 1969, p 165 and in Poulantzas, 1973, pp 58–60). The implication here, then, is that business or capitalist power translates into ideological power, and this helps to shape values and interests within capitalist societies including those of labour and the state.

Viewed in this way, the reproduction of ideas is part of the political struggle between capital and its opponents, which takes place through agency, and this emphasises the important connections between these two forms of power. Through agency, business contributes to the development of ideas while structural mechanisms constrain national debates on plausible alternatives to business-centred politics; dominant ideology renders pro-business policies normal and others deviant (Block, 1990, p 306). If this is an accurate picture, it is likely to have real implications for the political engagement of rational actors. Organised labour is unlikely to pursue what it considers to be unrealistic aims given the dominant ideological and political context at any one time and business need not utilise its own resources in order to steer policy agendas that are institutionally biased towards it.

Political and economic structures, then, define the context for action. Whether and how various agents act within the political arena, and the scope they have to influence policy making, is influenced by the signals that such structures emit. These signals are read by business and other actors. It is to business agency, and its political engagement in policy processes, that we now turn.

Business agency power

Two key forms of agency power are commonly identified in the literature. First, business is able to exert influence through its political lobbying activities. Individual firms or business associations apply political pressure on policy makers or, alternatively, employ one of a growing number of professional lobby organisations to do so on their behalf (see Jordan, 1991). Such is the size and importance of many firms and business organisations that they are seldom denied an audience with even the most senior politicians (Offe and Wiesenthal, 1980; Bonnett, 1985, p 96). Moreover, it is common for business people and business organisations to be co-opted into formal decision-making networks by policy makers (Useem, 1990; Rhodes and Marsh, 1992). Policy networks are important both to business actors, keen to promote a pro-business perspective, and to policy makers, keen to get an insight into the views of this most powerful group in society. Accordingly, the most important business actors and representatives of the largest companies are often involved in several networks and are consulted regularly by policy makers for their expertise or insight (Smith, 1993, p 61).

Networks also have an indirect impact on policy makers since they foster intra-class homogeneity. Such processes are especially important, according to Miliband (1973) and Scott (1991), to the formation of a common 'capitalist' class position within government and the wider state. For both authors, the promotion of class and other elite alliances through such networks is the most important factor to understanding the dominance of business perspectives within the state.

The second mechanism of business agency power is achieved through its command over resources. Business is able to use its access to financial resources to fund business-centred interest groups, boost the electoral standing of sympathetic political parties and gain access to politicians (Fisher, 1994, p 699). Political donations made by firms have been used in the past to help prevent the election of unsympathetic political parties, most notably the Labour Party in the UK, although the more business-friendly party that emerged under Tony Blair's leadership has succeeded in attracting increasingly large amounts of corporate sponsorship (Osler, 2002). This is testimony both to how comfortable business is with New Labour and how business donations can be used to reward political parties as well as nurture close relationships with parties in power.

Business' funding of think tanks has also gone a long way to establishing and promoting sympathetic public and political opinion. The Institute for Economic Affairs and the Centre for Policy Studies, for example, were particularly important in propagating Thatcherite ideas (Desai, 1994, pp 28–9). Leys (1989) found that donations to 'union breaking' organisations such as the Economic League, Common Cause and United British Industrialists, which specialised in infiltrating and destabilising unions over the 1980s, were equally important strategies aimed at weakening the Left during this time. For New Labour, the Institute of Public Policy Research (IPPR) has been especially influential in promoting Third Way ideas.

These, then, are the various mechanisms through which business is able to influence policy making in theory. As the following section illustrates however, in practice, power and its application are seldom uniform and straightforward.

The variability of business power

Business is clearly an important and powerful interest in capitalist democracies, yet business demands are not always met, and capitalist states appear to succeed with widely variable state–business relations (Pierson, 1995, p 9). In any analysis of the impact of business on policy makers it is important not to exaggerate the omnipotence of business or the impotence of the state. Several factors help to keep business power in check. First, business power, especially agency power, is dependent on the level of policy agreement and coherence between divergent parts of the business community and its ability to organise collectively. Yet on many issues, a clear, coherent, unified business view fails to emerge. Cleavages exist between sectors, notably between manufacturing and finance, between organisations of different sizes, for example large versus small business, and between firms within different nation bases (Mann, 1993). Without coherence and unity, the capacity for business to organise together is reduced and the potential for the state, or any other institution, to act in the interests of business as a whole is diminished.

Second, the nature and operation of the state is important to the realisation of business power. State-centred theory maintains that it is wrong to reduce the state to economic or other class interests; the interests and goals of state actors themselves are important determinants of policy outcomes (Skocpol, 1985). According to Skocpol, it is wrong to reduce the state simply to dominant class interests and negate the role and importance of state actors themselves, primarily politicians (Skocpol, 1979). While state actors may be constrained by certain imperatives to create the right economic conditions, institutional factors, such as large departmental budgets and previous policy promises, may afford policy makers a level of autonomy (Block, 1977, pp 22, 24). In such circumstances, policy may well go against the interests of business.

Third, the activities and relative power of rival interests, particularly the labour movement, are important. Non-governmental organisations (NGOs) and the wider labour movement are capable of offsetting and challenging the power and dominance of business. Similar factors to the ones that bind self-interested politicians to favouring business interests, also encourage politicians to steer policy towards the interests of their particular constituencies. Hence, over time, through the democratic process, rival interests have been able to extract favourable policy outcomes that do not directly serve the interests of business; especially in the sphere of social policy and employment regulations (Korpi, 1989; Esping-Andersen, 1990, p 16) and governments have been able to follow distinct pathways in managing capitalism (Esping-Andersen, 1990; Hall and Soskice, 2001).

The labour movement is also able to challenge the domination of capital in an alternative and, some would argue, more effective way, through collective organisation and direct political action. Strikes, demonstrations and workplace disruptions can all be used, and have been used effectively, in order to obtain concessions from individual capitalists, and the capitalist class more generally. Whether these concessions are in the form of welfare reform, or greater employment rights, they can then be used in order to further the interests of the labour movement (Piven and Cloward, 1979; Jenkins and Brents, 1989, p 896). It is also the case, however, that past victories tend to be reversed once agitation and unrest subsides, which again illustrates the way that policies naturally swing towards the interests of business (Piven and Cloward, 1979, ch 5).

Fourth, since one of the most important mechanisms of business's structural power is control over investment, it follows that the extent of this power will relate directly to its mobility and possibilities for exit. Put another way, the extent to which capital is able to apply pressure on the state is largely dependent on how genuinely mobile capital is. If capital is immobile, then the threat of exit is reduced or even removed. A number of factors can affect the mobility of capital: it is clearly easier for capital to shift investment within rather than between states; larger firms may find it easier to shift investment than smaller ones; and mobility is reduced or eliminated where access to materials or markets is geographically tied to a particular location, for example, in the extraction and service industries. The following sections assess how the above factors have shaped the political fortunes of British business since the 1980s.

Business and British politics

As elsewhere, the policy fortunes of British business have waxed and waned over time with political and economic changes. The relative importance of agency and structure to policy outcomes has also varied over time.

Structural dimensions

The ability of most countries to control financial capital has become extremely weakened under globalisation, but the UK is especially distinguished in this regard by a decisive move towards opening its economy and deregulating capital controls since 1980 (see Farnsworth and Gough, 2000; Farnsworth, 2004). The UK has one of the highest levels of inward and outward Foreign Direct Investment (FDI) rates, as a percentage of Gross Domestic Product (GDP), among OECD countries. In 2000, for instance, the UK's outward FDI was almost double the rate of the next highest country, Canada (UNCTAD, 2002, B6). The UK is also relatively highly exposed to transnational industry, as foreign manufacturers now account for more than 30 per cent of total production in the UK, which is higher than for most of its competitors (Coppel and Durand, 1999, Table 6). This, together with the fact that the UK has historically had relatively low absolute levels of domestic business investment (Gamble, 1990; Bond and Jenkinson, 1996), creates disproportionate dependency on mobile capital. In the

UK, successive governments, particularly since the 1970s, have placed a great deal of store on the importance of maintaining high levels of foreign investments, partly to make up for failing domestic industry and historically low levels of indigenous investment, where this competition has been based primarily on cost factors. Central to this strategy has been the view that the more policy is geared towards the needs of employers and the economy, the higher national income will be, and the lower will be unemployment and its associated problems. Thus consecutive governments have sought to introduce policies that encourage greater levels of inward investment that are geared towards the maintenance of indigenous investment. Competing for investment with other EU countries has been a key feature of policy making in the 1980s and 1990s – facilitated by the free movement of capital within Europe, but a relatively weak state at the federal level. Faced with these types of pressures, the UK has endeavoured to 'sell' itself as a country with low labour regulations, low taxation, low wage costs and low social costs, facilitated by a significant weakening of trade unions. The 1982 Green Paper *Corporation Tax* stated that:

> The UK system of company taxation must be capable of application to multinational concerns, overseas shareholders and so on. It must also command a degree of acceptance from the international community ... Any major change in the level or incidence of tax on company profits would affect the balance of advantage between the United Kingdom and other countries. (HMSO, 1982)

Later, in 1993, the British government placed an advertisement in the German business press that encouraged firms to take advantage of:

> Lower wage costs in Great Britain ... [where] wages and social charges are significantly lower. [T]he labour costs index for Britain is 100 compared to 178 for Germany. (Cited in IDS, 1993, p 8)

The following speech by Tim Eggar, Minister for Energy and Industry in 1994, reiterated the message:

> Today, the United Kingdom attracts more FDI than any other country in Europe ... We have a pro-business environment that is unequalled in Europe. Commitment to deregulation has played a major role in securing the

level of inward investment ... We have no foreign exchange controls, nor restrictions on spending profits abroad. We have a transport infrastructure that provides fast and easy access to the rest of Europe ... the English language ... [and] the best available combination of a skilled and flexible workforce, with lower production costs than our neighbours. By coming to Britain, inward investors get access to the single European market *without the costs of the Social Chapter* ... UK non-wage labour costs are below those of nearly all other European Union countries ... Inward investors also know that they can negotiate single and non-union agreements with an adaptable workforce that is ready to learn new skills and willing to work flexible hours ... The UK strike rate has been below the EU average for each of the last nine years. (Eggar, 1994)

Despite the fact that the Labour government has subsequently signed up to the Social Chapter, introduced a national minimum wage and made the joining of trade unions easier, they have not seriously altered the general sales 'pitch' used to sell the UK to foreign investors. The Labour government has tried to assure business that, taken together, its labour market, taxation and social policies continue to make the UK a better place to invest. The Labour's Party's *2001 Business Manifesto* spelled out the government's thinking on the central role that tax competition continues to play in UK strategies to attract inward investment:

The taxation system is one aspect of a country's environment of relevance to inward investors and others. We have created a tax framework which encourages investment and enterprise by reducing the rate of corporation tax, making capital gains tax more pro-enterprise, introducing incentives for R&D and making permanent the capital allowances available to small firms. Taken overall, UK business taxation levels, including employers' social security contributions and corporation tax, are competitive with the rest of the European Union. This is a situation we intend to maintain. ... We will continue to make the case for fair tax competition, not tax harmonization. (Labour Party, 2001, p 7)

Today, almost all countries have resources devoted to encouraging inward investment, and the UK has led the way in this regard. UK Trade and Investment (UKTI) exists to 'sell' the UK to foreign investors and increase investment opportunities abroad for British companies. Its sales pitch illustrates clearly how successive governments have responded to the growing structural pressures that have accompanied globalisation. In 2007, UKTI explained to potential investors that:

> The United Kingdom is the most favoured inward investment location in Europe, attracting around 40 per cent of Japanese, US and Asian investment into the EU. [I]t has a great deal to offer overseas companies. Fast, easy access to the EU single market (the world's largest market with 380 million consumers), a highly skilled, flexible, English-speaking workforce, and an environment which allows business to prosper ... The UK has 28 million skilled and adaptable workers, and high standards of education with a strong emphasis on vocational education and training. Labour market regulations in the UK, including working hours, are the most flexible in Europe, and staffing costs are highly competitive ... It has the lowest utilities costs in the European Union ... one of the lowest main corporation rates of the world's major economies, and there are no additional taxes on profits. (UKTI, 2007)

Thus, successive British governments since the late 1970s have responded to structural pressures by lowering corporate taxation and deregulating labour in order to compete for inward investment. Neither would it have been possible for any incoming government to drastically shift away from this. Any change to the UK's industrial strategy in the short to medium term would have proved very difficult. As Rhodes puts it:

> Low corporation taxes and social charges are vital, not just for sustaining Britain's FDI dependent manufacturing sector, but also for meeting the demands of the large low-wage, low-skill, low-productivity sector of the economy. (Rhodes, 2000, p 21)

At the same time, competing in this way has amplified structural power, as dependence on those forms of capital that are attracted by low-cost, flexible labour and low taxation increases, forces governments to constantly review their fiscal and regulatory competitiveness. KPMG, in its 2003 survey of corporate taxation, for example, stated that:

> Whilst the figures show that the UK's corporate tax rate
> is at a respectable 30, this is only just below the EU and
> OECD average rate. And with increasing competition from
> countries such as the Netherlands, Belgium and Ireland ...
> there is no room for complacency. (KPMG, 2003)

Such reductions in corporate taxation do not benefit all businesses, of course, and some companies may even suffer as a result of such policies. For instance, indigenous firms may face tax increases in other forms besides taxes on profits in order to make up for lost revenue from taxes on profits and, by contrast, some firms may benefit from more extensive public provision. Some commentators have suggested that this fact weakens the argument that states act in the interests of business under the conditions of globalisation (Yeates, 1999). It is probably more accurate to argue, however, that governments can and do react to structural and agency pressures under globalisation but they do so in different ways at different times. Moreover, the ways in which they act and react to corporate power impacts on subsequent levels of corporate power. Responding positively to structural pressures will often serve to reinforce and amplify structural power in future. To be clear, the more that states react to structural power – willingly or otherwise – the more likely they are to experience and have to respond to structural power in the future. As Cerny (1997) points out, those states which deregulate their economies in response to global pressures, will find it very difficult to re-regulate them.

This is something that is often forgotten by those who stress the freedom and autonomy of states to resist globalisation and corporate power. In the British case, given the UK's high level of dependence on foreign investment, and given that the strategy to try to attract and retain mobile capital continues unabated, it is clear that it would experience far greater structural pressure from any future attempts to regulate labour or increase taxation on employers than Germany or even France. While many commentators stress the fact that states still have choices under globalisation, it is probably more accurate to say that some states have more flexibility and more policy options than others.

Under these conditions, we would expect to see an expansion in those parts of public policy that contribute most to profitability and competitiveness – education, training, public transport infrastructure, and so on – along with the simultaneous withdrawal of those services which undermine, or at least do not promote, private markets, and this is precisely what has happened in the UK (Cerny, 1997; Farnsworth,

2004). Rather than forcing spending cuts, therefore, increased structural power steers public spending towards provision that promotes the interests of business. These changes are not inevitable; the greater the dependence of a state on mobile capital, the more likely it will be forced to compete for mobile capital by introducing these types of reforms. However, the extent to which a state is dependent on mobile capital is also an outcome of past decisions and power struggles played out between labour, state agents and organised business.

If a future government wanted to try to resist corporate structural power in the UK, therefore, it would first have to transform the British economy to one which is less dependent on mobile capital, low labour costs and regulation. Companies attracted to the UK because of low-cost labour might reduce investments if the government tried to impose greater regulations or higher taxation. Radical changes would, therefore, take a huge amount of political determination, though quite how much would depend on other countervailing forces to business, including the organisation and determination of labour. At the time of writing, however, the government appears to be going in the opposite direction – reinforcing rather than challenging corporate structural power. Even where policies have been introduced that are opposed by business, New Labour have gone out of their way to stress the cost advantages enjoyed by employers based in the UK. In a speech to the CBI in 1998, Blair appealed to business to see the bigger picture:

> Even where you may have doubts about certain parts of policy – a minimum wage or trade union representation – remember: that we are consulting business every step of the way; and that taken altogether, the entire changes proposed would still leave us with a labour market considerably less regulated than that of the USA. (Tony Blair, speech to the CBI Conference, 14 April 1998)

Structural pressures have been enough to persuade Labour of the need to maintain high levels of investment in the UK. However, Labour has also sought to set in place a good dialogue with British business since 1997. The last section of this chapter considers changing business agency in the UK since the 1980s.

Agency dimensions

As already indicated, the potency of agency power is determined by institutional factors, primarily business access to the policy arena, as well as the willingness of governments to grant such access to business. The position of UK policy makers towards business lobbies has been uneven: both Labour and Conservative governments prior to 1979 bemoaned the fact that British business was divided and difficult to engage with. For this reason, the Labour governments of the 1960s and 1970s put in place various measures to establish European corporatist-style measures, where the representatives of employers, employees and government would regularly come together to form opinions and reach agreements on a range of relevant issues. Moreover, both Labour and Conservative governments tried to establish a stronger, or at least more coherent, national voice for business; the former, in the 1960s, encouraged the establishment of the Confederation of British Industry (CBI), the UK's only real peak level business organisation, and the latter helped to set up the Devlin Commission in 1971, which pushed for a new Confederation of British Business, although this never came to fruition. Both governments were frustrated by their inability to obtain good data on business activities and the absence of a clear, unified business voice that could negotiate on behalf of all employers.

The post-1979 Conservative government approached British business and the economy in quite a different way. They felt that strong representatives of industrial capital would weaken their plans to transform the British economy and that the type of cosy exchange fostered by Labour with industrialists was actually undermining the economy by protecting old-fashioned and inefficient firms. As a result, the Thatcher government was more selective about which business voices they were prepared to listen to. The early Thatcher government in particular tended to favour financial above industrial interests and the interests of sympathetic entrepreneurs above organised interests. As a result, the CBI, the UK's largest employers' association, which tended to be critical of Conservative economic policy, was excluded from the national policy arena during the early 1980s in favour of the more sympathetic Institute of Directors (IoD) (Grant and Marsh, 1977), and actually consulted less after the election of the Conservatives in 1979 than it had been under the previous Labour administration (Grant, 1993). The relative cost to the CBI of exercising its voice at the national level became apparent early on, forcing the organisation to examine new ways to more effectively concentrate its resources on influencing government. One solution was to place greater emphasis on mechanisms of business influence that were relatively inexpensive (Farnsworth, 1998). It sought to improve its lobbying techniques through the production of clear and concise policy statements and made more efforts to communicate the view of business direct to the general public through the greater use of press releases and by staging its high-profile annual conferences. It also sought to make use of newly introduced government measures designed to better integrate business representatives into local decision making. The 1970s' Labour government placed pressure on schools to consult with business people, and a raft of measures, most importantly those introduced by the 1984 Rates Act, required local authorities to consult with local business people before setting taxation rates. Later, in a whole range of areas from local planning to educational provision, services would be forced to incorporate business interests into their decision-making structures so that provision more closely reflected the needs of business. From the early 1980s, the CBI encouraged the creation of such openings for consultation and partnership with business, and sought to encourage its members to make better use of these opportunities in order to push local business views. In contrast to the national situation, such changes reduced the relative cost of exercising agency at the local level.

For the Conservative government, business engagement in this way formed a crucial element of their managerialist revolution, which sought to inject into state management cultures a firm dose of private sector discipline (Clarke and Newman, 1997; Cutler and Waine, 2000). This revolution involved the removal of elected representatives from local services and their replacement with business people and, as a result, the private sector came to assume greater responsibility and leadership roles in areas previously monopolised by local authority representatives such as education, housing, care services and transport (Oatley, 1998). Senior business people were guaranteed, by statute, a majority presence within the Training and Enterprise Councils (TECs), for example. In other areas, most notably public health bodies and state schools, the government replaced local government representation with business people and other 'stakeholders', and replaced locally administered financing with direct central government grants, backed up with increasingly large amounts of private funding. By the time Labour came to power in 1997, therefore, business needs were already shaping public policy outcomes and business people had been well integrated into key services. The Labour government enthusiastically built upon Conservative policies by seeking to further embed business people, firms and values still further into public services. It has since created the opportunities for the increasingly formal engagement of business people and companies into state bodies, including regional development agencies, schools and hospitals.

Under New Labour the voice of business has grown still stronger. Business has been consulted more frequently and co-opted into various decision-making bodies in a deliberate attempt to increase the voice of business in Britain (Farnsworth, 2006). Blair outlined Labour's priorities clearly at the CBI conference in 1997, which was the first time the employers' organisation had been addressed by a sitting Labour prime minister:

> When I last addressed the CBI's National Conference, I promised a new partnership between New Labour and business. Six months into office, we have laid the foundations of that partnership. There are business people bringing their experience and expertise by serving in Government, on Advisory Groups, leading task forces, all contributing to the success of Government policy. But there is also great commitment and enthusiasm, right across the Government, for forging links with the business community. That this is the approach of a Labour government is of historic importance. It demonstrates we are entering a new era in British politics. (Blair, A., speech to the CBI Conference, 11 November 1997)

So successful was this strategy that the outgoing president of the CBI, Clive Thompson, explained to the *Financial Times* that the working relationship between the CBI and the Labour government was, in 2000, 'probably closer than at any time in the last 25 years' and certainly closer than under the Thatcher or Major governments (Brown, 2000).

Reaching out to business in this way would, Labour felt, lend legitimacy to the New Labour project; business was viewed as an important ally against entrenched interests within the public sector (Falconer and McLaughlin, 2000, p 122). Moreover, business actors were thought to have valuable experience that might be utilised in order to devise innovative solutions to institutional problems within public services. These pressures, coupled with the government's desire to steer public services towards the needs of business, led to a concerted effort to create new opportunities for business people to fill strategic decision-making positions from the highest levels of government down to individual services. Even more radically, business has been invited to bid to take over the running of essential services, including schools and hospitals.

Thus, in many respects, there has been little need for organised business and firms to seek to influence public policy during recent years since, in most ways and in most areas, policy has been steered in a pro-business direction by politicians. Governments have responded to structural pressures in different ways, but in the UK context they have increasingly led to cuts in spending on unproductive services and expansion in productive services. Business interest in public policy has been triggered wherever it has perceived provision as either harmful to firms or where it felt that provision could be better steered towards the needs of employers, for example, in the areas of taxation policy, public expenditure, labour regulations and education and training provision (Farnsworth, 2006).

Where it has exercised its voice, business has pushed for a more corporate-centred public policy: public provision funded through taxation on labour rather than business; deep spending cuts, especially at the local level; cuts in corporate taxation, especially local business rates; the increased targeting of social provision; an increased emphasis on vocational skills within education; increased participation in post-compulsory education and training; the establishment of tighter educational targets; increased business involvement in key services; an increased reliance on outsourcing; increased targeting of social provision and reliance on private provision; and increased private sector inputs into services (see Whitfield, 2001; Farnsworth, 2004, 2006; Pollock, 2004). This renewed agency capacity has been complimented by increased structural power and a sympathetic international discourse so that British business has not had to battle as hard as it might otherwise have had to in order to promote these kinds of reforms. For the most part, it has been enough for business to limit its campaigns to issues of central importance to business: regulations, tax reform, access to markets and labour costs.

Conclusion

Business is one of the most powerful forces in the policy process. However, as the above discussion has illustrated, its ability to shape policy outcomes varies over time, between states and between different policy areas. Business' structural power helps to shape policy decisions and the policy context by precluding certain issues from ever making it onto the policy agenda. Where it does resort to agency, business also occupies an advantageous position as a result of its access to financial resources, privileged access to policy makers and membership of influential networks. However, both agency and structural power vary in relative importance from state to state and from policy to policy, according to institutional setting. Although business has probably never been as powerful as it is today, this has more to do with the transformation of political institutions than the deliberate agency inputs of business itself into the policy process. Respective British governments since the 1980s in particular have responded to wider economic pressures by cutting expenditure and transforming public services so that they better fit with a more global competitive environment.

Where it has exercised its voice, business has responded positively to government initiatives and, has itself, pushed for a more business-centred policy environment. Businesses and business people have also taken advantage of the new opportunities for policy engagement offered to them in a series of Conservative and Labour initiatives. As a result, the scope for business influence over the policy process and over provision has increased and the process of the embedding of business into policy structures shows no sign of waning. The two main political parties in the UK appear to be equally committed to ensuring that business remains centre stage in policy making and the other major institutions of the state.

SEVEN

(Social) Policy and politics at the international level

Bob Deacon

In a globalising world within which time and space has shrunk, no attempt to understand the policy process is complete without an excursion into *international policy making* (Deacon, 2007). International policy has two dimensions. One is about the influence of international policy processes on national policy. The other is about policies at the supranational level such as the regional or global. This chapter explores these two dimensions of international policy through the example of social policy. How do we understand the ways in which international actors impact upon national social policy and how do we understand the emergence of a supranational social policy of global social redistribution, global social regulation and global social rights? The chapter first reviews some of the conceptual and analytical frameworks drawn from the international relations, policy transfer and political economy literature. It then explicates the complexity of the international institutional framework and density of the set of international actors involved in international social policy making. The chapter concludes with an overview of this multilayered and multi-actor international policy process, and with comment about what this implies for any political strategy wishing to engage with international social policy making.

The approach taken in this chapter is to emphasise the importance of discourses about policy choices at the international level, but it does this within an actor-centred analytical framework within which discourses are one 'weapon' in a complex struggle of interests. This chapter is also written from a 'value standpoint' that favours supranational policies that secure greater global social justice. Better understanding might further this policy objective. In that sense the chapter starts from the standpoint that international social policies are *real* and have concrete impacts on the well-being of people. It is, however, acknowledged that at times it does appear (following Lendvai and Stubbs in Chapter Ten) that the global policy discourse taking place between transnational actors is an epiphenomenon, having little to do with the interests of anybody other than those engaged in the process.

Approaches to understanding international social policy making

To begin to understand the international social policy-making process, we must draw upon international relations and international organisation theory, policy transfer and diffusion literature, global social movement studies, and concepts of hegemonic struggle, as well as some new work around the ethnography of global policy. Within this complex intellectual framework certain conceptualisations emerge as being of particular use. Among these are the concepts of *complex multi-lateralism* (O'Brien et al., 2000), *global policy advocacy coalitions* (Orenstein, 2005) and the *politics of scale* (Clarke, 2004, 2005a; Gould, 2005; Stubbs, 2005b).

Complex multi-lateralism

Political scientists writing about international relations in the context of globalisation are divided in their analysis between the two extremes of realists and cosmopolitan democrats. For realists we still live in a world of sovereign states. They use the Principal–Agent theory to show how International Organisation (IO) policies are nothing but the products of inter-state bargaining. For cosmopolitan democrats, the management of the world is transforming in the direction of a system of global governance with an emerging system of global regulations that are influenced by other global processes and actors (Held et al., 1999). Between the extremes of the state-centric realists and the cosmopolitan dreamers, most international relations theorists give much attention to the ways in which a large number of non-state, and often private, actors have entered the space we shall call the *contested terrain of emerging global governance*. Josselin and Wallace (2001) include transnational corporations, global knowledge elites or networks, organised criminal syndicates, the Catholic church and global Islamic movements, international trade unions and private armies in their review. To these should be added international non-governmental organisations such as Care International, Oxfam and Médicins Sans Frontiéres. It is not just that these actors enter the global political space and argue, but they also take on, in a private capacity, international regulatory activity not yet undertaken by the underdeveloped system of formal global governance.

Thus firms evolve private international regimes of self-regulation in many spheres such as labour and environmental standards (Hall and Biersteker, 2002). Global, or at least transnational, social movements from below, have become a major force in the global politics of globalisation, arguing to shift globalisation from a neoliberal to a more socially responsible form (Kaldor, 2003; Scholte, 2005). Issues like world poverty, global taxation, international labour standards, and access to pharmaceuticals in poorer countries can no longer be discussed at meetings of the G8 or the World Trade Organization (WTO) without there being a major presence on the streets of international campaigning groups on all of these issues. The World Social Forum attempts to provide a global organising space for these activities to match the organising space provided to international business by the World Economic Forum.

One study that focused on the ways in which global social movements (GSMs) interacted with and influenced the policies of multi-lateral economic institutions (MEIs) (O'Brien et al., 2000) is particularly instructive. Their examination of the relations between the World Bank and the women's movement, the WTO and labour, and The World Bank, WTO and the environmental social movement drew important conclusions:

> Our study has stressed the link between forms of international institution and social movements in which the state is just one area of contact and struggle (albeit an important one). The MEI–GSM relationship can be direct and need not be mediated by the state. Social forces with and across state borders are a factor in determining the nature of international order and organisation. (O'Brien et al., 2000, p 234)

They coin the term '*complex multi-lateralism*' to capture this reality within which the realist's concern with state–state interaction sits side by side with a new set of transnational power dynamics, within which IOs, and the social movements that confront them, have a degree of policy autonomy at a global level. It is this framework which is particularly useful in explaining some aspects of the ways IOs influence state social policy, and also how GSMs influence IO social policy.

This conclusion, that there might be a terrain of contestation about global social policy, and that IOs and GSMS, as well as states, are actors, is one that we shall return to. For now it is useful to note how this view might lead us to challenge an otherwise important recent contribution to the literature at the interface of development studies and international relations. Boas and McNeill's study of the policies of several IOs including the World Bank, the WTO and the OECD concludes, rather pessimistically, that:

> Powerful states (notably the USA), powerful organisations (such as the IMF) and even powerful disciplines (economics) exercise their power largely by 'framing': which serves to limit the power of potentially radical ideas to achieve change. (2004, p 1)

While I think this captures an aspect of the process, I would suggest that a more nuanced and more accurate conclusion might be that powerful states (notably the US), powerful organisations (such as the IMF) and even powerful disciplines (economics) contend with other powerful states (notably the EU, China, Brazil), other powerful organisations (such as the ILO) and other disciplines (such as social and political science) and engage in a war of position regarding the content of global policy. This alternative conclusion echoes John Clarke's recent attempt to capture the sense in which we live in, and against, a neoliberal global order:

> The work of constructing a neo-liberal hegemony is intensive, deploys different strategies, and encounters blockages and refusals. It has to engage other political-cultural projects – attempting to subordinate, accomodate, incorporate or displace them. To obscure such intense political-cultural work confirms the neo-liberal illusion of inevitability. If, on the contrary, we draw attention to the grinding and uneven struggle to make the world conform – and recognize the limitations and failures of this project – questions of conflict, contestation, and the 'unfinished' become rather more significant. Living in a neo-liberal world is not necessarily the same as being neo-liberal. Attention to the different sorts of *living with, in and against* neo-liberal domination is a necessary antidote to 'big picture' projections of its universalism. (Clarke, 2004, p 102)

Global policy advocacy coalitions and global knowledge networks

This bridges nicely to the concept of *global policy advocacy coalitions* used by Orenstein (2005) to analyse the development and worldwide selling of the global pension policy preferred by the World Bank since 1990. What is important here is the identification of both private and formal international actors and an account of the ways in which global policy is first put on the agenda and then campaigned for. Earlier work (Haas, 1992, p 10) on the role of epistemic communities noted that:

> How decision makers define state interests and formulate policies to deal with complex and technical issues can be a function of the manner in which the issues are represented by specialists to whom they turn for advice in the face of uncertainty ... epistemic communities (networks of knowledge based experts) play a part in ... helping states identify their interests, forming the issues for collective debate, proposing specific policies, and identifying salient points for negotiation.

The same can be said of the ways in which international networks of knowledge-based experts play a part in helping international organisations shape the issues for collective debate. Indeed, since 1992 the world has witnessed a proliferation of kinds of international knowledge-based experts or knowledge networks (KNETS) (Stone and Maxwell, 2005). Whether understood in any of their forms as listed by Stone (2005): as 'epistemic communities' who share a codified form of 'scientific' knowledege about an issue (such as pensions); or as 'discourse coalitions and communities' who use symbols, language and narrative as a source of power; or as 'embedded knowledge networks', who possess authority because of their track record for problem solving, KNETS are now an integral part of the emerging forms of global governance. As Stone puts it, 'KNETS do not simply crystallize around different sites and forms of power, the network is a site and form of power' (Stone, 2005, p 100). In a globalised world devoid of any effective global democratic processes, these KNETS substitute for other forms of policy making. Stone notes that:

> Global or regional networks are ... not subject to the usual reporting and accountability requirements of public bodies in liberal democracies. The public – even the well informed and politically literate of OECD countries – are still largely

> unaware of the roles, reach and influence of global networks
> ... Combined with the technocratic character of many such
> networks, the public is excluded and political responsibility
> is undermined. (Stone, 2005, p 103)

In the case of the global pension policy story told by Orenstein (2005),
the agenda setting was very much in the hands of a global knowlege
network based on economists educated in the Chicago School of
neoliberal economics. This network had a global reach in terms of its
links to Milton Friedman, Friedrich von Hayek and others (Valdes,
1995). It then became centred upon work in the World Bank initiated
by Larry Summers, the then chief economist, which was eventually
published in 1994 as *Averting the Old Age Crisis*. A transnational advocacy
coalition was then developed to further the adoption of these reforms.
This coalition included the World Bank, USAID, the Inter-American
Development Bank and other actors (Orenstein, 2005, p 193).

This analysis, which argues that global policy becomes shaped by
global knowledge networks, and then argued for by global advocacy
coalitions, has echoes in, but is somewhat different in emphasis to, other
work based upon world society theory. Adopting a more sociological
approach to the subject, Meyer et al (1997), among the founders of this
approach, argues that global society rests on and reinforces universalistic
definitions with which science gains more authority. Meyer argues
that many features of the nation state derive from worldwide models
constructed and propogated through global cultural and associational
processes. The approach within world society theory is to start not
from the nation state as a basis for sociological analysis but rather to
start from an already-existing global society that transcends borders.
Cross-border professional associations act to spread policy ideas and
practices wherever there are members. Education policy and practice,
healthcare procedures and practices become the same everywhere in
conformity with professional standards. While clearly this has some
explanatory value with regard to how policies in one country become
transposed to another country, it lacks a sense of contest and conflict
about policy options. It has echoes of the functionalist sociology of
Talcott Parsons whereby every social phenomenon is understood as
serving a higher societal function. Conflicts of interest and conflicts of
policies are missing. A glance at the policy transfer and policy diffusion
literatures (Dolowitz and Marsh, 1996) reveals accounts of policy
transfers across borders where it is clear that 'choices' are being made
by some countries to borrow the policies of another. These 'choices' are
often made because the country is being coerced into the choice by

powerful global actors, or because the choice is in conformity with its particular ideological goals, or is a better fit to sets of national cultural assumptions. In other words, national social policy choices reflect globalised policy options and contestations about them.

The politics of scale

Finally, in this review of aspects of the international relations literature which might inform our understanding of how global social policy is made and implemented, we turn to the *politics of scale.* This refers to the idea that it is not enough to attempt to capture the complexity of policy making in a globalised world by thinking only in terms of layers of government or governance. An account of policy making that speaks only in terms of the taken-for-granted levels of sub-national, national, regional and global is seen as lacking an important aspect of policy making in a globalised world. It is important to note that policy making is not only taking place at different taken-for-granted levels of governance but that key policy players are transcending each level at any one moment. The policy making process is multi-sited and multilayered as well as multi-actored all at one time. Within this context also, individuals as change agents and policy translators can act in the spaces between levels and organisations (Stubbs, 2006; see also Lendvai and Stubbs, Chapter Ten).

Thus, in attempting to understand policy making in developing countries such as, for example, Tanzania, we have to appreciate that the World Bank is *in* Tanzania; it has its office there and its consultants engage with the Ministry of Finance. Care International, a mega-INGO, is *in* Tanzania; it provides some of the social services off-budget. The consultation process between the Bank and the Tanzanian civil society about social policy involves local NGOs informed by international consultants. To understand something of the complexity of social policy making *for* Tanzania one needs to examine actors and activities at the Bank, in the government, in INGOs, in international consulting companies and in donor government international development sections. The idea is that the 'global' is in the 'local' and the local in the global captures a little of this politics of scale. Policy spaces open up in the dialogue between IOs and national governments, and those who are better able to travel between these scales, consultants, INGO experts and policy entrepreneurs, are better able to influence policy. Within this context the national policy-making process can become distorted. Indeed, Gould (2005, p 142) has argued that 'transnational private agencies [find] themselves brokering and, to some extent, supplanting local civil society representation in policy consultation'.

These policy spaces opening up between the international and the national create possibilities for individuals and individual companies to operate under shifting identities. In this sense, the insights provided by Janine Wedel, based on her case study of US aid to Russia in the early 1990s, offers a number of highly pertinent middle-range concepts in order to study these processes. While she prefers the metaphor of aid as a 'transmission belt', her focus is on 'the interface between donors and the recipients' in terms of 'what happens when differing systems interact' (Wedel, 2004, pp 154–5). She addresses the importance, in these encounters, of multiplex networks (2004, p 165), where players know each other and interact in a variety of capacities, with multiple identities (which she terms 'transidentities'), and in a variety of roles. Her tale is one of shifting and multiple agency, promoted in part by what she terms 'flex organisations', which have a 'chameleon-like, multipurpose character', with actors within them 'able to play the boundaries' between national and international; public and private; formal and informal; market and bureaucratic; state and non-state; even legal and illegal (2004, p 167).[1] At the extreme, this leads to the possibility of individuals playing a large role in global policy making. Jeffrey Sachs, a 'villain of the piece' in the Wedel story of Russian privatisation, becomes reincarnated as the author of the report of the World Health Organization's Commission on Macro-Economics and Health, and subsequently head of the UN task force on the Millenium Development Goals Project.

This review of the international relations literature has stated that certain concepts and approaches are of value in trying to make sense of global social policy. These included the concept of *complex multilateralism*, that suggests states still matter but that IOs and GSMs matter too; *global policy advocacy coalitions*, that suggests international coalitions of actors are formed to influence global policy; *global knowledge networks*, that suggests international policy is more open to the influence of unaccountable experts; and the *politics of scale* approach, that suggests such experts are better able to travel between the local and the international to influence policy. When combined, these concepts enable us to understand global social policy making as multi-sited and multi-actored.

Back to class, gender and ethnicity

It may be objected that this account of how international social policy is made takes us a long way from the conceptual framework provided by the notion of class, gender and ethnic struggles, which many have found useful in offering explanations of national welfare state development and variation. Class struggles can and do take on cross-border dimensions; the social movements of women have become globalised; organisations that represent the interests of different ethnic groups have taken on an international dimension too. The analytical framework provided by Williams (1989, 2001), of a racially structured, patriarchal capitalism, which was used by Ginsburg (1992, 2004) to understand why the social policies of Germany, Sweden, the USA and UK were so different, can be adapted to contribute to our understanding both of national social policy within a global context and of emerging global social policy.

In terms of national social policy in a global context, it is generally agreed that one consequence of the neoliberal globalisation project has been to strengthen the power of capital over that of labour. Capital is free to move across borders, labour is more restricted. Constructing cross-border trade union solidarities in defence of national welfare provision is not easy. As a consequence, the share of income going to profits rather than wages has increased (Wade, 2004). This is not to say that there has been a full-blown undermining of national welfare state provision in developed countries as a consequence of trade union weakening. This has happened but only in some places (for example, Germany) in small measure. By contrast, in other middle-income countries, an increased presence of trade unionism has lead to universal welfare gains (for example, South Korea).

Any summary assessment of the impact of globalisation upon the capacity of women to organise within countries to defend their gendered welfare interests must be more nuanced. While women *as workers* may have suffered some of the same effects of globalisation upon their capacity to defend and improve pay and working conditions, organisations of women *as women* have been strengthened by globalisation's easing of transnational networking. UN conferences, such as the Fourth World Conference on Women in Beijing in 1995, facilitated the growth of a global women's movement that empowered women in many developing countries, in particular, to confront issues of patriarchy and women-unfriendly development policies for the first time. Since then it has been argued that there has been 'much to celebrate' in progress towards gender equality (UNRISD, 2005).

In terms of the impact of globalisation upon inter-ethnic struggles, the story is less well documented. There is some suggestion that while neoliberal globalisation is spreading a global western culture, at the same time local and ethnic identities have become more important. Cross-border movements of people may have led, in part paradoxically, to an increased identification, and networking, with one's country of origin. Care chains and remittance link Philippino workers in New York to extended families in Manilla. Post-war diasporas have become an important factor in the policy making of some countries. Reaction in some developed welfare states has been to restrict welfare benefit access to new migrants. On the other hand, it has been suggested (Chau, 2004) that globalisation's push towards markets and democracy everywhere has had the effect of stimulating oppressed ethnic majorities to wrest power and resources from hitherto market-dominating ethnic minorities (Indonesian against Chinese, for example). Globalisation may have therefore increased the importance of inter-ethnic struggles in shaping national social policy.

Can the framework of capitalism, patriarchy and a racially structured imperialism, with its concomitant global social divisions of class, gender and ethnicity and associated struggles over work, family and nation, be applied to the shaping of a supranational global social policy? How are the new global actors that have been identified as playing a role in shaping global social policy influenced by these global conflicts of interest? First, in terms of class struggle this has a global dimension. At one level the entire range of international organisations, the policies they formulate and the intellectuals working within and around them might be understood according to Sklair (2002, p 99) or Soederberg (2006) as fraction of the global capitalist class. These are the 'globalised professionals' seeking to legitimate and shore up a globalised *capitalism* to prevent it becoming a globalised *socialism*.

For me, on the other hand, what is important is whether the 'globalised professionals' are formulating a global neoliberal social policy or something that we might recognise as a global social-democratic social policy, so that the global economy serves a global social purpose. In this context then, I interpret the contest between the more neoliberal pension policy ideas of the World Bank and the more social-democratic pension policies of the ILO as one reflection of a global class struggle. Global business is well positioned to influence global policy and global trade unionism rather less so (Farnsworth, 2005). Moves to bring global business into partnership with the UN through such devices as the 'Global Compact' are variously interpeted as the UN selling out to global business, or as a means of imposing a global social responsibility upon business. Equally important in terms of the impact of globalisation upon the relative balance of class forces at the transnational level are the ways in which global interconnectedness appears to be detaching the middle class of developing countries from a focus upon the national state-building or developmental project into a search after their own interests within a global marketplace (Cohen, 2004; Gould, 2005).

In terms of the global gender struggle, we have already referred to the ways in which some parts of the UN system have enabled a global women's movement to organise and influence across borders. Within the World Bank, however, as Sen (2006) has shown, the arguments about the positive developmental effects of putting women at the centre of development by, for example, ensuring equal opportunity for girls' education and by micro-credit for women, are now accepted as mainstream. The question of ethnicity and struggles on the part of the largely non-white global south to undo the huge global inequities left over from the imperial epoch, within which the whites were the beneficiaries, lies at the heart of the battle for global economic and social policies. Whether and how the global division of labour laid down in the period of empires can be altered, whether and how there can be restitution for past (and indeed continuing) exploitation of the south by the north, whether and how the debts incurred by the south to the north can be written off, whether and how a systematic policy of global transfers of resources from the global north to the global south to fund education, health and social protection might be made to work are *the* crunch issues. Here the Bank and the IMF are clearly owned by and still acting for the global north. The UN and WTO (which has a majority membership from the south), are forums for the continuing playing out of these issues. In the past two decades the global south has found a new voice and strength in these meeting places. Almost every global social policy issue becomes one of heated controversy between the EU bloc, the USA and the G8, or some alliance of the developing countries such as the new G20 led by Brazil, China and South Africa. At issue are such matters as the price of essential drugs to combat the AIDS epidemic in Africa and the needed increase in Overseas Development Assistance to support the funding of primary education in poorer countries.

Global actors, global institutions, global contest, global impasse?

We can now attempt to apply the complex analytical framework developed above, within which the concepts of complex multi-lateralism, global policy advocacy coalitions, global knowledge networks and the politics of scale play a part, together with struggles of class, gender and ethnicity, to make sense of the existing system of global social governance. It will be suggested that there is something of an institutional and policy impasse in the existing formal 'system' of global social governance, which in turn has led to international policy actually being shaped and progressed by informal actors in the spaces between the formal international organisations.

Paramount among the formal global actors influencing national and international social policy, are the *intergovernmental organisations* such as the UN social agencies (ILO, WHO, UNESCO, UNICEF), the World Bank, the IMF, the OECD and the WTO. These contending and overlapping agencies present us with a picture not of the slow diffusion of agreed social policy ideas and practices across the globe, as the world society theorist might have us expect. Rather the picture is one of a contest of ideas and principles in each sector of social policy (Deacon, 2007). The disputes take place between agencies and within them. The disputes about pension policy have been the most heated, but that concerning the proper role for the private sector in health and education provision comes close second. While there has been more consensus between some parts of the Bank and the UN system around the intellectual case for universal public provision, the activities of the International Finance Corporation (IFC) within the World Bank Group, the impact of the WTO General Agreements on Trade in Services (GATS) and the Millennium Development Goal (MDG) targets may conspire to continue to push countries towards limiting public expenditure on services only for the poor. Certainly we are faced with a complex set of formal global agencies all contending for the right to influence national policy and for the content of that policy. Moreover the agencies have differential capacity to influence national social policy in terms of (a) the instruments at their disposal: the World Bank's and IMF's conditional lending versus the UN's moral persuasion, (b) their command of resources: the richer Bank versus the poorer UN, and (c) their organisational links to international epistemic communities and think tanks: for example, the World Bank's Institute versus the United Nations Research Institute for Social Development (UNRISD).

But it is not, as explained earlier in this chapter, just these formal intergovernmental organisations that have a say. The part that *informal non-state international actors* are increasingly playing in world politics and global governance has been recognised by a number of international relations scholars. Josselin and Wallace (2001) usefully reviewed this literature. Hall and Biersteker (2002) also covered a similar terrain but with more of a focus on how such actors were increasingly involved in the actual practice of international regulation. Stern and Seligmann (2004) argued forcefully for the 'partnership principle' whereby a part had to be played in governance in the twenty-first century by business and civil society in fields such as poverty and disease eradication, human rights attainment, peace and security, and the economy.

In terms of global think tanks, knowledge networks, policy advocacy coalitions and epistemic communities within the sphere of international social policy, it is clear that the contest of ideas and policies articulated by the *formal* IOs, is reflected within, and shaped by, the contest between these *informal* actors. Significantly, Asuncion Lera St Clair (2006, p 59) explores this contest of knowledge claims in the field of global poverty analysis. She argues:

> Expert claims are usually determined by the interrelations between audiences, experts and the legitimacy of knowledge. But in most cases these interrelations are a mere circular process where experts seek legitimacy of their knowledge claims among audiences that have been created by or are dependent on the same experts that seek legitimacy in the first place.

As a result she suggests: 'The most we can say about the current state of knowledge about global poverty is that it reflects a "consensus among certain scientists" rather than a "scientific consensus"' (2006, p 60).

A resolution of this problem she agues, is to establish a more open and accountable mechanism where contesting scientific (and value) claims made by the World Bank, the UN and other stakeholders are assessed within a transnational body (St Clair, 2006, p 72) 'where research on global poverty could be reviewed and coordinated in analogous ways as knowledge about climate change is managed by the Inter-governmental Panel on Climate Change and its Subsidiary Body for Scientific and Technological Advice'. The alternative, she says, is to leave it as now to a situation where the most powerful actors 'win' the argument.

INGOs such as Oxfam, Christian Aid and Care International have come to assume importance within the global social policy-making process, in the sense of being policy advocates, often arguing for improved international and national commitments to welfare, but also, paradoxically, of being agents for the delivery of aid, and hence often substituting for government welfare provision. Stubbs (2003) has described these actors as intermediate organisations falling between genuine civil society organisations and formal intergovernmental organisations. They are important not only for their policy influence and service provision, but also because their presence in a country can distort the actual delivery of welfare in unintended ways. The higher pay of the INGO workers distorts the local labour market and undermines lower-paid public civil servants. INGOs are then part of the welfare mix that makes up the agents of welfare provision and policy in many countries in the context of globalisation.

Multinational or transnational corporations are important too. Transnational corporations (TNCs) can shift capital and production around the globe and consequently drive down wage rates, and affect labour rights and social security entitlements. Taxation and social reponsibilities can be avoided. Moreover global business is poised to take over the provision of national public services everywhere, whether these are in the education, health or social care sectors. Farnsworth (2005, p 219) concluded that 'The bottom line for international capital is that state provision is justified only if it contributes directly to economic growth or at least does not undermine it, and is affordable only if it exists in an environment populated by profitable and successful firms'. Given this, the Business International Advisory Committee (BIAC), for example, has urged the OECD to address impediments to job creation that include too generous social provision. Apart from education and training expenditures with which the BIAC is more in sympathy, international business favours reducing expenditures and taxation (especially on corporations). The BIAC pushed for a greater role for the private sector in service delivery and, in this context, pushed for the liberalisation of trade in services, which it sees as a great opportunity for expansion.

In terms of global social movements, the rise in the 1990s of an anti–globalisation movement, which has been symbolised by street protests at major world conferences of the WTO, the G8 and the World Bank and IMF, gave rise to the idea that there was a globalisation from below, which needed to be studied. It too was an actor shaping global policies. It took organisational form in the shape of the World Social Forum, mirroring the World Economic Forum for business. However, it is the general agreement of those who have attempted to make sense of the World Social Forum process (Hardt, 2002; Sen et al., 2004), that beyond the founding principles which assert that the Forum is a space within which movements opposed to neoliberalism and imperialism might come together to discuss the proposition that an 'alternative world is possible', the Forum has not begun to attempt to fashion any common or collective view about what that alternative at national or global level might look like. Patomaki and Teivainen (2005) and Glasius et al. (2006, p 84) report, however, that at the 2005 event a 'manifesto' signed by 19 intellectuals was produced, which restated familiar demands of the anti-globalisation movement: debt cancellation, adoption of currency transaction tax, dismantling of tax havens, promotion of equitable trade including the exclusion of health, education and services from the GATS, permitting countries to develop their own food policy, the establishment of a universal right to social protection and a pension, protection of the environment, enforcing anti-discrimination conventions and the democratisation of international organisations including the physical relocation of the UN to the south.

Thus, at the global level there are a number of competing and overlapping intergovernmental institutions and private players, all of which have some stake in shaping global policy towards global social problems. This struggle for the right to shape policy and for the content of that policy is what passes for an effective system of international social governance. The fragmentation and competition may be analysed in different groupings of contestations. The World Bank, and to a lesser extent, the IMF and WTO, are in competition for influence with the rest of the UN system. The Bank's health, social protection and education policies for countries are not always the same as those of the WHO, ILO, or UNESCO, respectively. While the world may be said to have one emerging Ministry of Finance in the shape of the IMF (with lots of shortcomings), and one Ministry of Trade in the shape of the WTO, it has two Ministries of Health, two Ministries of Social Security and two Ministries of Education. Then again, the UN social agencies (WHO, ILO, UNICEF, UNESCO) are not always espousing the same policy as the United Nations Development Programme (UNDP) or the UN Department of Economic and Social Affairs. Moreover, the Secretary General's initiatives, such as the Global Compact or the Millennium project, may bypass and sideline the social development policies of the UN's Department of Economic and Social Affairs (Deacon, 2007).

We have to add to this list of actors the variety of non-governmental or non-state actors we have just reviewed. Business, broader civil society organisations, INGOs and other private actors are increasingly involved in the processes of global social governance and global social policy determination. We are faced with a complex architecture of global governance that 'is characterised by a high degree of diversity and complexity ... The heterogeneous and at times contradictory character of global governance presents a challenge to any attempt to understand its operation and evolution in theoretical terms' (Koenig-Archibugi, 2002, p 62). Within the specific field of global health governance the same complexity can be noticed. Concluding a major study of global health governance undertaken within the German Overseas Institute, Hein and Kohlmorgan (2005, p 35) note: 'The new institutional setting of global health governance due to networks, partnerships, and increased private activities strengthens social rights to health, but tend to circumvent the formal and democratically authorised UN organisations like the WHO.'

Policy making at the international level, at least in the sphere of social policy, is, then, a contest of policy ideas taking place within and between intergovernmental organisations, backed up by contending global policy alliances involving numerous global private players. One element of this process is the flexible and multifaceted nature of many of these actors, sometimes the same agency is both policy advocate and service provider. Another is the variety of the networks and alliances struck, usually temporarily, between international public, international private and international civil society actors to address particular global welfare issues. Within the sphere of global social policy we might even describe the situation as a frozen institutional landscape within which policy is increasingly made within the spaces between the formal organisations by networked private actors accountable to nobody. We return to this point below.

Implications for those wishing to influence international social policy

What does all of this imply for practice? How might international policy be influenced? To answer this we need to remind ourselves that it is the multi-sited, multilayered, multi-actored nature of the policy-making process that emerges from this account. If this is correct, one thing is certain about the character of the political process that will shape the social policies of the future at national, regional and global level, and shape the future structures of global and regional social governance. It will also be multi-sited, multi-actor and multi-levelled. To put this another way, from a normative standpoint, to make the world a fairer place, better able to meet the social needs of more of the world's population, political struggle will need to take place at a number of sites and involve a number of different actors.

That is not to suggest that any neatly ordered system of multi-level governance is at work, where progressive social policies simply have to be won first at the local, then at the national, and then at the supranational regional level, and finally in the debating chambers of global social governance! Rather as Clarke (2005a, p 413) has put it:

> This cannot be simply grasped as multiple tiers or levels, since sovereignties overlap and collide in the same space (with jurisdictional claims being the subject of conflict and negotiations). Different polities or sovereignty-claiming agencies are constituted differently – most obviously in terms of their representative base.

Indeed, this has led us to argue that it is precisely in the spaces between such contending and overlapping (partial) authorities that the most effective moves to make transnational policy might take place. Thus, because there are now so many loci of action and initiatives on global social issues, we may be witnessing a shift in the locus and content of global policy debate and activity, from those more formally located within the official UN policy-making arenas and focused on UN/Bretton Woods institutional reform, to a set of practices around networks, partnerships and projects. In some ways, they bypass these institutions and debates, and present new possibilities for actually making global change, in particular social policy arenas (see also the work of the Global Public Policy Institute www.globalpublicpolicy.org for a similar conclusion in relation to other public policies).

In terms of the multi-level and multi-actor policy process, then, what will matter will be:

- struggles between neoliberal and social solidarity agendas within countries, perhaps none more important than that in the USA;
- debates about best social policies for countries within and between global epistemic communities;
- the work of global policy advocacy organisations and international think tanks;
- the winning over of international corporations to socially responsible practices;
- debates within the anti-globalisation movement about what actually are the prospects for, and actual policies of, alternative globalisations;
- the work of international civil servants within the UN meetings, struggling to keep the main lines of meeting declarations on a progressive track;

- individuals as policy translators and intermediaries working both in and against the international organisations and in the spaces in between them;
- but eventually success, if there is to be any, will depend on the construction of a global political alliance that embraces most of these actors and sites. Back to the politics of class, gender and ethnicity within and across borders!

In sum, taking issue with those who might see global policy discourses as concerning only those engaged in the discourse, it is being argued here that the contests over policies matter. Policies do have impacts even when they appear as 'mere' discourses taking place at a reified and abstract international level. The policy contests taking place within and around and between international organisations, by informal international actors, are, in the terrain of social policy, contests of values that matter for diverse interest groups. The contest of international social policy paradigms is surely in part a contest about ways of seeing the world; of giving it meaning. But at root, however reified and remote the debate, the interests of social classes, genders and ethnicities, every bit as much as the self-interest of the global policy actors and intermediaries are at stake.

Note
[1] I am indebted to Paul Stubbs for this summary. It is to be found in Stubbs (2005b).

Part Three
Practices

Introduction

The emphasis in this final part of the book is on ways of researching the practices of policy as much as it is about studying policy in practice. Policy studies texts mainly present a juxtaposition between policy and practice where what is laid down in thought (formulation) and what actually happens in deed (implementation) are compared. This type of analysis is useful in revealing the nature and form of implementation 'gaps', the trials and tribulations of policy execution at street level and the complexity of politics and ideology as they operate at different levels of organisation. At the same time, however, there is a risk in investigating 'policy in practice', that boundaries are respected and linearity assumed (whether from the top down or the bottom up), when these aspects of policy in action also need to become part of the processes being explored. Michael Hill (2005, ch 9) makes a clear case that not only is 'policy' a 'slippery concept', but that putting it (whatever 'it' turns out to be) into practice is an interactive process that requires attention to context. Earlier chapters in this book demonstrate that attention to meanings is also required in order to gain a fuller understanding of policy processes, and the chapters in this section are intended to present examples of ways in which the idea of 'policy practices' can be understood in a broader sense than the simple result of implementation.

Within these chapters, three newly emergent frameworks for policy analysis are demonstrated: Cowburn emphasising the centrality of ethics; Boxall, Warren and Chau contextualising the rise of the 'user' and Lendvai and Stubbs drawing on the sociology of translation (after Callon). As Cowburn warns, however, we must always bear in mind the origins and bases of all analysis. Any research on policy practices should not only consider how policy gets used, but how research gets used too. In the same way that policy does not simply travel from A to B, from statement to implementation, so research and the outputs of research cannot take a straight route from researcher to policy information. Policy research practices are as questionable as any other aspect of policy-related study and can easily lead to policy structures built on sand rather than the assumed bias-free bedrock. Thus research goals as well as policy goals need to be made explicit, since the evidence base that underpins formulation necessarily impacts on practices. Both Cowburn and Boxall et al. raise issues of science, objectivity and rationality, and highlight the limited mileage of these ideas in practical situations. They also point to the possibilities for resistance: resistance to conformance within hegemonic structures and institutional ways; and resistance to normativity (or categories, of people, of practices, of research).

As indicated in Chapter One, the contexts of policy making are shifting, and have been described as a general movement from government to governance. Clearly, analysis of governments or politics alone will not do much to illuminate this shift; we need to study the emerging contexts of, and the new influences on, policy work. Boxall, Warren and Chau chart some of this ground through a focus on the rise of the 'user' in research and practice. 'Users', and their rhetorically close relatives, 'stakeholders', have brought into being a whole new language in and for policy. New practices of engagement are called for, new routes to inform policy – to be 'involved' and to have a 'stake'. Concurrently, fresh analyses of these new policy relationships are required. As Boxall et al. observe, 'participation' in policy making is not unproblematic, but the mobilisation of policy subjects, whether spontaneous or manufactured, reiterates Richard Jenkins's conclusion, in Chapter Two, that policy is not simply a passive element of life's scenery, it enmeshes the script, the direction and the opportunity for active improvisation. The interrelationships between meanings, politics and practices are nowhere more clear than in the intricacies of international policy development and exchange. In the closing chapter of this section, Lendvai and Stubbs draw the three arenas together by tracing lines of communication and paying attention to loci of translation, showing how policy can be studied as a form of complexity. In Lendvai and Stubbs's account, meanings, in the study of practices, become absolutely central in understanding politics. Their work provides an important counterpoint to much policy analysis, which separates issues of practices, politics and meanings into clearly demarcated boxes, and it also illustrates the alternative avenues for policy exploration that a different perspective can bring to light.

EIGHT

Ethics, research and policy

Malcolm Cowburn

This chapter addresses the relationships between what have become dominant forms of knowledge and the policy this knowledge informs. It suggests that in both the conception and process of (policy) research, ethical issues construct the project, influence the findings and shape subsequent policies. This points to the inextricable links between ethics and epistemology (as well as between ethics, outputs and policy products). A research project embodies or antagonises dominant forms of knowledge; the choice between these alternatives, I suggest, is an ethical choice.

Policy also relates to forms of knowledge and how these are embodied in practices (Colebatch, 2002, p 20). Colebatch (2002, p 8) has noted that '"Policy" is a way of labelling thoughts about the way the world is and the way it might be, and of justifying practices and organizational arrangements ...' However, as he also points out, there are a range of ways of understanding the world and governmental policies draw attention to a *particular* way of understanding a (social) problem while, at the same time, obscuring or ignoring alternative ways of understanding the same phenomenon (Colebatch, 2002, p 19). As the editors of this volume have pointed out (Chapter One): 'Policy provides the practical framework for the expression of political messages and the achievement of social goals. The use of policy as a governmental device is central in maintaining social, political and economic relationships.' Being aware of the political nature of the framing of social issues in policy statements, and of the existence of alternative interpretations of social issues, leads to a consideration of the relationship between knowledge, interpretations, policy and ethics.

Generally, discussion of the relationship between ethics and policy concentrates on the ethical implications of particular courses of (policy-directed) action, and is usually illustrated with reference to morally contentious issues such as IVF or euthanasia. Little attention is given to the ethical implications of a particular epistemological standpoint. However, in order to develop these points, I will focus on research relating to the sexual offending of men. This area starkly highlights the problems involved in both conceptualising and conducting research that seeks to inform policy aimed at protecting the public. As shown later in the chapter, most men who are convicted of sex offences are only convicted on one occasion. Thus, most new sex offenders are men who have no previous convictions: yet research aimed at understanding and reducing the harm caused by male sexual violence concentrates on the convicted population. This raises ethical questions about the focus of such research. Such questions cannot, however, be addressed in a vacuum. Issues related to the social construction of knowledge and, importantly, the social construction of policy need to be considered within a context that focuses on knowledge and power. Initially, I outline the main approaches to thinking ethically in relation to developing research and policy. I then consider the socially constructed nature of knowledge (and policy) and develop the notion of hegemonic discourse. Thereafter, I develop the case study used in this chapter to illustrate the arguments presented. Understanding and responding (via policy) to sexual violence provides a vivid opportunity to explore the interrelated nature of epistemology, power and ethics. Finally, I consider wider issues for the development of ethical research that seeks to inform policy.

Ethical perspectives

Banks (2006, p 4) describes two distinct and different usages of the term 'ethics'. As a technical and philosophical discipline, ethics is more usually referred to as 'moral philosophy', and it incorporates *meta-ethics*, *normative ethics* and *descriptive ethics*. However, Banks (2006, p 5) also notes that the other usage of the term ethics: 'is as a plural term referring to the norms or standards of behaviour people follow concerning what is regarded as good or bad, right or wrong'.

It is this usage that she suggests is employed interchangeably with the term 'morality'. This chapter is primarily concerned with this second usage of the term, in that it focuses on the construction and conduct of research rather than the esoteric intricacies of moral philosophy.

Kvale (1996, p 121) suggests that there are three major philosophical theories of ethics that provide help in thinking about moral issues in research. These are: a utilitarian ethics of consequences, duty of ethics principles and virtue of ethics of skills. Banks (2006) considers that the first two of these approaches are 'principle based'. 'Principle-based' approaches are derived from abstract sets of principles designed to guide/shape ethical behaviours. Virtue of ethics skills is different in its focus, and fits within Banks's (2006) broad category of 'character and relationship-based' approaches. In relation to developing a policy-related research topic, principle-based approaches are primarily involved in identifying the research question – the area to be explored – whilst character and relationship-based approaches inform the conduct of the research process.

Principle-based approaches

> Principle-based theories of ethics usually construe ethical reasoning and decision-making as a rational process of applying principles and derived rules to particular cases and/or justifying action with reference to relevant rules and principles. . . . (Banks, 2006, p 28)

The two principle-based approaches to ethical reasoning are utilitarian ethics of consequences and Kantian duty of ethics principles. Utilitarian ethics of consequences are concerned with the outcome(s) of specific actions, and judge them to be more or less ethical on this basis. Drawing on the work of the philosophers Bentham and Mill, the utility principle is variously described as indicating the right action as being the one that brings about the 'greatest good over evil' or 'the greatest happiness of the greatest number' (Banks, 2006, p 36). As a general rule, utilitarian ethics are the ostensible guidelines for much policy. Duty of ethics principles focus on the nature of the act itself, rather than on the consequences of the act (Kvale, 1996, p 121; Birch et al., 2002, p 5). Moral actions live up to principles such as respect for the person, honesty and justice. They focus on the nature of actions rather than their consequences: 'So act as to treat humanity, whether in your own person or that of any other, never solely as a means but always also as an end' (Kant, 1964, p 32).

As such, duty of ethics principles are more likely to be involved with the detail of the conduct of research and are, therefore, strongly linked to character and relationship-based approaches to ethics. I explore this approach more fully below where I consider issues of confidentiality. Principle-based approaches, particularly but not exclusively utilitarian approaches, inform the construction of policy-oriented research. However, how the greatest benefit to the greatest number is construed is not without its problems. Issues pertaining to how the social problem is constructed, and thus responded to in policy, have their roots in thinking about how knowledge itself is constructed, and this inevitably leads to a consideration of knowledge and power.

Epistemology, hegemony and discourse

The dominant framework for understanding the social world within Western academic disciplines is developed from the natural sciences (Nicolson, 1995). The object of study is observed, and from these observations general 'laws' are derived. Proponents of a natural science approach to social data suggest that empirically-validated data can be 'discovered' through systematic observation, measurement and collection of facts which, when analysed, reveal laws about the physical and social world (Van Langenhove, 1995). These laws form the basis for predicting future events: personal behaviours, social movements and so on. Van Langenhove notes that:

> Within the natural sciences model for social sciences, the idea of explanation is copied from the models of explanation used in the classical physical sciences such as inorganic chemistry and Newtonian physics. These models are aimed at generating law-like predictions based on causal relations. (Van Langenhove, 1995, p 14)

Within this paradigm, the most important feature of this manner of conducting enquiry is 'objectivity'. It is not necessary to describe in any detail the debates surrounding the possibility or not of value-free, objective research (see Bhaskar, 1989; Harding, 1991). However, Harding notes that the conventional approach in natural science:

> fails to grasp that modern science has been constructed by and within power relations in society, not apart from them. The issue is not how one scientist or another used or abused social power in doing his [sic] science but rather where the sciences and their agendas, concepts, and consequences have been located within particular currents of politics. How have their ideas and practices advanced some groups at the expense of others? (Harding, 1991, p 81)

The key issue for ethical consideration here, for Harding, is 'where the sciences and their agendas, concepts and consequences have been located' politically and whose interests are advanced by adopting such a standpoint. For example, Hearn (1998) has pointed out that what often stands as 'objective' social science is in effect the worldview of a socially and economically dominant group of men. The power of this grouping is embodied in 'scientific' discourse where its worldview masquerades as the objective truth: in effect it has created a hegemonic discourse. In the exemplar used in this chapter, the hegemonic discourse that shapes research and policy in relation to male sexual violence concentrates attention on those men convicted of sex offences, and also constructs them, as a group, in particular ways (see also Britton, Chapter Four).

The term 'hegemony' has its origins in structural understandings of power. It is derived from the Greek verb meaning 'to lead', and referred to the holding of political power. Antonio Gramsci is recognised as a key exponent of this term (Bocock, 1986; Clegg, 1989). He (Gramsci, 1971) used the term to describe the dominance of one social class which was not only manifested politically and economically, but also *culturally*. Bocock has offered this (much cited) definition:

> [hegemony occurs] when the intellectual, moral and philosophical leadership provided by the class or alliance of class and class fractions which is ruling, successfully achieves its objective of providing *the fundamental outlook for the whole society*. (1986, p 63, emphasis added)

However, structural approaches to understanding power, such as that taken by Gramsci, are questioned by post-structuralist thinkers (Clegg, 1989; Purvis and Hunt, 1993). While structural approaches are concerned with hierarchical power and sovereignty, post-structural approaches are concerned with the operation of power in a variety of locations, at historically specific moments.

For post-structuralists, power is not hierarchically located or held, but discursively present; it can be contested in a variety of settings and at different times. Clegg (1989) identifies the key feature of this tradition as being the focus on the *exercising* of power rather than merely *holding* power. Whitehead (2002) designates this tradition as 'discursive' and identifies the work of Foucault as being of key importance. Here, the word 'discursive' is taken to mean pertaining to discourse(s). Burr notes:

> A discourse refers to a set of meanings, metaphors, representations, images, stories, statements and so on *that in some way together produce a particular version of events*. (1995, p 48, emphasis added)

Referring specifically to Foucault, Bell comments:

> For Foucault, it is both less and more than 'language'. It is less in that discourse is not a description of the whole language system ... it is more in that it is not just speaking and writing, but entails social and political relations: *one cannot dissociate discourse from a social context where relations of power and knowledge circulate.* (1993, p 42, emphasis added)

While Burr's definition of discourse potentially implies that all discourses have equal/no power, Bell's interpretation highlights the relationship between knowledge and power (see also Gregory, Chapter Five).

Although Foucault avoided any associations of his work with explicit structuralist analyses of power, he clearly did not conceive of power as being apolitical. In *The History of Sexuality, Volume One* (1984), he provides a vivid and pertinent example of the interplay between power and knowledge in creating a hegemonic discourse concerning sexuality and sexual behaviours. He highlights the role of medical science in providing an intellectual structure of justification for the attitudes and values of the dominant group in a society (1984, pp 53–73). Medical science is clearly a form of knowledge that sustains the power of a particular social group. It is the shaping impact of 'expert' knowledge with regard to sexual coercion that provides the example used in this chapter. The experts, in this case, are particularly drawn from forensic psychology and criminology, and their concerns are largely with the convicted sex offender, yet their 'expert' knowledge is given a wider field of relevance in, for example, policy and popular media (Cowburn and Dominelli, 2001). However, although discourses provide an inclusive framework for understanding, inevitably, discourses also exclude items, experiences and voices – as such they can be said to serve a hegemonic purpose. Purvis and Hunt (1993, p 485) note:

> Discourses impose frameworks which limit what can be experienced or the meaning that experience can encompass, and thereby influence what can be said and done. Each discourse allows certain things to be said and impedes or prevents other things from being said. Discourses thus provide specific and distinguishable mediums through which communicative action takes place. (Purvis and Hunt, 1993, p 485)

Thus, although there are a variety of discourses, within these discourses are a range of narratives/stories some of which will carry more power than others and thus be hegemonic. The use of the words 'narrative' and 'story' are not intended to belittle or relegate certain accounts to the realms of fantasy or fiction. Rather, such usage highlights the constructed nature of all accounts. Burr notes that the term 'narrative' can be used in ways that move the focus beyond individual personal accounts. Referring to the work of Gergen and Gergen (1986) she comments:

> narrative structure applies as much to the accounts of science and social science as it does to personal accounts ... we address ourselves to the task of understanding how theorists use narrative criteria to enable them to formulate powerful and compelling accounts of human functioning. (Burr, 1995, p 136)

A key part of developing understanding of human functioning is the social contexts in which narratives are produced. Again, referring to Gergen and Gergen (1986), Burr emphasises that it is important to recognise 'the historical and social contexts of experience, and indeed the historical, social and therefore political contexts of our theories about human life' (1995, p 136). Highlighting the political dimension of narrative draws attention, again, to the operation of power in knowledge creation. Thinking specifically of discourses in which male sexual coercion is construed, feminist commentators have persistently drawn attention to the widespread nature of harmful male sexual behaviours that are beyond legal definition (see for example Jackson [1984] for an account of early feminist activity in this area, and also Liz Kelly's [1988] elaboration of a continuum of male sexual coercion). Yet these voices are mostly ignored within policy responses to male sexual violence: governmental policy is, by definition, inevitably hegemonic and thus adopts hegemonic discourse in the formulation of policy.

Hegemonic discourse relating to sexual coercion ensures that only certain acts of sexual coercion are considered and incorporated into the development of penal policy and practice in response to the perpetrators of sexually coercive acts. Other acts – the coercive sexual behaviours of a wider (unconvicted) group of men – I suggest, are excluded and ignored. This has implications for research and the associated development of policy. Research that is uncritically located within the hegemonic discourse may be more attractive to policy makers (and funders) than research which challenges dominant understandings of social problems.

Researching male sexual violence – towards a safer society?

Research focused on male sexual violence that seeks to influence policy is motivated by a utilitarian ethic of promoting the greatest good of the greatest number. Policy in relation to sexual crime is explicitly concerned with protecting the public (that is, securing the greatest 'good' for the majority of citizens). The Explanatory Notes to the 2003 Sexual Offences Act (HMSO, 2003, para 7), for example, state that one of the purposes of the Act is 'protecting the public from sexual harm'. This prompts questions about how 'sexual harm' is constructed.

Media coverage of sexual violence is a key part of the hegemonic discourse relating to male sex offending. It has shifted from focusing on the rapist to 'the paedophile' (Cowburn and Dominelli, 2001), and the emphasis is strongly on the danger posed by the unknown 'stranger' who is a dangerous, calculating and ruthless sex offender from whom the public must be protected (Kitzinger, 1999; Cowburn and Dominelli, 2001). Research has highlighted that newspaper reportage characterises 'the paedophile' as an ungendered being whose offences occur in the public domain (Cowburn and Dominelli, 2001). Such reportage fails to address offences that occur in the domestic sphere thus perpetuating the notion of a generalised danger only in the public arena. More recently Chris Greer (2003, p 40), in his study of reportage of sex crimes in Northern Ireland, has noted that many practitioners within the criminal justice field are concerned that:

> the narrow and highly emotive coverage of sex crime in the press identifies the wrong areas of risk. As a result ... it may actually undermine measures taken by those trying to ensure the safety of children in their care and increase the likelihood of sexual victimisation.

Greer (2003, p 39) also notes that:

> The representation – and condemnation – of sex offenders [in the media] ... serves to establish a common enemy against which all 'decent' people can unite. It denotes a criminal type that is wholly distinct from respectable society.

However, a key feature in these constructions is that the sex offender is *known* by his convictions. Emphasis in the popular press on knowing/recognising the threat of sexual harm through having knowledge of criminal convictions and crime reports has, in recent years, reached almost fever pitch. During the trial of Ian Huntley in England (in 2003) for the murder of two children at the school where he was the caretaker, it was discovered that between 1995 and 1999, there had been four crime reports against him, related to alleged sexual offences against girls aged between the ages of 13 and 15; there was also a crime report for an offence of burglary. None of these reports resulted in a conviction.

Following the government inquiry (known as the Bichard Inquiry) into the circumstances of this case (Bichard, 2005), there have been many changes in relation to the employment of (ex-)offenders in jobs where they have contact with children (Department for Education and Skills, 2005; Department of Health, 2006a) or vulnerable adults (Chartered Institute of Personnel and Development, 2004; Department of Health, 2004). However, these initiatives have not caused public concern to abate. During 2005/6, criminal convictions in relation to the teaching profession featured in debates in the British press and in the UK Parliament. Concern focused particularly on the discovery that a number of convicted sexual offenders were employed in schools in the UK (Kelly, 2006; Kirkup and Peev, 2006; Naughton, 2006; Pascoe-Watson, 2006), and that the employment of these people had been authorised (in some cases) by central government. The UK government is now planning to tighten further the vetting and barring processes in relation to people with convictions seeking employment involving work with children or vulnerable adults (Department for Education and Skills and Department of Health, 2006b).

The popular view that most sex offenders are aberrant men/beasts who invariably reoffend (Cowburn and Dominelli, 2001) is contradicted by research findings. In a review of 61 studies undertaken in Europe and North America between 1943–95, Hanson and Bussiere (1998, p 357) noted that, as a group, sex offenders have a low rate of recidivism:

> Only a minority of the total sample (13.4% of 23,393) were known to have committed a new sexual offense within the average 4–5 year follow-up ... even in studies with thorough record searches and long follow-up periods (15–20 years), the recidivism rates almost never exceed 40%.

To set this figure in context, a recent reconviction study in the UK noted that two years after conviction the recidivism rate for people who have offended sexually against a child is 14.3 per cent, whereas the rate for domestic burglary is 72.8 per cent and for theft the overall rate is 78.7 per cent (Shepherd and Whiting, 2006, p 17). However, as Hanson and Bussiere (1998) point out, offenders may be reoffending and not being caught. This is an unknown, but Soothill (1998) and his colleagues have suggested that, given the length of time of follow-up in many recidivism studies (10–20 years), it is unlikely that the reoffences of a known sex offender would remain concealed for this length of time.

Low recidivism rates, however, are more marked in the population known as 'first offenders'. Soothill and Gibbens (1978) found that 12 per cent of first offenders were reconvicted within ten years. Similarly, Phillpotts and Lancucki (1979) noted that within a six-year follow-up period, only 1.5 per cent of sex offenders with no previous convictions were convicted of a further sexual offence. Many other commentators (Quinsey et al., 1984; Howard League Working Party, 1985; Quinsey, 1986; Furby et al., 1989) have also drawn attention to this feature of sex offender recidivism. West (1987, p 18) notes that:

> It is a common misapprehension that sex offenders are very liable to repeated convictions. Certainly some of them are, but that is not the general rule. The typical sex offender appears in court once only and never again.

Linked to the low conviction rate of sex offenders is the rarely commented-upon feature that *the majority* of sex offenders *do not* have previous convictions for sexual offences. This finding has been consistently affirmed in a number of studies over a period of time (Cowburn, 2005, pp 215–31).

To summarise, these data offer a picture of low reconviction rates for convicted sex offenders, and very low rates for offenders with no previous convictions. This is at odds with the dominant media construction that highlights the prolific offending paedophile, and it raises questions as to why policy designed to protect the public from sexual harm, and research into male sex offending, concentrates so heavily on this convicted population. If there was clear evidence that showed that the number of sex crimes reported correlated more or less exactly to the number of convictions recorded for sex crime, then focusing the vast majority of research endeavour (and associated funding) on the people who committed these offences would appear to be a rational and ethical way of using research to ensure the greatest good of the greatest number. Unfortunately, there is no research that supports this picture and there is much that undermines it.

It is important to make clear the distinction between offences reported (crime reports) and convictions secured. After a crime is reported to the police a series of decisions and actions determine whether the crime report becomes a criminal conviction. Initially, a judgement is made as to whether or not to investigate the crime; thereafter decisions are made depending on whether or not perpetrators are identified, and whether or not there appears to be sufficient evidence to justify prosecution. Not all criminal investigations result in a prosecution and not all prosecutions result in a conviction. For example, in 1991 in the UK, the total number of sex offences reported was 29,423, and in 2001 it had risen to 37,311 (Home Office, 2001, 2002). However, in 1991 the total number of sex offence convictions was 8,843, and in 2001 it had fallen to 5,042 (Home Office, 2001, 2002). It emerges from these data that two clear and overlapping populations are reported for acts of sexual coercion: the perpetrators and the offenders. It would appear that sex offenders comprise approximately one per cent of a larger population of people who allegedly commit acts of sexual coercion. This is the *visible* population that is identified and subsequently punished, and it is research on this population that informs social policies that are designed to protect the public from sexual harm (such as the 2003 Sexual Offences Act).

Further indications of the larger invisible population of sexually coercive men are to be found in prevalence studies, and in self-report studies. These studies investigate the prevalence, and experience, of unwanted sexual acts within given populations. The great variety in the findings of these studies (due largely to differences in definitions of sexual acts and in the populations being investigated, with higher prevalence rates found in studies undertaken in psychiatric clinic and hospital settings), indicate clearly that there are many more sexually harmful acts committed than there are convictions. On the basis of their extensive review of prevalence studies, Percy and Mayhew (1997) have estimated that there are 15 times more unreported sex offenders than reported ones.

Studies that ask men to report the likelihood of their committing sexual offences if they were free from any adverse consequences, reveal a disturbing picture (see Cowburn, 1998; Hanson and Bussiere, 1998 for a review of the relevant literature). Most of these studies have used American college students, a population that is assumed to be 'normal' (Stermac et al., 1990, p 146), the majority of whom are from white middle-class socioeconomic groups and unrepresentative of the general population made up of wider social class and ethnic groupings. These studies demonstrate that a significant proportion of the 'normal' male population believe it acceptable to carry out a sexual assault and report the likelihood of doing so if they could be assured of not being detected or punished. In one study around 28 per cent reported having actually carried out forced sexual assaults against women (Rapaport and Burkhart, 1984), while 10 per cent claimed to have engaged in coercive sex with children (Finkelhor and Lewis, 1988). Whatever the relationship between claims and reality these disclosures indicate disturbing propensities in a wider non-forensic population.

Crime reports (as opposed to criminal convictions), prevalence studies and self-report studies all point to the threat of sexual harm being wider than the population of convicted sex offenders. And yet the dominant social construction of the sex offender that appears in the media and seems to guide much policy thinking is based on this latter group. Ethical thinking in the construction of a research project in this area has to engage with these issues.

Ethical reflections on conceptualising research with men convicted of sex offences

This section reflects on ethical issues involved in the development of a life history research project with nine men who were convicted of sex offences. They were serving sentences of between four and ten years. Six of the men had offended against children and three had offended against adults. Only one of the men had any previous convictions for sexual offences. All of the men were white and aged between 25 and 61 years old at the time of the interviews, which all took place in prison. The men told their life stories from their earliest memories to their current situation, using life transitions (for example, entry to school[s], and work) as prompts for memories.

In reflecting on the ethical issues raised above, it could be said that the research colluded with the hegemonic discourse in relation to male sexual coercion by choosing to focus on men who were convicted of sexual offences, rather than looking more widely at problematic male behaviours in an unconvicted population. However, additional ethical issues shaped the decision to concentrate on this group. Practically, it would be very difficult, if not impossible, to identify a group of men who would admit that they had behaved in a sexually aggressive and coercive manner but had not been convicted of such behaviour. If such a group could be found, maintaining confidentiality where men were disclosing ongoing sexually abusive behaviour would be seriously problematic (see below and Cowburn [2004] for a fuller discussion of these issues), and, thus, the significant area of unreported and unconvicted sexual coercion is precluded from study here.

Although media attention, criminal law and penal practice are principally and primarily concerned with knowing about the detail of the sex offender's crimes, I deliberately chose life history research as a means of understanding each man within a context wider than that of his offending behaviour. This decision was rooted in Kantian respect for the individual and challenged the dominant constructions of the (male) sex offender that defined him solely by his criminal behaviours. Having decided to interview a group of men convicted of sexual offences, the issues of whether the group should be composed of men living in the community or men in prison was subjected to ethical scrutiny. In-depth personal reflection on life history is a sensitive issue (Lee, 1993) and has the potential to cause distress to the research participant. From a Kantian perspective of respect for the individual it was essential to minimise the harm to research participants and to ensure that they had help to cope with any distress. Additionally, it may be that intense reflection on some life events may be sexually arousing and such arousal could be the precursor to further offending. From a utilitarian perspective it was important to not knowingly put the general public at risk of harm. From both ethical standpoints, interviewing men who were living in the community seemed to be problematic. I could neither ensure that distressed men received help and support nor that they would not reoffend as a result of arousal experienced during the research interview. However, both these problems could be more effectively managed with the prison population. Not only would prison separate them from the community at large, but their response to the interviews could be more closely monitored and some help could be provided for them to manage distress.

While the above ethical considerations affected the conceptualisation of the project, other issues impacted on the conduct of the research and on the nature of the research findings. Thus ethical and epistemological issues are intricately interwoven at both the macro-level in designing a research project and also in the micro-level of the conduct of the research itself.

Ethical reflections on the process of research with men convicted of sex offences

Much of the discussion so far has focused on principle-based approaches to ethics and how they influence the shaping of a research project. 'Character and relationship-based' approaches to ethics (Banks, 2006, p 54) are more concerned with the detail of ethical conduct. Banks has noted that:

> Principle-based approaches ignore important features of moral life and moral judgements including the character, motives and emotions of the moral agent, the particular contexts in which judgements are made and the particular relationships and commitments people have to each other. (Banks, 2006, p 54)

Banks (2006, pp 54–71) has identified three main character and relationship-based approaches to ethical thinking and, more particularly, practice: all of these approaches share a focus on the detail of *relationship* and *context* (time, place and persons). In his discussion of research ethics, Kvale identifies an alternative to principle-based ethics that focuses on active reflection. He calls it 'a contextual ethical position' and describes it thus:

> Ethical behaviour is seen less as the application of general principles and rules, than as the researcher internalizing moral values. The personal integrity of the researcher, the interaction with the community studied, and the relation to their ethical values is essential. The emphasis is on the researcher's ethical intuitions, feelings and skills as well as on negotiations between actors in a specific community. (Kvale, 1996, p 122)

Contextual or character and relationship-based approaches are directly concerned with the conduct of a research project, but they inevitably relate back to principle-based approaches for (competing) guidance in practical situations. In relation to researching sex offenders and other criminological and 'sensitive' research, the issue of confidentiality is of key concern (Cowburn, 2004, pp 49–63). However, the issue is not easily resolved by reference to one or other of the principle-based ethical approaches; for example, how does a researcher deal with the issue of undisclosed offending behaviour coming to light during an interview? On the one hand a utilitarian approach would suggest that the fuller the picture of offending behaviour that can be obtained the greater the benefit to the majority because this information can inform subsequent developments of policy. However, a Kantian approach would seek to balance respect for the individual(s) against a duty to protect individual members of the public from harm: 'So act as to treat humanity, whether in your own person or that of any other, never solely as a means but always also as an end' (Kant, 1964, p 32). Thus, if a research participant disclosed that they or others were harming or intending to harm another person, a Kantian approach would have to balance the duty to:

- maintain confidentiality;
- protect the identified victim from harm;
- protect the research participant from harmful consequences of their disclosure.

Elsewhere (Cowburn, 2004), I have suggested ways of reconciling these apparently irreconcilable ethical positions in the process of a research project, through the adoption of a contextual ethical position. However, the purpose of this chapter is not to repeat this discussion but to consider how ethical dilemmas in research may or may not impact on policy formation.

Knowledge, policy and ethical conduct

The issue of confidentiality and in particular the issue of dealing with disclosure of sensitive material (Lee, 1993) potentially impacts on the research project and its relationship to policy formation in two ways. First, in the area of knowledge development it could be argued that by adopting a utilitarian standpoint (and guaranteeing complete confidentiality), a fuller picture of deviant/harmful behaviours might be obtained and this may then be used to develop an informed policy response to difficult issues. Second, however, in obtaining individual detailed information about a person's past, current and intended harmful actions, and taking no actions to prevent harm to specific individuals, may well be viewed as a failure to act ethically, from (one version of) a Kantian perspective, that would require consideration of the well-being of individual (potential victim) as an end in itself. Thus a failure knowingly to protect the well-being of either the individual being studied or potential known victims may also be viewed as a failure of ethics.

The issues raised by the utilitarian standpoint to the process of research link back to two issues discussed earlier: the social construction of knowledge and the ethics of methodological choice. It could be argued that allowing licence for offenders to disclose unreported offences and planned offences allows for the development of a fuller knowledge about sex offenders. However, as this knowledge relates only to convicted sex offenders it may not be particularly helpful in developing social policies aimed at protecting the majority (of the population) from sexual harm. That is not to say that such information is valueless. Abel et al.'s (1987) ground-breaking study into the unreported sex crimes of convicted sex offenders revealed much that was not previously known about the (previously undisclosed) offending proclivities of men convicted of sexual offences. This study challenged the notion that the risk sex offenders posed could be identified by their pattern of convictions, and is clearly of importance in developing policy in relation to the convicted population. The study avoided the issues of disclosure discussed above by surveying a large sample of men who were asked questions about their unreported sexual behaviours. The survey was anonymous and the researchers went to extreme lengths to protect the identities of their respondents. Ethically, this study did not have to face the issues of interview-based research: neither the offenders nor their potential/current victims were identified.

Conclusion

Colebatch (2002, p 19) has highlighted that an important part of policy development is dialogue between contesting forms of knowledge. The issue for him is not necessarily to choose one interpretation over another but rather to see how different interpretations cast light on social problems. This chapter has highlighted the importance of addressing ethical issues in research at a theoretical level of constructing the project and considering how it relates to dominant constructions of knowledge and how these influence and shape policy. It has also considered the impact of ethics in the process of research and how these also influence and shape the findings/knowledge constructed by research. The relationship between research and policy is never simple. The decision to design a research project within the terms dictated by hegemonic knowledge may mean that the research is more accessible to policy makers (and more likely to be funded), but inevitably the epistemological choices made are also ethical choices. Ethical research practice that is linked to the development of governmental policy needs to address the issue of how the project contributes to the greater good of the general public – this may mean challenging dominant notions of how governments construe these terms – whilst also ensuring that research participants are not compromised by their participation in research. Explicitly adopting ethical standpoints provides a starting point and a monitor for the conduct of research.

NINE

User involvement

Kathy Boxall, Lorna Warren and Ruby C.M. Chau

Introduction

Public service and research arenas are currently witnessing strong pressures to 'involve' service users in social care research, policy and practice. These pressures come from policy makers and the providers of services but also, as Peter Beresford (2001) has argued, from the users of welfare themselves; thus the involvement agendas of both the 'makers' and the 'subjects' of policy appear to coincide. This apparent consensus, however, belies the complex nature of the relationships and processes of user involvement and the strong feelings that can be aroused. It is these relationships, processes and feelings which form the focus of our exploration of user involvement in this chapter. Although we include discussion of user involvement *policy* – part of the broader UK government agenda to promote more participatory forms of governance – our primary concern here is user involvement in *research*; albeit research for policy and practice.

The different parties to user involvement are frequently presented as discrete groups: 'service users' who are the 'recipients' or 'subjects' of welfare policies and 'researchers' and 'policy makers' who are the 'architects' of those policies. Indeed, the notion of involvement assumes a separation between 'service users' and the research and policy-making processes in which, increasingly, their involvement is required. As with other participatory methodologies (see, for example, Reason and Bradbury, 2001), user involvement presents challenges to more traditional approaches to social research in that it is carried out 'with' (rather than 'on') those who are being researched. The challenges of such involvement extend to the realm of epistemology/ies and positivist assumptions about the separation of 'knower' and 'known'. They also prompt reconsideration of the personal and political dimensions of social research and the extent to which user involvement can be meaningfully conducted without reinforcing the separations on which it is based. Drawing on our own work in this area (Boxall et al, 2004;

Warren and Cook, 2005; Chau, 2007), this chapter illustrates some of the complexities of user involvement in research, which become apparent when 'users' and 'university researchers' work together. Thus, our discussion is concerned with the meanings and politics of user involvement in research as well as the methods and practices of such involvement.

Such discussion is particularly relevant to this volume's reconsideration of the processes and practices of policy. As we highlight later, service users are not new actors in the policy process. However, it is only relatively recently that public involvement has become part of the policy agenda and changes in policy/service structures put in place to encourage users' regular engagement. This entails an intended power relocation; but at the same time there are tensions among policy makers and service providers as to how far and in what form power should be relocated to users – if at all. Similarly, in relation to evidence-based policy and practice, questions about how far evidence generated from user-involved research processes would be accepted and whether users' views of 'what works' would count, have tested policy makers' and service providers' commitment to the practice (or rhetoric?) of user involvement (Hanley, 2005).

We begin our discussion by briefly exploring the category 'service user', and consider processes of 'participation' and 'involvement' and the meanings of these terms for those involved. We then consider the historical background to service provision and the development of service user involvement in services, policy and research. We argue that the methods and practices of user involvement present a number of challenges to conventional social policy research and to researchers who seek to work in this way. In particular, we highlight tensions between conventional expectations of researcher 'neutrality', 'objectivity' and 'professionalism', and ways of working, which welcome and accommodate the personal lives and experiences of service users in the methods and processes of research.

We conclude by arguing that service-user involvement, which is meaningful and useful for both service users, researchers and policy makers, necessitates approaches to research and policy which diminish, rather than reinforce, conventional separations of public/private, researcher/researched, knower/known, policy maker/policy subject.

Service users

As Jo Britton argues in Chapter Four, terms of categorisation tend to be overlooked in critical evaluations of policy as they are often assumed to be unproblematic; this is particularly so in relation to the term 'service user'. Although, at first sight, it may appear that people who receive health or social care services can be assigned straightforwardly to the category 'service user', such categorisation risks presenting people in 'passive, consumerist terms' (Beresford, 2005, p 469), and also gives rise to a number of anomalies. For example, disabled people, older people and others may be assessed as 'insufficiently severe' to warrant service provision (Greaves, 2006). Conversely, mental health services may be regarded as neither welcome nor useful by the 'service refusers' (Pembroke, 1994) for whom they are intended. Additionally, people using disability services at key stages in the life course – for example, when approaching adulthood or older age – may suddenly find themselves recategorised and no longer eligible for services to which they were previously entitled (Greaves, 2006). Despite these differences, the term 'service user' is used indiscriminately to refer to ex-users of services, people who 'refuse' or have been 'refused' services as well as those in receipt of services, whatever their route to designated need. As Beresford (2005, p 469) has noted, even people 'who are unhappy about this terminology nonetheless find themselves using it, or it being used about them'.

There is also the issue of *who* decides who 'counts' as a service user. Traditionally such decisions lay within the remit of welfare professionals (Wilding, 1982) and researchers frequently deferred to service providers' expertise. However, given the anomalies identified above, it may prove far from straightforward to decide who should, or should not, be 'involved' in user involvement initiatives and, indeed, whose responsibility it is to decide. In relation to membership of their own organisations, for example, the disabled people's movement has rejected professional assessment and has instead adopted a principle of self-definition as disabled people (Campbell and Oliver, 1996). Beresford (2005) appears to be advocating a similar position in relation to service users more generally when he argues that many long-term service users object to a broader understanding of the term 'service user', which embraces everyone who has contact with services:

> being a service user as they understand it, tends to be a very different matter from occasional routine use of mainstream acute health care, or having a short-term experience of social care. For them, service use may play a very significant part in their life and have a strong bearing on their identity and self-perception. (Beresford, 2005, pp 475–6)

The term 'service user' also encompasses a range of other professionally imposed categories, many of which have found their way into everyday understandings of welfare and its subjects. Peter Clough and Len Barton (1995) discuss the impact of these categories on those to whom they are applied:

> They are the recipients of powerful professional categories. These envelop their identities. They are the 'lunatics', the 'idiots', the 'mentally handicapped', the 'subnormal', the 'spastics', the 'cripples' and 'level-one child'. The point is: *We* know who *They* are. (Clough and Barton, 1995, p 2, emphasis in original)

Indeed, such categorisation extends to those who are not actually using services because they are 'hard to reach' or 'look after their own' (SSI, 1998). The recipients and subjects of the professional and administrative categories to which Clough and Barton refer have, however, voiced their own opinions and acted upon this issue themselves. Rather than accepting professionally imposed identities as passive recipients of social care, or subjects of social policy, they have reclaimed categories such as 'cripple' (Hunt, 1998) and 'mad' (Campbell, 1996) translating them into positive and forceful political identities which highlight social exclusion and oppression rather than deficit and difference. They have demanded 'rights, not charity' and the opportunity to represent themselves rather than accept prescriptive professional assessments of their 'needs' (Beresford, 2001). Members of supposedly 'hard to reach' minority ethnic communities have responded to their categorisation by setting up their own support groups and alternative welfare services (Chau and Yu, 2001; Chau, 2007). Instead of being passively defined service users, they have proactively redefined themselves as service providers.

As Beresford (2005, p 470) observes, service user organisations usually focus on specific groups (for example, mental health service users, people with learning difficulties) rather than service users in general. A problem with the term 'service user' is that it includes a range of groups and individuals without acknowledging the differences between these groups. Older people, for example, have not achieved the same kind of strength or prominence as disabled people in organising and speaking out for themselves, subject as they are to ageism as well as the stigma of disability (Warren, 1999). Beresford (2005, p 473) suggests, however, that all service user groups and individuals share experience of 'services which are historically associated with stigma, segregation, poverty, exclusion and restricted quality of life'. As researchers with a particular interest in user involvement, we work with a range of service user organisations (older people's groups, including Chinese older people's organisations, and self-advocacy groups of people with learning difficulties), all of whom place particular emphasis on the need to challenge negative perceptions and stereotypes of service users. Our view is that unless we seek directly to challenge such understandings in our research work, we risk further constructing and perpetuating dominant views of service users in passive, consumerist and stigmatising roles. However, as Clough and Barton (1995, p 2) argue, we cannot work in or inhabit the field of welfare without being 'in some way conditioned by [its] categorical hegemony'.

Research has played a key part historically in the identification and definition of those viewed as 'different' (Ryan and Thomas, 1987; Bytheway, 1995) and the academy provided 'powerful academic support' for their institutionalisation (Radford, 1994, p 15). Yet a growing number of the leading researchers in the field of welfare research and user involvement are themselves users, or ex-users, of services, adding another layer of complexity to, but at the same time opening up, the issue of categorisation. Peter Beresford for example describes himself as qualifying, in tabloid speak, as a 'nutter', 'psycho', 'crazy' and 'loony' (Brown, 2005). But he is also a university professor who, as an 'out' 'mental health service user', is bringing to higher education experiences that have been excluded in the past. Traditional social science research was founded on ideas of neutrality, objectivity and distance (Stanley and Wise, 1993; Beresford, 2003), and although more recent methodological approaches encourage reflexivity and the situating of researchers in their own work (Warren, 1990), the personal lives of researchers had no place in historical research with service users. Researchers, like the staff working in welfare services, were expected to maintain a 'professional distance' from the service users 'on' whom they undertook research (Morris, 1991).

For Beresford (2005), what is crucial is challenging the prejudice of categorisation. He argues for a reappropriation of the term 'service user' as a means of highlighting shared experiences of discrimination, and recommends that all user groups work collectively towards improving the status of service users. Although we share Beresford's aim, at the same time, we also have concerns about over-focusing on service users' 'difference' (Clough and Barton, 1995). Thus, one aspect of this chapter is to consider some of the similarities and parallels in the lives and experiences of 'university researchers' and the service users with whom they undertake research.

Participation in service development and policy making

Many people identified as service users today would have faced institutionalisation during the first 60 years of the twentieth century (Oliver and Barnes, 1998). The Mental Deficiency Act 1913, for example, was largely successful in its aim to remove undesirable 'social inefficients' from mainstream society (Race, 1995, p 49), and it was not until after the Second World War that public opinion about the institutions began to change and organisations such as the National Council for Civil Liberties started their campaign to reform the long-stay hospitals (Thomson, 1998). Changes in legislation from 1959 onwards signalled a willingness to release people from hospitals but the majority had to wait several decades before being discharged to their communities of origin. The situation for people with physical and sensory impairments was slightly different in that many were accommodated in residential homes run by charities or local authorities, and some residents were able to make use of British housing association schemes which offered disabled people a way out of (often large-scale) residential accommodation from the 1980s onwards (Oliver and Sapey, 2006).

In the late 1960s and 1970s, a series of inquiries into scandals in long-stay hospitals for older people, people with learning difficulties and those deemed mentally ill revealed overcrowding, squalid conditions and abuse (Martin, 1984). Despite public outcry, the process of 'resettling' large numbers of people from long-stay hospitals began very slowly. David Race (2002, p 44) points to the Thatcher government's paradox of 'expensive long-stay hospitals on valuable land', which, if they were sold, would release considerable resources for the 'resettlement' process; and the government's commitment to 'run down the power of the Local Authorities'. However, because of the spiralling costs of private residential care places funded by the social security system, the government eventually supported the recommendations of the Griffiths Report and implemented the Community Care Act 1990. This charged local authority social services departments with responsibility for assessing vulnerable individuals' suitability for residential care and also transferred central government funding to local authorities. Under the new system, a 'mixed economy of care', supported and encouraged by local authority social services departments, was put into place.

Although the idea of participation in service development and policy making was not new at this time, Suzy Croft and Peter Beresford (1989, p 5) linked growing interest in *user involvement* to these late

1980s' developments, arguing that 'the discovery of the social policy consumer ... coincided with the market's increasing appropriation of welfare'. However, as they also point out, 'user involvement' had different meanings for the different parties involved. They argue that for service providers, user involvement had strong overtones of 'welfare consumerism', and was tied in to particular service provision; whereas for service users, user involvement was often underpinned by the philosophy of 'self-advocacy', which extends beyond the boundary of services, to 'having a greater say and control over the whole of our lives' (Croft and Beresford, 1989, p 5).

More recently, New Labour's modernisation agenda has promoted 'active citizenship' and public involvement across a range of policy areas. The Local Government Act 1999, for example, requires local authorities and other local service providers, including police and fire authorities, to consult service users about the services they provide (Marinetto, 2003). National programmes such as 'Better Government for Older People' have also sought to include older people's views and contributions. The *Valuing People* White Paper (DH, 2001) has put into place new structures and arrangements for the coordination of services for people with learning difficulties through Partnership Boards, which include service users and carers in local planning and policy making. Thus, there has been a shift in expectations of service users: rather than just being 'users' or 'choosers' of services, they are now expected to engage in 'making' and 'shaping' services and policy (Cornwall and Gaventa, 2000).

These heightened expectations of service user involvement have, however, been criticised on a number of fronts. Service users have highlighted poor access to consultation events, confusing terminology, lack of responsiveness or feedback and concerns about their knowledge and experience not being taken seriously (Carr, 2004). Service providers have questioned service users' 'subjectivity' or lack of representativeness (Beresford and Campbell, 1994; Parkinson, 2004). Commentators have argued that rather than 'active citizenship', user involvement can be viewed as 'active management' (Milewa et al., 1999); 'a consultation industry' or 'technology of legitimation', which serves to reinforce professional and managerial power under the guise of pluralism (Harrison and Mort, 1998); or as a means of avoiding engagement with structural issues by focusing attention on the individual concerns of those service users in attendance (Hodge, 2005). As Mike Williams (2004, para 2.13) has observed, while the shift in expectations of service user involvement has increased the *symbolic importance* of service users' views, there has been 'no accompanying reform of the formal decision making procedures that would guarantee those views more influence'.

Despite heightened interest in service user involvement, from the late 1980s onwards, it is sobering to note the similarities between service users' requests and demands then and now (Croft and Beresford, 1989; Branfield et al., 2006). The fact that recent inquiry reports have uncovered conditions not dissimilar to those highlighted in the hospital scandals of the 1960s and 1970s (Martin, 1984) is also a sad indictment of welfare provision for vulnerable groups. At the same time, there have also been substantial improvements in service provision (Wistow, 2005) some of which have been influenced by the disabled people's movement (Beresford, 2005). Notwithstanding these positive developments, service users have a range of outstanding concerns, many of which centre on the power of welfare professionals and support personnel to control or influence their lives (Carr, 2004).

'Ordinary' citizens (who are not long-term service users) can attempt to influence policy- and decision-making processes in a number of different ways. They can, for example, participate in interest and pressure groups, express views to elected representatives or those with decision-making powers, or campaign to change public opinion. They also have opportunities to vote and to participate in party politics. There may, however, be obstacles to their active participation; for example, barriers related to education, class or ethnic background. For people visibly identified as service users, these barriers may be compounded by attitudes (public and professional) towards older people, disabled people, mental health service users, people with learning difficulties and so on, and the devalued status assigned to 'welfare dependants' (Wolfensberger, 2000). Service users may also be disenfranchised (Scott and Crooks, 2005), their views may be dismissed because of perceived 'incapacity', other groups (for example, large national charities or carers' organisations) with whom they may not be in agreement, may campaign more respectably on their behalf, and the professionals' power to know what is best for them may leave little room for negotiation. Ultimately, they may fear having services removed or being victimised by service providers as a result of voicing their views (Warren and Maltby, 2000).

Historically, the welfare professions claimed that their professional ethics and expertise equipped them to act in the interests of both their 'clients' and the public (Wilding, 1982). Public faith and confidence in the professions has, however, been shaken by a range of high-profile national events, including the organ retention scandals at Bristol and Alder Hey children's hospitals, the Victoria Climbié inquiry and the murdering of patients by general practitioner Harold Shipman. The demise of the long-stay hospitals and their replacement by community supports may also be viewed as diminishing the power of the professions. However, although new funding arrangements for community based support have undoubtedly resulted in increased opportunities for some service users, they have also further complicated already complex funding structures and in order to qualify for such support, service users are still subject to professional assessment of need (Means et al., 2003). Helen Carr (2005, p 404) has argued that the introduction of programmes such as 'Supporting People', which is an ambitious 'strategic and dispersed framework of welfare governance' aimed at supporting people to live in their own homes, has served to enhance the strategic power of a range of welfare professionals at regional and national levels.

As Chris Drinkwater (2005) has observed, power is also exercised by the support personnel who provide assistance in people's own homes. Such power may extend to providing, or withdrawing, support to attend user involvement activities and assisting, or failing to assist, service users to register on the electoral roll and vote. Despite its emphasis on the involvement of health and social care service users, New Labour's goal of active citizenship and community involvement may, therefore, be beyond the reach of those service users whose participation is mediated by welfare professionals and support personnel.

Service users and the academy

Before discussing user involvement in research, we wish first to consider the historical relationship between service users and the academy. During the twentieth century, academic research was used to legitimate a range of policies and interventions in the lives of people who would today be identified as service users. John Radford (1994) argues that:

> The most powerful academic support was given during the lamentable denouement in the first half of [the last] century: the custodial incarceration, sterilization and even extermination of many people diagnosed as 'feebleminded' on the basis of a perceived eugenic threat. (Radford, 1994, pp 15–16)

Bill Hughes (2002, p 58) similarly argues that 'the long historical partnership between modernity and medicalization produced a hegemonic conception of disability as an outcome of physical or mental impairment', resulting in the 'disposal' of those with 'broken bodies' and 'faulty minds' whose presence offended the rationality and reason of the modernist project. The 'science' of medicine and other associated disciplines thus identified, removed and then controlled the lives of disabled people. Aileen Wight Felske (1994, p 183) suggests that the deficit 'way of knowing' inherent in the positivist research of the academy, continued to influence later community-based services where social science behaviourist responses 'emulated the rules of natural science observation and replication' and instituted damaging regimes of punishment and control. Radford (1994, p 23) also argues, however, that research underpinned by positivist approaches was used to 'undermine much of the eugenic argument' on which institutionalisation policies had been based.

The positivism of the nineteenth-century academy was the methodology of the natural sciences and medicine. Twentieth-century researchers adapted positivist techniques in order to study the social world of service users. These social science approaches, however, continued to be underpinned by individualised medical understandings of disability (Oliver, 1990). Feminist critiques of positivist social science (Stanley and Wise, 1993) have been echoed by disabled people and other service users, who have questioned the supposed neutrality and objectivity of such approaches, arguing that they serve the interests of the dominant group research community and powerful professionals (Beresford, 2003). Later studies of service users adopted qualitative or interpretative approaches to social research; these were viewed as offering greater possibilities of respect for the people being researched in that their aim was to understand their perspectives. However, qualitative studies have also been criticised by service users both for interpreting their realities and because they involve 'a relatively small group of powerful experts doing work on a larger number of relatively powerless research subjects' (Oliver, 1992, p 106).

Until recently, research considering the circumstances of service users has tended to be research 'on' rather than 'with' or 'by' service users. There has been little expectation that service users will themselves be researchers or that they (or their families) will have access to published research reports which refer, albeit anonymously, to their lives and personal experiences. The academic community has thus controlled knowledge and ideas about service users within the literature (Morris, 1991). As Chris Jones (1996, p 197) has observed, the historical knowledge base 'reveals startling continuities, such as social work's construction of clients as generally unworthy and manipulative individuals' who have been 'written off'.

Unlike developments in services and policy outside the academy, social policy as a discipline has been slow to involve service users and their organisations (Beresford, 2001, p 508). There is, however, some evidence to suggest that this exclusion of service users is beginning to change. Access to the Internet through public libraries, and the commitment of organisations such as the Joseph Rowntree Foundation (www.jrf.org. uk), INVOLVE (http://www.invo.org.uk) and the Disability Archive UK at Leeds University (http://www.leeds.ac.uk/disability-studies/ archiveuk) to placing research reports and policy documents in the public domain, has significantly increased access to research findings. Service users are becoming increasingly aware of academic literature, and some user organisations are now undertaking and publishing their own research and developing their own understandings of their experiences (Turner and Beresford, 2005a). Policies of widening access to higher education have also supported 'non-traditional' students, some of whom are now working as researchers (Hurst, 1995) and requirements to involve service users in research have led to their increasing presence in the academy (Boxall et al., 2004).

Methodological developments relating to the involvement of service users in academic research can be linked to participatory approaches where research is undertaken 'with' rather than 'on' those whose experience is being researched (Reason and Bradbury, 2001). Service users may be involved in research design, data collection, data analysis and/or dissemination. They may have very limited roles as consultants or advisory group members or more active roles as user-researchers who carry out interviews, participate in analysis and present at conferences alongside 'university researchers' (Warren and Maltby, 2000). Involvement may also vary from lone service users who have no affiliation to user groups but are somehow expected to represent a 'service user perspective', through to representative groups or committees from democratically constituted organisations of service users (Beresford and Campbell, 1994).

As with user involvement in service development and policy making, the meanings of 'involvement' may differ for the different parties involved and expectations may vary between research funding bodies, service users and 'university' researchers, as well as across different research projects. The Joseph Rowntree Foundation, one of the major funders of social research in the UK, has for a number of years required that applicants demonstrate the involvement of service users in research design and process. Requirements may also extend to making research processes more accessible to service users; for example, the Social Care Institute for Excellence commissioned research into people with learning difficulties' transition from childhood to adulthood. This stated that since people with learning difficulties were to be involved in the evaluation of submissions, '*the tender response should be in accessible format*' (SCIE, 2003, p 13, emphasis in original). On their part, service users and their organisations may have requirements in relation to access (including accessible information), and payment for their time and expertise (Turner and Beresford, 2005b).

Academics developing an interest in user involvement in research often find themselves on a steep learning curve in terms of gaining an understanding of service users' starting points and agendas and, as a result, may adopt narrow approaches to user involvement research. The failure of academic researchers to use more creative ways of working (see, for example, Barnes, 1999) may be a reflection of the failures of 'mainstream' user involvement theory and practice to accommodate emotional experience, story-telling and diverse debates (Barnes, 2002).

Methods that are radical or untested in research with one user group may be common practice with other user groups or may still carry questionable restrictions in relation to the aim to share responsibility and control. For example, Lorna Warren, Joe Cook and Tony Maltby (Warren and Cook, 2005) wanted to recruit older women to conduct life-story interviews with other older women. However, in contrast to the area of physical impairment where such an approach is not unusual (Campbell and Oliver, 1996) they could find no existing examples of where this had been done in policy-related research with older people. At the same time, the process of making a project video raised ethical issues, which ironically restricted control for some members of the group (Warren and Cook, 2005).

Currently, there are arguments for research which is controlled by service users themselves (Turner and Beresford, 2005a) and for a distinct 'service user identity' (Beresford, 2005). User controlled research has links with emancipatory disability research and the social model of disability. Research based on a social model understanding of disability takes as its focus the barriers experienced by disabled people, rather than their individual 'functional limitation' or 'deficit' (Barnes, 2003). Sarah Carr (2004, p 6) points to the broader influence of the social model among service users, and argues that non-disabled service users 'who are disempowered by social, cultural and physical structures' have also used social model ideas as a means of making sense of their experiences. In emancipatory disability research, researchers also 'have to learn how to put their knowledge and skills at the disposal of their research subjects, for them to use in whatever ways they choose' (Oliver, 1992, p 111).

Michael Turner and Peter Beresford (2005a) suggest that user controlled research is particularly useful in enabling service users to describe their experience and develop shared understandings which may challenge academics' constructions of service users. In practice, support for user controlled research is limited and despite the importance currently placed on user involvement, service users' organisations have to compete for funding alongside universities and research institutes, and receive only a very small proportion of available research funds (Turner and Beresford, 2005a). Our experience is that the 'us' and 'them' of service users and academic researchers is still present and indeed, it could be suggested, is being reinforced by arguments for a distinct 'service user identity' and for service user controlled research.

Implications of 'user involvement' for research practice

The impetus for service user involvement in research comes from a number of different sources including service users themselves, government departments and those responsible for funding and administering research. There is also some acknowledgement of involvement approaches from within the research establishment, in that the social policy and administration and social work panel collated information about service user involvement in research in the 2001 Research Assessment Exercise. Thus, in principle at least, this way of working is being recognised. Our own experiences, however, suggest that there are significant challenges and barriers for academics who wish to involve service users in research. These include ethical concerns about exploiting the same over-researched or 'over-involved' service users and ways of ending intensive involvement, as well as the time commitment required to work in this way, coupled with the pressure to publish. Additionally, the same status is not accorded to participatory research with service users as to more 'scientific' or 'scholarly' work (Goodley and Moore, 2000). These concerns are, we suggest, indicative of a mismatch between academic and service user cultures; a mismatch which, as we discuss below, lies at the heart of service user involvement in academic research.

A review of published reports of user involvement studies (Tarpey, 2006) found that service users give a range of reasons for getting involved in research. These include motivations linked to personal or family needs in the area of research, the desire to 'have a say' or influence services and policy, the need to do something with the anger and frustration they feel about previous bad experiences of services, as well as perceived benefits in terms of personal development and opportunities for social and emotional support. Some service users also welcome the opportunity to enter the ivory tower (Warren et al., 2003).

Service users who are not involved in research have suggested that those who do get involved are probably 'gullible' or have 'nothing else to do' or have questioned user involvement agendas, suggesting that they are motivated by the need to 'pacify growing complaints about the state of the provision' (Tarpey, 2006, p 6). Indeed, some users have refused to become involved unless subsequent changes can be guaranteed, levelling the charge of 'lip service' at projects without concrete outcomes (Warren et al., 2003). Those service users who do get involved want to challenge public perceptions about people who use services and improve future service provision; they also have 'a strong sense that something tangible and useful will result from their involvement in research' (Tarpey, 2006, p 5). However, concern about the lack of impact of research has been raised by disabled people's organisations for a number of years (Oliver, 1990). Similar concerns have also been identified in relation to user controlled research where service users have highlighted the importance of the research *process* as well as outcomes:

> I think that the very process of the research has got to be not only enjoyable, but it has got in itself to be empowering, for want of a better word. So that when people come together and discuss things they feel better about themselves in some way. (Disabled person, Discussion Group D, Turner and Beresford, 2005a, p 63)

Evidence of the intrinsic benefits of research has been captured in various forms including poems (Warren et al., 2003). Service users have also produced their own guidelines and principles for research (for example, Faulkner, A., 2004). These include involving everyone from the start, communicating clearly, providing training, attending to people's needs (for example, arranging transport) and making sure resources are adequate. Comparable guidelines for user involvement have been produced from within the academy (for example, Cormie and Warren, 2001); these share many similarities with those produced by service users with an emphasis on practical matters.

However, some service user-researchers with experience of working in universities highlight a conflict between the competing interests of professionals/academics and service users, which may be more or less visible within the research arena: academics are viewed by some service users as 'chasing the money' and putting their own agendas and careers before service users' interests. Service users raise concerns about the amount of money being spent on research and question whether it could be better spent directly improving services (Turner and Beresford, 2005, pp 25–6). More fundamental concerns about the nature of knowledge and its production also come into play when university researchers and service users work together (Beresford, 2003, Boxall et al., 2004).

Although the imperative to involve service users in research comes from research funders and policy makers, it is being played out mainly within the academy, a place from which service users and their knowledges have been traditionally excluded. Historically, academic knowledge production has prioritised researcher 'neutrality', 'objectivity' and 'professionalism' and the expectation that researchers maintain a professional distance between themselves and their research 'subjects'. User involvement, however, is founded on the expectation that service users bring to the research process knowledge that comes from experience, and also work alongside university researchers as colleagues or peers. This fundamentally changes the research relationship, and also blurs both the researcher/researched and public/private boundaries on which, historically, professional research practice has been based.

The working methods and practices of the academy leave little space for the personal experience. 'Objective' research processes derived from positivist science were designed to remove the personal and political. Later interpretative research has been criticised for using people as 'objects' of study and even 'post-modernist' approaches prioritise the voices of academics over those of service users (Wilson and Beresford, 2002). Service users bring the personal and political dimensions of their lives into research practices, which were originally designed to 'factor out' such dimensions. We cannot just 'step back' and observe, comment upon or analyse the personal and political concerns of service user colleagues; they are present in the work we undertake together. They impact upon our working arrangements and force us to re-evaluate research practices which dehumanise relationships and devalue the 'less academic' contributions of service user colleagues (Boxall et al., 2004). Our work with service users has also caused us to revisit debates about the separation of public and private lives (Pateman, 1989), and to question the lack of space for our personal lives within research practices, which create space and time for the service users with whom we work. The clash of expectations regarding the time requirements of ethical research practice with service users, and the output demands of the academy is particularly keenly felt in work of this nature; more so because of the lack of regard for research outputs based on service users' knowledges (Goodley and Moore, 2000).

Service users' knowledges challenge notions of objectivity, and separations between knower and known (Hekman, 1997). It is precisely because they have experiences *as* service users, that their perspectives are being sought. It is, however, difficult for service users to challenge existing understandings of themselves and their experiences because of the dominance of academics' ideas. As Jenny Morris has argued: 'the views which become part of the general culture are those of the academics and professionals working in our field' (1991, p 133). Service users, like women, in general, may seemingly be viewed as being rightfully subordinate because of an 'appeal to nature' and their 'naturally' dependent status (Brown and Smith, 1989; Pateman, 1989).

> This plays out in many forms: from the basic ontological premise that one must have a certain degree or type of reason to even be considered human in any morally significant sense to the more political incarnation that an insufficient degree or type of reason excludes one from being a citizen or having significant legal status ... All of these ideas can be found at the very core of the Western intellectual tradition – in the work of Plato and Aristotle. (Stainton, 2001, p 452)

Although Stainton's discussion refers specifically to people with learning difficulties, it is not difficult to see how such ideas might be applied to other service users including people with dementia, mental health service users and older people from minority ethnic communities who speak little English. These people are now being expected to participate in the knowledge production processes of an academy, which worked historically to exclude many of them from mainstream society. Through their involvement in research, they are expected to contribute to a policy-making process which barely recognises them as citizens. Viewed in this way, the radical nature of user involvement in research becomes apparent. We should not be surprised, therefore, if we encounter resistance to the research practices of user involvement or if the findings of user involvement research are deemed to lack 'validity'. Ideas about validity may be viewed as a means of shoring up the reality and interests of the dominant group within the research community, and resisting deviations from established ideas (Stanley and Wise, 1993). Research findings are frequently viewed as 'valid' if they conform to the predictions of members of the research community, produce the same (expected) findings as colleagues or peers or conform to the theoretical expectations of the construct(s) within which the research community is working (Clough, 1995).

Although it may be possible to work within alternative counter-hegemonic constructs, there may be few incentives for the powerful within the research community to accept such constructs (Seller, 1988) and the system of peer review, where established members of the research community review and judge the research of new members, works to resist such change (Clough, 1995). It is not common practice to involve service users in peer review of academic research reports though service users are themselves challenging this convention (Hanley, 2005). Implementation of such a practice would raise a whole host of questions about the status of knowledge that comes from one's own experience, relative to that of knowledge, which comes from the experience of others. Related discussions argue that such decisions would need to rely on ethical considerations such as prioritising previously silenced voices, the challenging of injustice or the 'transformative potential' of the knowledge produced (Bar On, 1993; Collins, 1997; Barnes, 2003). Though it is difficult to imagine such a system in practice, it is important to remember that the conventional system of peer review, where respected academics review research papers, has also been identified as problematic (see, for example, McCarty, 2002).

Working alongside service users in user involvement research projects challenges conventional distinctions between the roles of researcher and 'researched'; we have found ourselves in situations, which we have never had to think through before or for which there are no obvious protocols. For example, in earlier research projects, while we underwent checks by the Criminal Records Bureau (CRB) ourselves, it simply did not occur to us that service users working as user-researchers would also need CRB clearance prior to interviewing 'vulnerable adults'. Clearly, at this stage, we were still viewing service users as 'service users' rather than colleagues or, at best, as 'token researchers'. It now seems obvious that these checks need to be carried out in order to comply with the law, although lack of clarity remains regarding universities' responsibilities towards user-researchers who may themselves be 'vulnerable adults'. We have also found ourselves taking other support roles and tasks including personal care, support for people with health conditions such as epilepsy, which may need immediate attention, and intervening in situations where there is concern about the personal safety of service users.

Conclusion

Ultimately, user involvement in research prompts us to examine the very foundations of social policy (research) and to reconsider the epistemological basis of welfare provision (Beresford, 2001). It also prompts us to question the situating of user involvement research within the academy (Turner and Beresford, 2005).

We do not wish, however, to argue for the removal of user involvement research from universities but rather for a reconsideration and theorising of the role of academic researchers who support and facilitate such approaches. Central to this reappraisal is the inclusion of service users' voices and concerns, as well as consideration of the personal/political dimensions of both service users and academic researchers' roles in user involvement research. We suggest that theorising user involvement research within the academy should draw upon the existing work of service user researchers, methodological discussions of user controlled research, critiques of user involvement within service development and policy making as well as debates concerning situated knowledges and the academy.

Finally, we welcome initiatives by research funding bodies (such as those mentioned previously) to encourage the involvement of service users and carers in research design and process; and to enhance their access to research outputs. However, the traditional policy studies ground has left little space for theoretical contributions from policy's subjects (Beresford, 2001). We look, therefore, to funders, research councils and academic colleagues to support the further involvement of service users in policy studies debate – for policy analysis by its subjects surely would be policy reconsidered.

Acknowledgements
We wish to acknowledge the support of the Economic and Social Research Council for the projects, Older Women's Lives and Voices: Participation and Policy in Sheffield (ref L480254048) and Partnership Research: Negotiating User Involvement in Research Design (ref RES-333-25-0002); and the Joseph Rowntree Foundation for the Involvement of Chinese Older People in Policy and Practice: Aspirations and Expectations project.

TEN

Policies as translation: situating transnational social policies

Noémi Lendvai and Paul Stubbs

Introduction

A constructivist 'anthropology of policy' 'treats the models and language of decision-makers as ethnographic data to be analysed' (Shore and Wright, 1997, p 13) so that policy is viewed as a process rather than a fact. This approach is more concerned with *how* policy means rather than with *what* policy means. It reverses a traditional anthropology of 'making the strange familiar' with a commitment to 'making the familiar strange' (MacClancey, 2002, p 7). In addition, policy has become internationalised, with important policy-making arenas existing at levels beyond those of the nation state; transnationalised, as policy models and frameworks travel across time and place; and even globalised through the formal conditionalities of international financial institutions and the 'soft' power of 'global public policy networks' (see Stone, 2003). This chapter, essentially, explores some of the implications of developing an anthropology or ethnography of the transnational dimensions of policy, that is, those dimensions of policy which encompass levels beyond the individual nation state.

This is framed, theoretically, in terms of the notion of transnational policy not as *transfer* but rather as *translation*. It is addressed, contextually, in terms of our own work on understanding changes in social policies in a number of post-communist countries in transition in Central and South Eastern Europe as a somewhat dramatic, although perhaps not unique, site of a decade and a half of 'symbolic hyperinflation' of 'symbols, metaphors, language and emblems' (Scott, 2002). A complex conceptual architecture has emerged, under the umbrella of 'reform', constructed in the encounter with supranational bodies including the European Union, the World Bank and the United Nations and its agencies, as well as in and through encounters with a range of international non-state actors, including international NGOs and private consultancy companies.

In this sense, our work is part of an emerging tradition of international social policy research which replaces a notion of international actors as all-powerful with a much more complex, contextually-rooted understanding of the interactions within and between supranational and national actors. We adhere to ethnographic accounts of policy change processes which emphasise policy mediation, dialogue, translation, compromise and resistance. We focus on social policy in terms of its 'deep uncertainties' or 'displacements' of the taken for granted (Rustin and Freeman, 1999, p12). We situate this in the context of a new internationalisation in which countries compare their social policies with those of other countries and in which notions of 'European social policy' and even of 'global social policy' suggest reform models and benchmarks which are beyond those of the nation state.

The first part of this chapter outlines the basic conceptual apparatus, in terms of policy as meaning-making. The second part examines policy as translation and explores the implications in terms of the transnationalisation of policy and, in particular, seeks to contrast policy translation with more orthodox notions of policy transfer. The third part explores policy translation through a reflexive ethnographic approach developing two vignettes based on our own practical involvement in, and intellectual understanding of, social policy reform in parts of Central and South Eastern Europe. The fourth part draws some brief conclusions, and notes some theoretical and ethical objections that can and should be raised concerning our approach.

Our work is an encounter between two scholars, travelling between sites and across disciplinary boundaries. One of us (NL) is a Hungarian living and working in the UK, the other (PS) is British, living and working in Croatia. Schooled in more empirical and normative traditions in social policy and social administration we have, each in our own way, struggled to find our anthropological voices, and to explore new relationships between research and praxis as part of a process of re-examining our own work on globalisation, Europeanisation and social policy in Central and South Eastern Europe.

Policy as meaning-making

Framing policy as a meaning-making process is to acknowledge that policy is always 'layered by implicit meanings' (Innes, 2002) which involves, in Stone's terms, 'a constant discursive struggle over the definitions of problems, the boundaries of categories used to describe them, the criteria for their classification and assessment, and the meanings of ideals that guide particular actions' (Stone, 2002, p 60). In a sense, policies are always meaning-making and claims-making processes (Yanow, 1996), which have to be 'studied through' in terms of 'tracking policy discourses, prescriptions and programs and then linking them to those affected by the policies' (Wedel, 2005, p 37). In other words, a series of interesting, and sometimes even surprising, disturbances can occur in the spaces between the 'creation', the 'transmission' and the 'interpretation' or 'reception' of policy meanings.

Policy, in Fischer's terms, 'is not only expressed in words, it is literally "constructed" through the language in which it is described' (Fischer, 2003, p 43). We would go beyond this notion of language as 'descriptive', to assert that policy is inscribed through language and cannot exist outside of language. This is, however, never neutral or technical, but rather, as Bourdieu and Wacquant assert:

> linguistic relations are always relations of symbolic power through which relations of force between the speakers and their respective groups are actualised in a transfigured form. Consequently, it is impossible to elucidate any act of communication within the compass of linguistic analysis alone. Even the simplest linguistic exchange brings into play a complex and ramifying web of historical power relations between the speaker, endowed with a specific social authority, and an audience, which recognises this authority to varying degrees, as well as between the groups to which they respectively belong. (Bourdieu and Wacquant, 1992, pp 142–3)

Bourdieu and Wacquant suggest that linguistic relations are 'unintelligible' outside the 'totality of the structures of power relations' (1992, p 143) although whether, as they suggest, these are usually rendered invisible in linguistic exchanges is a more open question, particularly in the case of transnational policy encounters and discourses. For Yanow, policy is fundamentally an interpretive process, which 'focuses on the meanings of policies, on the values, feelings, and/or beliefs which they express, and on the processes by which those meanings are communicated to and "read" by various audiences' (Yanow, 1996, pp 8–9). In her work, she demonstrates convincingly how the meaning of policy is never singular, but always plural and contested, involving an 'active readership' by various policy actors and policy relevant publics, who are both interpreters as well as creators of 'new' meanings. Policy in this sense is always multiple and changing, transforming both the content as well as the context of policy, from formation to implementation.

In a number of languages, including all the Slavic languages and Hungarian, the same word usually serves for both the English words 'politics' and 'policy'. Recently, in Croatian, the word *'politika'* for policy has been partially replaced by the word *'mjere'* (literally *'measures'*) in order to capture the difference between policy and politics. In addition, the word 'policy' is almost inevitably framed by a number of other words: consider 'public policy', 'social policy', 'family policy', 'gun-control policy', 'equal opportunities policy', and so on. This suggests that the word policy is, in and of itself, insufficient in order to 'map' or 'frame' that which is being discussed. Of course, meaning-making in policies is never an apolitical or technical process, although a cadre of 'policy makers' and 'advisers' seek to suggest that this is the case. As Shore and Wright have argued, the political nature of policies is often 'disguised by the objective, neutral, legal-rational idioms in which they are portrayed' (Shore and Wright, 1997, p 8).

Central to this is the achievement and ascription of 'expertise' and 'expert knowledge' within the policy-making process. While a vast body of work on 'governmentality' points to the role of 'expertise' in fixing subjectivities, the dangers of this becoming little more than 'the functionalist accumulation of premise-confirming anecdotes dressed up in uniform conceptual garb' (Gould, 2005), are all too real. For this reason, while we continue to emphasise the importance of policy technologies, including statistics, standards, contracts, terms of reference, logical frameworks and the like, we insist on the historical and contextual specificity of these technologies. Perhaps even more importantly, we take a keen interest in the complexity of 'expert domains' and the creative need for 'experts' to deal with 'contradiction, exception [and] facts that are fugitive' (Holmes and Marcus, 2005, p 237).

Policy translation and the transnational: beyond policy transfer

Translation as a concept has, itself, travelled a long way from its origins in linguistics and translation studies, to a situation in which 'today an increasing number of scholars are aware of both the conceptual complexity and the politico-ethical significance of translation', in terms of its 'complicity with', or, as we would prefer to state, inseparability from, 'the building, transforming or disrupting of power relations' (Sakai, 2006, pp 71–2). A long-standing 'sociology of translation' emphasises the fluid and dynamic nature of 'policy', where meanings are constantly transformed, translated, distorted and modified (Latour, 2005).

The notion of translation problematises policy, which is seen as a continuous process of 'displacement', 'dislocation', 'transformation' and 'negotiation' (Callon, 1986). 'Translation' occurs in a complex web of social actors, and non-social actants, called actor networks, because all those enrolled in the network are active members and mediators shaping and transforming claims, artefacts, discourses and interpretations according to their different projects (Latour, 1987), 'actively paralleling and even displacing those of political authorities' (O'Malley, 1996, p 316). Translation can be seen as 'a continuous process through which individuals transform the knowledge, truths and effects of power each time they encounter them' (Herbert-Cheshire, 2003, p 456).

An unpublished paper by Richard Freeman comes closest to our own sense of the use of 'policy as translation'. For him, translation transfers and transforms: it entails representing something in a new way and in a new place, inevitably changing what it means. It is a 'craft of compromise', an art not a science, and entails mediating between different claims. Above all, it is more than interpretation: it is active, productive and creative (Freeman, 2004).

Translation is, then, the very working of power. In postcolonial theory, recognising that a root meaning of 'translate' is 'to conquer' (Kiberd, 1995, p 624) so that 'cultural translation' is a significant site of a 're-ordering of worlds' (Loomba, 1998, p 101), there is a focus on representation, power and historicity (Niranjana, 1992). The sociology of translation considers the particular ways by which 'objects', 'knowledge' and 'facts' are produced through displacement or suppression of dissenting voices, or of those '*facts unfit to fit*' (Gebhardt, 1982, p 405, emphasis added). A recent text by Rada Ivekovic suggests that neglecting translation may contribute to 'the premature shutting down of alternative histories' and 'suppressing the diverse, constructing un-translatabilities and incomprehension, forcing separation between related idioms: constructing otherhood and striving to expulse it outside the "system", or outside the "good world"' (Ivekovic, 2005, p 1). She contrasts 'translation' with 'dialogue', where the latter implies symmetrical dichotomy and hides hierarchy, while the former is a form of resistance 'to the hegemonic lines of imposition of the meaning' (2005, p 1). In a broad sense, translation is used as a sensitising device, emphasising the traversals of meaning and the power relations that translation practices entail. Monaci and Caselli frame translation as:

> ... a result of a linked set of social and material processes
> that take place within a network of relations and that *modify*
> *knowledge at each stage*. Contrary to the diffusionist view of

the knowledge transfer process as akin to contagion by a virus or the flow of electricity, the metaphor of translation suggests that the production, circulation and sharing knowledge among different socio-cultural contexts should be analysed by investigating how its users change their cognitive and normative attitudes; but it also stresses the role of the cultural categories of those who 'en-act' and bring into being the knowledge transferred to local contexts of application by *mobilizing, mediating, distorting, exposing, ignoring* and so *recreating* it. (Monaci and Caselli, 2005, p 56, emphasis added)

John Clarke (2005b) considers translation as a useful metaphorical insight into three critical policy practices. First, translation illuminates some processes of policy diffusion and policy transfers in transnational forms. Here he argues that 'the Anglophone domination of policy expertise and policy networks, the passage of concepts into and out of "Policy English" may be a site of significant articulation and variation' (Clarke, 2005b, p 8). Second, translation sheds new light on implementation, or how policy moves from policy formation to 'front-line' practice. Finally, he asserts that translation as a conceptual framework can draw attention and indeed 'make visible' the work of 'translators', 'brokers', and 'mediators', 'those translocal agents who mediate languages, contexts, sites and levels' (Clarke, 2005b, p 8; cf. also Lendvai and Stubbs, 2006).

The transnationalism of policy as translation focuses on the attempt to render certain specific policies as universal and to 're-transcribe' (Venn, 2006, p 82) existing socioeconomic, administrative and cultural practices within its idiom. There is nothing new in the movement of ideas, institutional blueprints, discourses and knowledge claims between and across sites, scales and actors. However, in the last thirty years and, particularly in Central and Eastern Europe in the period of 'transition' since 1991, these processes have intensified.

Space precludes a thorough examination of the mainstream, objectivist 'policy transfer' approach which builds on earlier work on the international movement of ideas and practices, particularly utilising concepts such as policy diffusion and lesson-drawing (see Bennett, 1991; Rose, 1991; Hulme, 2004). The approach has been developed, in particular, by writers such as Dolowitz and Marsh, who define policy transfer as:

> The process by which knowledge about policies, administrative arrangements, institutions and ideas in one political system (past or present) is used in the development of policies, arrangements, institutions and ideas in another political system. (Dolowitz and Marsh, 2000, p 5)

In our view, their list of key questions: 'Why do actors engage in policy transfer? Who are the key actors involved in the policy transfer process? What is transferred? From where are lessons drawn? What are the different degrees of transfer? What restricts or facilitates the policy transfer process? and how is the project of policy transfer related to policy "success" or policy failure?' (Dolowitz and Marsh, 2000, p 8), appear somewhat linear, simplistic and, ultimately, normative.

Our main concern, however, is that the trope of 'transfer' catches much less that is important in the process than that of 'translation'. As Yanow has suggested:

> Translating is not the same thing as transferring knowledge. 'Transfer' suggests an objectification or commodification of knowledge, extrapolated from its context, with the translator serving as a mere conduit or channel through whom the meaning simply passes. Even this simple model of knowledge transfer, however, incorporates the problem of 'noise' – a distortion of the original meaning – which recognizes the likelihood of altered meaning. (Yanow, 2004, p 15)

'Noise' and the mediation, distortion, and recreation of transferred knowledge which it entails, is crucial, and points to one of the central contradictions of a universalistic understanding of both the policy process and policy transfer on the one hand, and the cultural, political and social particularities of their diverse meanings, interactions, consequences and resistances on the other. Table 10.1 illustrates the different registers or vocabularies of the two sets of literatures.

While the mainstream policy transfer literature with its realist ontology sees 'policy' both in the source and in the recipient context as a stable, pre-existing and uncontested 'reality', and the transfer as a more or less linear process, a sociology of translation works with a much more fluid and dynamic framework. For scholars using sociology of translation:

Table 10.1 The different 'vocabulary' between mainstream 'policy transfer' literature and a sociology of translation

Keywords for the mainstream policy transfer literature[1]	Keywords for the sociology of translation approach
Construction	Deconstruction
Policy transfer, diffusion, learning	Translation, transferability, displacement, 'normalisation'
Policy change/stability	Transformation, hybridity, fluidity, reflexivity
Adaptation, dissemination	Negotiation, enactment
'Goodness of fit'	'Unfit to fit'
Institutions	Knowledge networks, actor networks, agency, social relations, processes

[1] In particular applied by the Europeanisation scholarship

> policy does not exist somewhere else in finished form, but is finished/produced in the act of transfer. Policy is not available to be looked at and learned from, but is produced in the act of looking. Policy is the output of a series of communications, not its input. The issue is one of germination, not dissemination. (Freeman, 2004, p 2)

From this perspective, policy translation goes beyond policy transfer since the world cannot be reduced to binary notions of stability versus change, or adaptation versus resistance, determined by the 'goodness of fit' (based on the distance or gap between the original policy and policy in the recipient country). The mainstream literature operates within a perspective that has a narrow conception of power primarily in terms of institutional veto points or veto players, and their ability to block change. Most of the policy transfer literature adheres to a 're-hashed neo-pluralism in which societies are seen as composed of diverse interests, with power distributed along various dimensions' (Stubbs, 2005a, p 71). By reconsidering our understanding of the policy transfer process from the point of view of translation we would argue instead that the policy transfer process should be seen as one of continuous transformation, negotiation and enactment, on the one hand, and as a politically infused process of dislocation and displacement ('unfit to fit'), on the other hand.

Emphasising processes of formation, transformation and contestation implies that policy transfer is never an automatic or unproblematic, taken-for-granted, process. Rather, it suggests the need to pay attention to the ways in which policies and their schemes, content, technologies and instruments are constantly changing according to sites, meanings and agencies. In that sense, a sociology of translation provides 'a language by which we can begin to explore the interrelation of discourse and agency' (Newton, 1996, p 731), where social structure is seen not as a noun, but as a verb (Law, 1992), accentuating a relational approach that emphasises heterogeneity, uncertainty, fluidity and contestation.

One aspect of understanding policy as a translation process taking place within a transnational space is the notion of 'contact zones', which involve 'the spatial and temporal copresence of subjects previously separated by geographic and historical disjunctures, and whose trajectories now intersect' (Pratt, 1992, p 6). A contact zone is a kind of in-between or 'interstitial' space akin to Homi Bhabha's notion of the 'third space' which is never fixed but is, rather, always becoming (Bhabha, 1995, p 208), characterised by forces and directions rather than forms or dimensions. Pratt suggests that a 'contact zone' perspective 'foregrounds the interactive, improvisational dimensions of colonial encounters so easily ignored or suppressed by diffusionist accounts of conquest and domination' (Pratt, 1992, pp 6–7).

In other words, structuralist conceptions of the workings of colonial power are trapped by many of the automatisms of the mainstream policy transfer literature. While offering, in Bhabha's terms, the possibility of eluding 'the politics of polarity' (Bhabha, 1995, p 209), the concept of 'contact zones' emphasises 'copresence, interaction, interlocking understandings and practices, often within radically asymmetrical relations of power' (Pratt, 1992, pp 6–7) or, in James Clifford's terms, 'a power-charged set of exchanges' (Clifford, 1997, p 192). In the 'contact zone', encounters are rarely, or rarely *only*, about words and their meaning but are, almost always, more or less explicitly, about claims-making, opportunities, strategic choices and goals, interests and resource maximisation. In the 'contact zones', all kinds of complex negotiated interactions occur, on multiple stages, as well as off-stage.

It is, precisely, for this reason, that, while we recognise, in the domain of social policy, some aspects of both the 'homogenizing ambition of Anglo-American as (a) universal language' and the 'systematic attempt by neo-liberal discourse to colonize ... practice' (Venn, 2006, p 82), we remain highly sceptical of linear notions of intentionality and causality and, most importantly of all, critical of notions of total closure. 'Anglo-American' is, itself, a complex product of an encounter between two traditions, as indicated by the necessity of the symbol '-' joining two words, as in the case of 'Indo-China' or the language of 'Serbo-Croatian' (Hersak, 2003, p 132). Undoubtedly, the 'Anglo-American' of which Venn speaks is the lingua franca of the World Bank and the IMF, both of whom employ vastly more US and British citizens than those of any other country. But is it the dominant or hegemonic language of the European Union? One could, certainly, argue that whatever the EU's pretensions are to celebrating all member state languages as somehow 'different but equal', some are more equal than others and, as linguistic pluralism grows apace with new members, then English is becoming increasingly important.

However, this is a peculiar EU English the codes and terms of which are, perhaps, better able to be exchanged between a Portuguese-speaking and an Estonian-speaking EU policy maker, consultant or bureaucrat than between either of them and a lay, or even an academic non-policy-making, native English speaker. While various English-Croatian EU dictionaries exist, the least translatable word or phrase, in fact, appears to be French, namely *acquis* or *acquis communitaire*. Indeed, the EU's concern with 'social exclusion', not just as a concept but in the way in which it is framed and discussed, can be traced back to an earlier French discussion of *exclusion sociale*, and many other social scientific concepts and debates in a European arena are most understandable when their routes are traced to German writings. The term 'benchmarking' is one of the most difficult to translate. Indeed, in Croatian the term *benčmarkiranje* is still often used. Hence, there is not total closure, although the tendency for English to dominate is there, and we are far from real diversity in which, say, Slovenian or Polish come to have an influence beyond the confines of their own linguistic communities.

The idea of universalising neoliberalism is also problematic. The neoliberal project is by no means as unchanging, all-powerful and universal as some of the critics of neoliberalism suggest. On these lines, John Clarke has argued that, whilst 'neoliberal globalisation' is the dominant form of contemporary globalisation, any attempt to understand it as 'a hegemonic project' has to address 'both the logics and limits of neo-liberalism, and the different ways in which people and places live with/in – and against – neo-liberalism' (Clarke, 2004, p 89). He is profoundly interested, therefore, in 'uneven neoliberalisms', varying in space and time, and able to enter 'national-popular formations' only in and through alliances, 'assemblages of political discourses', which inevitably change shape, and produce 'hybrids, paradoxes, tensions and incompatibilities', rather than 'coherent implementations of a unified discourse and plan' (Clarke, 2004, p 94).

Global policy forms are always articulated in specific places and times, or as Collier and Ong would have it, 'territorialised in assemblages' which 'define new material, cultural and discursive relationships' (Collier and Ong, 2005, p 4). If, following Tickell and Peck's influential work on the topic, we consider neoliberalisation as a *process*, the outcomes of which are 'contingent and geographically specific – since they are working themselves out in a non-necessary fashion across an uneven institutional landscape' (Tickell and Peck, 2003), then what are needed are (ethnographic and anthropological) studies of policy as translation as part of the study of 'grounded globalisations' exploring 'forces, connections and imaginations' (Burawoy, 2000, p 344; see also Jenkins, Chapter Two).

Case vignettes: towards a reflexive ethnography of social policy reform

This text is underpinned by a commitment to reflexive ethnography as offering an intellectual base, and something of a privileged standpoint, for the analysis of policies as translation. This commitment is less to an ideal type notion of 'intensive fieldwork' as a kind of anthropological *rite de passage*, and more to Willis and Trondman's notion of ethnography as a 'layered and evocative … presentation of located aspects of the human condition *from the inside*' (Willis and Trondman, 2000, p 7, emphasis in original), as a corrective to over-theoretical, over-functionalist and over-structuralist explorations. The problem is, as Jeremy Gould has suggested, 'the range of things we can know first hand – the time–space coordinates we can physically occupy, much less learn to know well, within the scope of a research project or a lifetime – is extremely narrow', and transnational policies ('aid' more generally in Gould's formulation) are 'comprised of multi-sited, multi-level, trans-scalar … processes' which themselves necessitate trans-scalar observation as a 'translation device' (Gould, 2004, p 283).

Above all, our concern is to acknowledge and embody the need to research alternative research sites, breaking down some of the boundaries between the role of a researcher and other roles such as consultant, policy maker, activist, and the like. It is through the bending and the blending of different positions and perspectives that we are enabled to see 'policy' as a constant move between the formal and the informal, the institutionalised and unofficial practices, the paperwork and 'the reality'. In this sense, our commitment to reflexivity, notwithstanding justifiable critiques of its 'relativism' and lack of conceptual clarity (Lynch, 2000), involves, in Marcus' sense, 'cognitive and intellectual identification between the investigator and his variously situated subjects in the emergent field of multi-sited research' such that the ethnographer is located 'within the terrain that she is mapping' which serves to reconfigure any methodological discussion that pretends 'a perspective from above or "nowhere"' (Marcus, 1995).

As a part of this, we would suggest that presentation of fragments of research material in the form of short vignettes or case studies is useful, not least because it allows for a somewhat truncated, but no less intelligible, rendering of a 'peopled ethnography' which, following detailed participant observation, represents extracts from 'field notes, interview extracts and the texts that group members themselves produce' (Fine, 2003, p 41). Ethnography is highly sensitive to the issue of the construction of meaning, which is often neglected in structuralist accounts of political processes. It offers a way out of the agent–structure binary within mainstream social science although, of course, the issue of how to 'write up' vignettes remains complex and contested. Here, we offer both a multi-voiced ethnography and a privileged reading of certain encounters with policy from our own experience and practice.

Structural Funds in Hungary: from social policy to social cohesion

In 2000, one of us (NL) was working in the Ministry for Social and Family Affairs of the Hungarian government as a consultant on the preparation for the Structural Funds to be absorbed for social policy programmes. At the time, not many civil servants spoke or understood English, and since the Structural Funds' regulations were only available in English and French, those who spoke either of the two main EU languages were in key positions to move the programming forward. The preparation was also given a high priority, because it was offering substantial funds for generally underfunded social policy schemes. However, understanding the logic of the European Social Fund for a country that did not have a 'project culture' before, and interpreting the eligible types of activities for the funding, was immensely difficult. NL and her colleagues soon learned that nurseries are not nurseries, but 'reconciliation of family and work' (a label against which some heads of nurseries protested); that gender mainstreaming is more than just (re)training a few unemployed women; that regions and their inequalities are of concern, with newly established NUTS I I (Nomenclature of Territorial Units for Statistics) regions a key scale in public policy making; and that the notion of social cohesion funded by the EU is significantly different from a traditional understanding of social policy in Hungary.

There seemed to be a fundamental mismatch between eligible funding and existing social policy schemes at the time. Instead of talking about social needs, the Structural Fund wanted to see community initiatives, social development and innovative ideas to promote employment, gender equality and social inclusion. However, employment was not considered part of social policy; policy makers were not familiar with community initiatives; and 'innovation' constituted only a very small and fragmentary part of the social policy budget. Core domestic policy activities (social assistance and benefits, child protection and social services and institutions) were not included as eligible activities, and previously marginal policy domains (such as gender, Roma policy, innovation and community or regional initiatives) became the centre of attention. Yet, no week would go by without NL's boss asking: 'But what is social cohesion after all?'

The encounter and the (not necessarily equal) dialogue of two policy frameworks (the EU Structural Fund and Hungarian social policy) offer a reflexive space. On the one hand, the difference between the two policy frameworks results in a 'stretching' of the understanding and framing of 'social policy' in Hungary, and re-couples issues such as regional policy and social policy; employment and social policy; education and social policy; and so on. On the other hand, it creates new 'centres' and new 'peripheries'; it fosters new policy activisms (for example, in programmes promoting gender mainstreaming or Roma integration), while marginalising other agendas; and it forges new policy networks at the same time as weakening others. It both enables and delimits the activism of policy actors. The stretching process is both flexible and open, and because of the lack of a grasp of those 'EU' concepts, agencies such as ministries have a large manoeuvring and claiming space.

Yet, at the same time, meanings can only work on the basis of previous policy memories. This is the policy space where nothing can be taken for granted, and nothing seems to fit the classic policy studies dichotomy between policy change and stability. Everything is changing, yet, at the same time, resistance to change prevails and the possibilities are limited. New discourses, concepts, ideas and policy frameworks emerge; yet, in this intensified meaning-making, sense-making process, the institutionalisation of these ideas can only be limited. NL's experience in the ministry framed 'policy' and the 'policy process' as a constant puzzle, where meanings never settle into any stable entity, but rather are constantly contested, challenged and therefore changing. Certain imaginaries are rejected outright, some hit institutional barriers, and others are picked up as a political discourse, in a very fluid context. That is why dynamic and process-oriented approaches are so crucial for any claims towards understanding policies in practice.

Croatia's 'Social Protection Reform Project'

In April 2002, the first meeting of the main participants in the World Bank, UK Government DFID and Government of Japan funded Social Protection Project, took place in the conference room of the Ministry of Labour and Social Affairs in Zagreb. One of us (PS) had been recruited directly by DFID to be part of the 'social services' team, one of no less than nine consultancy teams or companies contracted to work on a broad blueprint for the reforms, including teams for: social assistance; labour and employment; fiscal issues and decentralisation; administrative strengthening, IT and database issues; poverty monitoring; as well as an overall team leader and a local resources team.

The supposed importance of the occasion, with introductions by the responsible Minister, the State Secretary charged with leading the reforms, the World Bank staff member, and the Team Leader, was challenged by an earlier discussion PS had had with a senior politician, the father of a close friend, who replied, on understanding the nature of the work, 'Oh, I see, it's one of those projects', before politely declining to intervene to speed up the start of the project. Fairly quickly, cracks and disagreements began to appear between the consultancy teams. A Croatian colleague, a lecturer in social policy at the University of Zagreb, surveyed the foreign consultants and noted the massive over-representation of British and US consultants asking: 'Is there no one from Holland here?'

The Team Leader, on his second visit to Zagreb, quickly alienated Croatian colleagues, and some of the foreign consultants, by insisting on exploring the project goals within a logical framework matrix and, indeed, delivering a very long and largely incomprehensible and certainly unnecessary lecture, on the virtues of the approach. By the midway point, relationships were at breaking point with one team already dismissed for late submission of work judged to be of a low quality. Consultants disagreed constantly regarding the contours of the reform in the context of a clear message from the State Secretary of the importance of advocating 'radical' change, and the equally clear message from career civil servants that nothing of the sort should, or could, be undertaken.

The Team Leader was dismissed prior to the end of the project, with the final composite report compiled by the fiscal and decentralisation team, best able to manage its informal relationships with key local stakeholders in part through its strong links to both USAID and the Croatian Ministry of Finance, advocating 'marketised' recipes for social protection reform. None of the reforms were implemented although, some time later, a loan agreement was signed between the World Bank and the new Ministry of Health and Social Welfare based, loosely, on some of the measures proposed.

The vignette shows the fragility of discussions about the content of policy in the context of project modalities; the taken-for-granted ways of doing a 'project' of this kind and problematic processes of systematic mis-communication in a projectised contact zone where encounters were highly power-charged in the context of emerging 'co-presences'. It quickly became clear that those teams who could manage relationships with key insiders would achieve more. Sometimes, the key part of this, however, was the ability to turn notes from group discussions into polished PowerPoint presentations, or to summarise discussions from participatory workshops in ways that privileged one reform option over others. Language issues were important as, indeed, an Anglo-American policy-speak and presentational style (bullet points preferred) met a more rhetorical Croatian style. Transnational complexities of communication rubbed up against, and interacted with, differences based on disciplinary perspectives, political leanings and prior memory and experience. In many ways, technologies of presentation and, to an extent, technologies of involvement (Haahr, 2004), in terms of somewhat constructed 'participatory workshops', came to dominate over judgements either of the quality of the work produced or over its ideological or political leanings. Echoing aspects of the first vignette, the possibilities of change and the limitations to change coexist, with an expansion of the range of available repertoires of meanings, concepts and ideas emerging but with limited coherence in terms of their interrelationship and no immediate prospects of their institutionalisation.

Conclusions

Beck and Lau (2005) in their latest manifesto for 'reflexive modernity' argue that we are witnessing a contemporary transformation where the dualism, and the 'either/or' principle, of the first modernity is replaced by the 'both/and' principle in the second or reflexive modernity. In this process, along with the breaking down of boundaries and distinction between categories, 'it is no longer possible to fall back on the tried and tested, usually scientific resources of rationalization, as these themselves have become ambiguous and uncertain' (Beck and Lau, 2005, p 527). In this process, which for Beck and Lau entails the discontinuous transformation of basic institutions, policy, and its claims and meaning-making processes, play a crucial role.

In this chapter we have argued that policies are not simply rationally engineered, linear processes. Rather, they are complex, multiple and fluid processes of knowledge production, meaning-making and claims-making that are taking place in multiple, including transnational, spaces. Drawing on our experience in social policy reform in Central and South Eastern Europe, we highlight and amplify four issues crucial to our reconsideration of policy: the role of language; the problematic of policy transfer; the importance of researching alternative or unusual sites; and methodological issues around how we produce knowledge about the policy process, through reflexive ethnography and multi-sited research.

In the context of the transformation of social policy in Central and South Eastern Europe, language, and as a result meanings, cannot be taken for granted. Linguistic representations are constantly and radically changing, with new concepts and discourses emerging and becoming (re)inscribed. In addition, the unprecedented transnational influence that accompanies and frames this transformation produces an encounter or clash between local and transnational languages, along with their implied representations, claims and norms. Language, then, becomes an important site for policy resistance and contestation. To an extent, language becomes a site for an exclusion/inclusion process depending on whether various policy actors are able or willing to speak the dominant language, be it Anglo-American, EU English or another.

The multiplicity of languages, meanings, representations, claims and norms in the transnational social policy space, foregrounds important questions around translation practices. In this chapter we have argued that policy transfers are complex cultural, political and social practices, and, as such, are far from mechanistic, top-down and exclusively formal processes. Instead, critical issues of distortions, displacement, negotiations and, as a result, transformation need to be addressed. Translation practices are always plural and multiple, and since our vignettes are as much about confusion and puzzlement as about domination and resistance, we contest the complete closure that grand narratives of neoliberal hegemony often seem to suggest (see Clarke, 2004 for a critique of this type of theorising). The trope of translation is to emphasise the alternatives and processes of re-transcription, which produces very diverse stories, voices and, as a result, meanings and practices in policy processes. Translation is also a dynamic framework to capture the fluidity of policy processes, with an emphasis on the constant (re)construction of issues, discourses and actor networks, as a part of real human agency.

Finally, any attempts to reconsider policy need to address methodological issues. In order to unfold complex translation practices, we argued that a more dynamic and open-ended framework is required to capture the complex interplay between discourses and ground-level practices, conflicting choices and pressures, between the 'political' and the 'technical', and indeed the metamorphosis of flexi-actors, criss-crossing sites, scales and spaces. Indeed, new hybrid concepts, terms and new theoretical perspectives are needed if we are to grasp important fragments of this complex transformation process. This suggests the need to reconceptualise politics, institutions and contexts themselves. Of course, the wider implications of this approach need to be developed in terms of multiple positionalities, no longer necessarily privileging either the nation state or the complex 'transition' setting as in these vignettes. Many problems remain, not least in terms of the situatedness of the reflexive observer and the dangers of overstating the creative nature of interactions between agents. There is much to recommend a translation approach, however, as worthy of exploration as part of an emerging reflexive ethnography of policies in general, and social policy in particular. The challenge is no less than the need to reconfigure understandings of the policy process, transforming our own vocabularies around it and, ultimately, producing new forms of knowledge that have meaningful theoretical and practical implications.

ELEVEN

Studying policy: a way forward

Susan M. Hodgson and Zoë Irving

We began a reconsideration of policy by setting out our intent to 'disturb some of the comfortable ground' (Chapter One). The rationale for the endeavour was based on theoretical, methodological and practical concerns including:

- changes in the wider landscape of social sciences, despite certain ongoing divisions of academic labour that confine some forms of study;
- radical shifts in how policy is informed, formed and implemented;
- the sense that much policy-related and policy-relevant research practice is exploring new questions, requiring a different conceptual apparatus to that currently available.

While the need to reassess policy in a sustained theoretical and practical manner was evident, the questions through which this reassessment could be conducted, and the range of perspectives that we could bring to bear on the analysis, was large. Hence, the themes of meanings, politics and practices were developed to shape and inform the work of all our contributors to a reconsideration of policy. While presenting a view on the changing form of politics remains important in policy work, analyses of meanings and practices are central to making better sense of those changes.

Rather than take 'policy' as a given, chapters have sought to expose the various occurrences and constructions of the term. In covering a range of positions including, realist, institutional, practice-focused and constructivist, the different authors have utilised the idea of 'policy' in differing ways. Indeed, these very labels serve to highlight the diversity of interests that underpin current work in policy studies, and they lead us to explore what differing perspectives can offer – in particular, if brought into close proximity, as here. The issue we attempted to address in this collection links into both the centrality of power and decision making, and developments in how this is understood. Thus, we each engaged with our tripartite division of meanings, politics and practices, while appreciating the problematic nature of these very distinctions. By employing these categories, we have enabled some issues to become visible whilst others have faded from view. Only by bringing multiple perspectives together, however, can we appreciate the range of interconnections and contradictions with which policy studies should engage.

To continue our 'disruption' of what are often taken as 'givens', our reconsideration of policy will now begin to extract themes that cut across the work already presented, primarily in order to provoke yet further thinking. This final chapter draws out some overarching ideas from the various contributors, in order to assess the implications of this critical exploration of policy for future policy-related study and research. The implications for the teaching of 'policy' and the training of social researchers and welfare professionals are also discussed as this seems key to ensuring future, critical policy thinkers. However, we start by posing a foundational question.

What counts as (social) policy?

Policy is changing because the world is changing. Thus, whether this book is about 'social policy' or just 'policy' has been left deliberately fuzzy. We stated at the outset that this divide, alongside numerous others, is artificial. Through this book we have attempted to problematise some of the boundaries often found in policy studies and want to explore a little more the implications of not taking such boundaries for granted.

Changing contexts, both of policy processes and of policy analysis, force us to question a range of boundaries. We need to question not only the boundaries open to conventional challenge, such as the divide between 'public policy' and 'social policy', but the non-conventional ones too, such as between these two categories and other policy monikers. For example, how are we to define a distinction or boundary between social and environmental policy, when the two are now seen as inextricably linked, or even fused? Continuing to neglect such boundaries seems unproductive. In light of changes in the policy arena that are beginning to foreground the whole notion of 'sustainability', for example, there comes a realisation that the key concern of social policy – who gets what – is now a question for everyone, not just social policy analysts. We would like to give just one example, in this regard, of how apparently non-social policy is indeed thoroughly social.

Social policy analysts may not usually view the remit of the environment and rural affairs as part of their terrain. However, the

UK Department for Environment, Food and Rural Affairs (Defra) has an explicitly social purpose, 'Defra's core purpose is to improve the current and future quality of life' (Defra, 2007), and perhaps ought to be a legitimate area of social policy study. In 2006, Defra proclaimed its overarching vision guiding all policy work as 'one planet living' – previously, 'sustainable development' was the pre-eminent tag-line: 'One planet living' is 'one of the greatest challenges facing our society today' (Miliband, 2006). Although sustainable development remains a key principle, the shift has significance in that it changes the meanings that can be attributed to what government (in this case) policies are about. If we are aiming for 'one planet living', and the values inscribed therein, a different kind of politics is required, 'an environmental contract that has the same transforming effect on society and the behaviour of individuals which the social contract had in the nineteenth and twentieth centuries' (Miliband, 2006).

In part, the shift is an attempt to individualise and personalise policy objectives and to encourage people to feel responsible for successful achievement. In order to meet Defra's policy objectives, individuals and groups are exhorted to change their practices (primarily of consumption) or otherwise risk humanity's demise. Globalising the policy goal and individualising responsibility for its achievement happens concurrently. 'Who gets what' has changed scale (it is now a planet-sized problem) and is no longer just about welfare resources but all the resources of the planet (including air, water, energy and so on). A change in policy language, therefore, is not merely a swapping of one set of words for another. The function of language, and the implications of the policy vision it espouses, run much deeper (see also Gregory, Chapter Five).

Brief consideration of the Defra position points to how 'environmental' and 'natural' problems – such as unpolluted air or access to clean water – become translated into thoroughly social ones. Indeed, an integrative and relational vision is being proclaimed. As noted in the introductory chapter, the use of policy is central in the management of relationships between agencies, organisations, collectives and individuals as well as the framing of social objectives. What does this imply then for policy not usually positioned as 'social policy'? To what extent is Defra policy not social policy? If previously taken-for-granted boundaries are being transgressed, in the policy rhetoric and elsewhere, then this should force us to challenge our own continued, intellectual boundary-making in policy analysis. It becomes problematic to differentiate easily between what counts as a 'social' policy, or an 'environmental' policy, or an 'economic' policy, save in our own disciplinary construction of a policy problem. Cahill (2001, p 2) has made moves to relate the social and the environmental, 'social policy is concerned with the satisfaction of human needs ... The meeting of need has an environmental impact.' However, this approach resolutely maintains the social–environmental division whereas we assert that these distinctions need questioning.

Attention to boundaries also suggests that we can attend to the study of policy work as the study of boundary work (Gieryn, 1999). To slightly misquote Gieryn (1983, p 781), policy 'is no single thing: its boundaries are drawn and redrawn, in flexible, historically changing and sometimes ambiguous ways'. As with all boundaries, policy-related boundaries enable some things to be included and others to be excluded. The intellectual terrain of social policy, sociology, public policy, social administration and so on, acts as both facilitator – of coverage of potentially relevant issues – and brick wall, as disciplines compete over who can define the 'real problem' of study. While we can accept that demarcating one area of work from another can serve particular purposes and enable certain ends to be met, we can too easily neglect the very processes of *boundary construction* as key to understanding aspects of policy work and its analysis. It should be no longer acceptable to draw neat boxes around 'the political system', 'social systems' and so on, nor to delineate uncritically between a 'social problem', a 'transport problem', a 'flooding problem' or a 'health problem' and carve these up into different academic disciplines. However, we recognise that this petition for boundary-crossing requires further conceptual thinking about processes of change than we have offered here.

The challenging of boundaries inevitably leads to yet other challenges, of conceptual, methodological and communitarian natures. That is, concerning the generation of potential new ways of thinking; sharing ideas on approaches to research design and output; and rethinking what we should be aiming for in terms of the next generations of policy analysts and makers. We deal with the first two ideas in the following sections on knowledge, classification and values. Turning to the future will come later.

Knowledge and evidence

Much work has described and analysed how the contexts and processes of policy have shifted in the last 10 to 15 years. Our understanding of knowledge generation processes has also moved on significantly (Pickering, 1992; Denzin and Lincoln, 2003). The post-modern turn in social science has, if nothing else, allowed us to reflect on how our past was constructed and realise that we never occupy a 'view from nowhere'.

Policy makers, policy actors and policy analysts are all situated, in time, in space and world-view. This would appear to render impossible the quest for 'objective information', 'generalised models' and 'universally-applicable laws'. The policy-producing world appears to still demand these, however, and so we must continue to ask, who informs policy making? And, what form does their information take?

One answer to the former, in the UK context at least, is individual organisations such as the World Wild Fund for Nature (WWF) who initialised the 'one planet living' approach referred to earlier. Clearly, a single organisation can have a seemingly large impact, even if the route between organisation and policy is more complicated than the word 'direct' might imply. The presence of a diversity of organisations and formations in policy work is not a new finding. Farnsworth (see Chapter Six) points to the increasing voice of business, and Deacon (Chapter Seven) signals the presence of policy actors that are notable for their mobility between contexts as much as their official institutional position. The range of *who* provides input and/or knowledge for policy is shifting and, therefore, our analytical gaze must shift around too. At the same time, a major shift, in the UK at least, is in the *form* of informing, for example in the rise of the idea of 'evidence-based policy'.

The shift to explicit claims of 'evidence-based policy' (or evidence-informed, evidence-supported, etc.) immediately requires us to ask, what is meant by *evidence*? This question has taxed philosophers for a long time and it remains subject to ongoing debate in other academic disciplines. In much policy rhetoric, however, evidence appears to be treated as unproblematic, as something that we would all recognise when presented with it. In addition, the movement from 'evidence' to policy can often be left unexamined. Some authors have pointed to policy developments that run *counter* to evidence. Indeed, Gregory (Chapter Five) uses the example of cognitive behavioural programmes in the criminal justice system to suggest that some policies rise to prominence despite a lack of evidence of their efficacy. The notion of evidence clearly has to be treated with caution.

There are more foundational reasons also for being circumspect. The problematic relationship between information/knowledge providers and policy makers (or between evidence and policy) is clearly highlighted in considering (natural) science as a source of policy advice (or scientists as policy advisers). As one example, we might consider the affair over whether or not to permit commercial planting of genetically-modified crops in the UK. On the surface, some 'straightforward' scientific evidence ought to provide sufficient grounds for making a policy decision (whether to grant licences for commercial planting).

This assumption is demonstrated in the quotations below, provided by the policy makers, for public consumption:

> We must proceed on the best scientific evidence. (Tony Blair, quoted in *The Independent*, 15/2/99).

> We need the accurate, scientifically based data on which we can make the judgement that the sowing of GM crops and the use of their accompanying herbicides does not cause significant damage to the environment. (Michael Meacher, Environment Minister, quoted in *The Independent*, 19/2/99)

> Let's proceed with caution according to the evidence. (Tony Blair, quoted in *The Times*, 21/6/99)

These quotations illustrate how scientific evidence is assumed to be rational, objective, clear, concise and obtainable. Upon this collective of assumptions, special trials were set up and a programme of experiments was specifically designed to provide the evidence required. In the event, conflicting responses were found; insufficient time for the trials was available; and only a limited number of variables affecting the environment – and a small number of animal and plant species – were considered. This case exemplifies that, 'the relationship between political authorities' need for advice and the generation of scientific insights is complex and indirect' (Yearley, 2005, p 160). In addition, the assumptions that enabled the setting up of the trials as the route to objective information are based on a normative prescription of scientific knowledge production long since disassembled by sociological studies of the practice of the sciences (Pickering, 1992), and also through critique from philosophy (Longino, 1990). Numerous (social) science research studies point to the messiness and contingency of science work (Jasanoff et al., 1995). The capacity of science to speak to policy has thus been probed and found wanting from a number of perspectives (Yearley, 2005). Arguably, in the case of the GM crop trials, public mobilisation against commercial planting held more sway at the time than the body of ten, peer-reviewed journal reports that the scientists produced.

If scientific evidence can be problematic in relation to evidence for policy, then under what circumstances can we take it for granted that social scientific knowledge/evidence will be more relevant, useful or meaningful to policy-making? Both Cowburn (see Chapter Eight) and

Boxall et al (Chapter Nine) question some of the underpinning notions of knowledge that inform policy research and policy expectations of research. The implication from this and other work is that the notion of 'evidence' is highly problematic. In the same way that 'scientific research is not normally carried out in order to give advice' (Yearley, 2005, p 160), to what extent is *social* scientific research designed to 'give advice': 'Political decisions about social policies rarely are the direct outcome of social science research' (Lee et al., 2005, p 21). Indeed, the question we need to ask is whether it should.

A further perspective on the evidence debate is introduced by a standpoint that emphasises that *policy is cultural*. In this formulation, policy is central to matters of social life and is not a backdrop to other processes (Jenkins, Chapter Two). From this perspective emerges the need to study policy ethnographically, that is, by immersion in the settings within which policy work is accomplished, and by doing fieldwork that addresses the practices and meanings of policy participants. By undertaking studies that focus on doing and saying, we can access parts of the policy process that other techniques cannot reach. We can observe and address the enactors of policy on a day-to-day basis, as noted by Gregory (see Chapter Five).

Despite various critiques of the relations between evidence and policy, there are numerous arenas in which the relationship between research and advice continues to be advanced. Formal means through which the relationship can be given direction now exist, for example the Cochrane collaboration in health research and the Campbell equivalent for social science (Young et al., 2002). In addition, the voice of 'the public' in the GM debate, pointed to above, leads us back to another aspect of the knowledge/evidence theme; that is, the accounting for '*who* informs?' In the past, processes of policy formation could be understood as drawing on 'policy experts' as the source of information for policy making. This remains the case, but the range and number of voices who may count as expert has increased and the notion of 'expert' has been expanded (Collins and Evans, 2002).

So, one of the ways in which the matter of evidence for policy making is being directly addressed is in the rise of 'user involvement', in both policy and research. This involvement can take a variety of forms that we will not rehearse here, but we need to note that the rise, in the past decade, of the 'user' agenda could lull us into a false sense of security, that everyone is now aware of the partiality of past work. The attention increasingly given to 'users' at all stages of the research is to be welcomed for a variety of reasons. At the same time, as 'users' become a requirement – a box to be ticked in a research proposal, in the 'relevance to user groups' section – we need to maintain our awareness of the socially constructed nature of the term and the sociopolitical context that has given rise to 'user' prominence (Woolgar, 2000). Caution also needs to be exercised as researchers may not want the eventual users involved, perhaps citing concerns over political interference or challenges to autonomy. Other concerns over user involvement include the worry that it builds false hopes of positive change (or any change), and that it creates unsustainable relationships, for example, what happens to the involved users when the research is finished? Alongside is the view that 'user' involvement in research is a calculated move by the research establishment, designed to add further to the illusion of consultation generated by the rise of 'stakeholder involvement' in government. In these forms of policy generation, the possibilities of allocation of blame for policy failure are multiplied and diffused.

Clearly, the whole notion of 'users' is deserving of further analysis – likewise the term 'stakeholders' – as they become ubiquitous phrases at the same time as defying definition. Urgent study is required as the 'up-streaming' of users and 'the general public' in policy work becomes more prominent in everything from the nature of service delivery to the future of nanotechnology (Macnaghten et al., 2005). Alternative ways to conceptualise the user agenda could be developed as a route to supporting future participatory approaches: for example, co-productionist frameworks for understanding knowledge production (Jasanoff, 2006); and the analysis of *networks* and *associations* (Latour, 1987). These latter suggestions are given as a way to refocus our attention on the dynamics of user–policy–research relations, rather than as an attempt at a post-modern upheaval. They offer conceptual food for thought when seeking to build additional frameworks for the analysis of policy, whatever the policy flavour.

Classifying, measuring and scale

The need to address methodological issues in any attempt to reconsider policy is of primary import. Several authors have brought out the fundamental role played by categories in the production and implementation, indeed the very foundation, of policy. As Britton (see Chapter Four) states, 'A critical understanding of policy processes requires that close attention be paid to how and why categories ... are chosen'. The drawing of lines, of boundaries around groups, is elemental to policy; the production of policy is the production of categories; policy is about boundaries. Inclusion, exclusion, who's in/

out, and, critically, who gets to say, are all issues that are raised when bringing the notion of categories to the fore.

This brings us back to the call above to reconsider the impact of boundary making as an integral aspect of policy work. It is not necessarily that old questions and concerns have now disappeared. The understanding and measurement of poverty, for example, remains a key task. The ways in which poverty is experienced, however, are always changing. So while traditional welfare concerns may remain, what comes into the analytical frame of welfare is expanded. The origins of social science, and its resulting problematic relation with science, mean that attention to numbers, statistics, aggregations and comparisons are the bread and butter of policy analysis. There remains a tension between counting and exploring the patterns that count. New inequalities do emerge over time, in relation to changing sociopolitical conditions; tracking these remains a key task of policy analysis. We suggest that by paying more attention to the key role of category construction in policy work we can confront this task more confidently. We can thus begin to distinguish the nuances, and the significance, of the lines that get drawn around the *un*categorised and the seemingly uncategorisable. Following from this, it becomes more likely we will understand better how to 'sort things out' (Bowker and Star, 1999).

To return to Defra briefly, and the matter of counting, the move to 'one planet living' as a way to structure policy provision can be interpreted as a move towards sets of practices and outcomes that are more easily measurable than progress related to the woollier notion of sustainable development. While the latter concept remains the subject of much deliberation, and an ongoing lack of a definition that can be operationalised, 'one planet living' is based on sets of calculations about resource-use per capita. There is an implication that a 'balance' can be achieved – between what we take and what we put back – and, therefore, policy success becomes a measurable possibility. Our progress towards living within our planetary means can be calculated and mapped. Our conjecture that policy aims to manage what can be counted, rather than what counts, needs to be probed further.

An additional matter that relates to measuring, indeed to knowledge production more generally, is the notion of 'scale' (see Marston, 2000, for an interesting overview). Put simply, what is the appropriate level at which to categorise and measure? Concurrently, what are the appropriate scales at which to analyse? Although scale can have geographical (spatial, physical) meaning, it also implies magnitude (as in the magnification of a lens). At different spatial scales, different kinds and a different number of actors can be taken into account. At different magnifications, some things are visible and others are out of focus, blurred from the analysis. This inevitably raises issues of 'representation' in an ontological sense. As Hill has stated, 'Some of the most important controversies in policy analysis have been among analysts who differ on what they observe and what they want to observe' (Hill, 1997, p 27).

Several authors in this volume address the matter of scale directly. Calls for consideration of 'global' and 'transnational' scales are not novel, and recognition of the proliferation of international actors, such as the IMF and WHO, does exist in analysis. But perhaps an enduring problem has been that the world of policy analysis has tended to prefer linear and hierarchical models and explanations for what goes on. Whereas, as Deacon noted (see Chapter Seven) and Clarke (2005a) has also observed, on the vertical axis of policy action, actors are moving up and down the layers, local to global and vice versa. And, as Lendvai and Stubbs have shown (Chapter Ten), on the horizontal there is no clear point A to clear point B form of transfer for policy – policy is transformed and remoulded through the journey.

To sum up briefly, categories may be constructed but they have consequences. To aim for particular outcomes, perhaps we need to rethink how we make categories (this being the corollary of 'categories have consequences'). By tracing back from the consequences we aspire to, is it possible to construct or formulate categories that enable us to reach them? This is not an outcomes-oriented approach we are advocating here, rather it is a desire to embed an appreciation of the *dynamic* nature of policy into the policy-making process. Can we only analyse what we can categorise? Or can we develop approaches and concepts that bypass categorisation as conventionally understood and instead tackle analysis as an exploration of associations and their effects?

The place of values in research and policy

Phillips (Chapter Three) describes how the idea of 'values' comes to prominence in the context of the Europeanisation project. Cowburn (Chapter Eight) illustrates how values function – in the guise of ethics – to shape policy making and research on policy, in ways that suggest 'this is how the world is' rather than in a way that implies 'this is one way the world could be'. We contend that these are not just matters of metaphysics, there are real implications for both policy making and policy research.

Often, 'values' are absent from policy analysis. Analysts fail to expose their own value base for example, making the deciphering of their subject position the job of the reader. The capacities of readers of differing constituencies to fulfil this task will be variable. Research on policy may be read uncritically, outside of the context of its production; or may be read too critically. Young et al (2002) point to a problem of research literacy in relation to the production of systematic reviews for evidence-based policy. Based on the assumption that systematic reviewing is a good thing (Gough and Elbourne, 2002), Young et al suggest that the way forward requires better indexing and informational retrieval techniques, and better trained researchers. However, we suggest this is somewhat missing the point and that 'values' are a key aspect missing from their consideration. There is the long-standing argument over the 'value-neutral' social scientist; a position that seems ever more untenable given the now widespread acceptance that all inquiry is value-laden. Here the job for researchers is to be able to recognise the values we bring to bear, and use these to work for explicit ends:

> Social policy analysts direct their attention to improving conditions. The problem with this is that there is no one scientific way of agreeing what is 'better'. Ultimately the debate cannot be resolved because it is based on values, not upon facts. (Erskine, 1998, p 14)

This raises the question of whose values? Phillips (Chapter Three) suggests that there is potential for a harmonisation of values between seemingly incompatible value frameworks, and that politics will decide whose values win out. The implications of the normalisation of particular sets of values that influence policy are pointed to by Farnsworth (Chapter Six). Although as both he and Deacon (Chapter Seven) also demonstrate, there is nothing straightforward about this – even within dominant groups of actors there is contestation of ideas and values, and conflict of interests. Lendvai and Stubbs (Chapter Ten) explored this area using the ideas of translation and networks, rather than seeing the process and outcome of value contestation as locatable in specific groups. And as Jenkins (Chapter Two) states: 'policy processes are hugely significant in the making of everyday life, for everyone. Policy is thus "cultural" through and through'. The matter of values requires our ongoing attention.

Circularity

Related to the matter of values is a concern raised by some authors of the inherent circularity implied by the generation of knowledge to inform policy, policy outputs, policy evaluation and further calls for knowledge/evidence. Cowburn, for example (Chapter Eight), has demonstrated how ethics are implicated in the construction of a project, which subsequently informs policy, which (inevitably) reinforces the underlying (original) ethics. Within this scheme of circularity – or *reproduction* or *reinforcement* of perspective – the capacity of the field to appraise policy critically is reduced. The field (Bourdieu, 1984) becomes closed to alternative perspectives because they are seen as outside the remit or interest of what usually gets done. Policy fields technocratise political processes and submit these for social sanction; analytical fields confine what are acceptable approaches to policy study. Gregory, for example (Chapter Five), alludes to how the policy apparatus can become attached to, or convinced by, what is possible rather than what works. This situation could be viewed as 'normal science' in a Kuhnian sense (Kuhn, 1970) – puzzle solving without the worry of whether the shape of the puzzle is correct. Unlocking the ways in which the reproduction of particular perspectives is maintained could be one objective of the ethnographic project offered by Jenkins. As Cowburn observes, it is not often that research funders support work that challenges the dominant (paradigmatic) perspective within a field. On the other hand, as Boxall et al show (Chapter Nine) there is room for manoeuvre as new approaches – such as user involvement – come to be seen as politically useful. In this way, possibilities arise to subvert or divert dominant paradigms from the inside, rather than necessarily through confrontation from the outside.

Are there ever any opportunities for radical change, either in the study of policy or within the policy world? Perhaps not; the history of policy development shows clearly that it is never radical and always incremental. There are always too many dimensions of resistance, from the 'institutional stickiness' identified within the political science literature, to electoral constraints perceived by politicians, to the strength of user/public pressure. But we can make some inroads. In line with our belief that the processes of policy analysis – as well as the processes of production and performance of policy – need to be made visible, we can speak more loudly about our work.

As first steps we need to get away from linearity, increase the number and range of voices that inform our knowledge production, and take account of diversity matters in a meaningful way, that is, one that accepts power is always present. Circularity itself can become the subject of analysis. For example, Farnsworth (Chapter Six) posits that business has not had to seek out influence over policy, but a lack of direct influence does not equate to an absence of influence. Business – and markets more generally – are part of the landscape of ongoing policy work. Actor interventions do not have to be deliberate to be present, which suggests that temporal and interactional aspects of policy need to be given more emphasis in policy studies work.

What else can be done to allow for – at least occasional – breaks of the circle? Currently, research training specifications for policy analysts encourage reinforcement of paradigmatic concerns and this seems a key place in which to intervene. While current arrangements will serve to develop disciplinary experts in line with current conceptions of the discipline, it is possible that today's policy issues – let alone tomorrow's – may need perspectives and analysis drawn from outside traditional boundaries. The work of Boxall et al. (Chapter Nine), for example, sets up a clear challenge to the educating of researchers; by calling for a realignment between the knower and what can be known, even 'knowledge' becomes reconfigured. If we recognise that new conceptual models are needed that can take into account the multilayered and multi-actored policy world, then we should refrain from promulgating the neat linear models and unidirectional flows of policy in teaching curricula and training programmes. We should be more explicit about the need for cross-disciplinary interaction. Lendvai and Stubbs (Chapter Ten) have suggested that 'new hybrid concepts, terms and new theoretical perspectives are needed if we are to grasp important fragments of this complex transformation process. This suggests the need to reconceptualise politics, institutions and contexts themselves.' We should take seriously this call to build new ways of thinking and working into the lives of future policy analysts.

In case this is sounding too post-modern for some tastes, let us remind ourselves that a lapse into relativism and 'anything goes' is unlikely, if not impossible, in the route and questions that we advocated. The very presence of values, as discussed above, ensures that policy and its study remain rooted in a non-relativist position. Additionally, the centrality of politics, highlighted by many authors, serves to ground the field in matters of power and interest. Our point, then, is to emphasise the need to build in mechanisms that will support the questioning, reassessment and reanalysis of the stuff of policy. Otherwise, the mutually reinforcing relationship between policy and its study leaves no way in for change.

Reconsidering the study of policy

Attention to the metaphysical aspects of policy is not a commonplace but has been one of the ways in which we have sought to reconsider policy. In this endeavour, our attempt does not add up to a lone voice (Lewis et al., 2000; Colebatch, 2002). In 2005, UNESCO published a report on the relations between social science and social policy, and the possibility of policy making (Lee et al., 2005). They advocated four elements to characterise a new relation between social science and policy, namely:

- a change in the unit of analysis to expand space and time
- an attention to theory and concepts that enable hype to be bypassed
- reassessment of the fact–value relation
- the role of actors in social change.

Although different in origin to our work here, the work of Lee et al. in questioning the capacity of social scientific disciplines and policy processes to make sense of each other, affirms our intent to question policy through deliberate awkwardness. Given the significance of policy as a means to organise and direct social, economic and political life, this book originated in the need for a critical restatement of policy origins, development and form. Without this, we risked being trapped by received wisdom, and caught up in a cycle of change without understanding the 'why' or 'how'. The main purpose of the work presented here then, has been to find ways to look at the 'why' and 'how' with renewed intent. We have suggested that future generations of policy analysts may have a restricted view of their remit if the existing disciplines that study policy do not challenge their own dominant forms of working. In this way, we could also highlight some issues of concern for the teaching of 'policy' and the training of policy analysts.

What we hope is clear from the preceding chapters is that the concerns of this volume are not marginal to the traditional concerns of policy analysis or the more general study of public and social policy. There are, of course, many aspects of policy studies that we have not covered in this book, and the case studies utilised by the contributors do not represent a complete range of policy areas, levels of policy making, social groups or theoretical perspectives. We have deliberately traded breadth for depth and rather than attempting to address every point to every level, the chapters have drawn out key topics within the policy arena and subjected them to sustained theoretical and practical reappraisal. There are sound pedagogic reasons for taking this approach. This volume is not intended as a textbook in the traditional sense, but its contents do address what ought to be the key concerns of any scholar with an interest in understanding the nature of policy. The analyses contained within the individual chapters have application beyond the specific case studies included: contested visions of 'the good society' are crucial to all attempts at regional governance as they are to national developments; the meaning and language of policy is central to all areas of public and social intervention and all statements of action. Similarly the reach of politics in policy making is endless and the questions of categorisation, power relations and scale are applicable at all levels and in all policy contexts.

The volume has explored the development of the meaning and language of policy, and examined the practice of policy from the micro- to the supranational levels, using illustrative case studies to demonstrate how policy is contested, shaped and accounted for. We believe that this approach demonstrates the gains that can be made from applying a multi-perspective lens to the study of 'policy'. 'Slicing through' these chapters in this concluding one has generated some new questions and shown the potential of subjecting the 'known' to new ideas. Inevitably some things are omitted; 'culture' has been touched on but not fully explored; classic services are completely absent, for example, housing and education; and traditional groups, such as children, are not discussed. In part, this is because we wanted to excavate some of the reasons why these categories are taken as classic or traditional in the first place. In part, it is to introduce ideas from further afield as valid to the study of policy. The contexts in which policy can be studied are many and multiplying. We hope that this volume has demonstrated the need to expose old terrain to new concepts and explore new terrain with conventional insights.

However, we must also ask whether our division of meanings, politics and practices is a useful one for the study of policy. Attending to a range of levels of understanding policy and new units of analysis involved the bringing together of differing epistemological bases, which are seen by some as irreconcilable. Indeed, there is something indelible in the arguments between the realist and constructivist stances taken by different authors in this volume. The approaches and forms of explanation they each employ make the collaborative act of reconsideration essential. The utility of our categories then becomes a way to provoke dialogue. 'Meanings' is not just about discourse analysis or how the idea of policy becomes meaningful, but is also about understanding what policy can and ought to do. Leading with this section was deliberate because traditionally it has not been a major concern of policy studies and yet it highlights why policy making is muddled and contested. Politics is obviously, and literally, central to explaining how and why things (do not) get done. The kinds of explanation that can be used, however, vary. Practices are important to address, and not only to show up simplistic 'gaps' between policy and practice. In the same way that 'implementation' used to be assumed to follow naturally and simply from 'formulation', practice is too often assumed to follow naturally from 'policy statement'. We have tried to show that there are different ways of practising policy, even before it gets 'made'.

It is inevitable that policy will continue to be made, and policy researchers will continue to analyse. Our aim in the work presented here has been to reconsider these inevitabilities. The frames of meanings, politics and practices have facilitated this reconsideration, opening new ground for debate, new readings of existing thinking and the application of new concepts within the policy studies field. Given our purpose in opening up the field, we conclude by asking some questions that we see as remaining central to further work in policy studies.

First, what constitutes the valid terrain of policy studies research? We need to appreciate that what counts as 'policy' for the purpose of policy analysis is open to debate. How is a boundary created between those aspects of policy that are subject to scrutiny and analysis, and those that are not? Who gets to define these boundaries? In other words, what gets taken for granted and what gets problematised, both by the policy makers and by the policy analysts? These questions can be asked within policy studies of conventional service areas and groups, but should not stop at the conventional. Late modernity, the risk society, the globalised economy, a planet on the brink of collapse – or however we choose to label the world – is too multifarious to be conventional.

Second, widening the frame of potential analysts has multiple benefits, and suggestions implied here have included anthropologists and other ethnographers, critical discourse analysts and science studies researchers. Governing society these days also means governing science and technology, not just the social (Ong and Collier, 2004; Jasanoff, 2005, 2006). We can reinvigorate policy studies through a dialogue with these other perspectives and this seems essential as the social, the natural and technological become ever more interwoven. The academic call for multidisciplinarity has a basis in everyday life. Drawing on the traditions of other fields will enable us to probe:

- national *traditions* of policy making and the idea of policy cultures;
- the policy process in *practice* – studying *how* it works rather than holding onto a normative view of the way it should work;

- the creation and crossing of boundaries, between policy objects and between policy subjects – furthermore, how power is implicated in boundary work;
- the potential for a policy-making process that can engage with the complexity, or socio-technical nature, or multifaceted character, of life.

Throughout this text, we have maintained the idea that policy is ripe for critical reappraisal – with the context for policy making constantly changing. We propose that this reappraisal be ongoing, that it should continue to address the enduring questions in new ways, and that, in the process, it claims new ground as our analytical terrain. Policy is too important for us not to step up to these tasks.

References

Abel, G.G., Becker, J.V., Mittelman, M.S., Cunningham-Rathner, J., Rouleau, J.L. and Murphy, W.D. (1987) 'Self-reported sex crimes of non-incarcerated paraphiliacs', *Journal of Interpersonal Violence*, vol 2, no 1, pp 3–25.

Acheson, D. (1998) *Independent Inquiry into Inequalities in Health*, London: The Stationery Office.

ACOP (Association of Chief Officers of Probation) (1988) *More Demanding than Custody*, London: ACOP.

ACOP, CCPC and NAPO (1987) *Probation: The Next Five Years: A Joint Statement by the Association of Chief Officers of Probation, Central Council of Probation Committees and National Association of Probation Officers*, London: ACOP, CCPC, NAPO.

Ahmad, W. (1999) 'Ethnic statistics: better than nothing or worse than nothing?', in D. Dorling and S. Simpson (eds) *Statistics in Society: The Arithmetic of Politics*, London: Arnold, pp 124–31.

Ahonen, P., Hyyrylainen, E. and De Salminan, A. (2006) 'Looking for governance configurations of European welfare states', *Journal of European Social Policy*, vol 16, no 2, pp 173–84.

Alber, J. (2006) *The 'European Social Model' and the USA*, Notestein Seminar Series, Princeton, NJ: Princeton University.

Anderson, B. (1983) *Imagined Communities: Reflections on the Origins and Spread of Nationalism*, London: Verso.

Arts, W. and Gelissen, J. (2002) 'Three worlds of welfare capitalism or more?', *Journal of European Social Policy*, vol 12, no 2, pp 137–58.

Aspinall, P. (2001) 'Operationalising the collection of ethnicity data in studies of the sociology of health and illness', *Sociology of Health and Illness*, vol 23, no 6, pp 829–62.

Aspinall, P. (2003) 'The conceptualisation and categorisation of mixed race/ethnicity in Britain and North America: identity options and the role of the state', *International Journal of Intercultural Relations*, vol 27, pp 269–96.

Balarajan, R. and Raleigh, S.V. (1995) *Ethnicity and Health in England*, London: HMSO.

Banks, S. (2001) *Ethics and Values in Social Work*, London: Palgrave Macmillan.

Banks, S. (2006) *Ethics and Values in Social Work* (2nd edn), Basingstoke: Palgrave Macmillan.

Barnes, M. (1999) 'Working with older people to evaluate the Fife User Panels Project', in M. Barnes and L. Warren (eds) *Paths to Empowerment*, Bristol: The Policy Press, pp 107-18.

Barnes, M. (2002) 'Dialogue between older people and public officials: UK experiences', in *Grey power? Volume 1: Political Power and Influence*, Les Cahiers de la FIAPA/Action Research on Ageing, 2, pp 166-82. (Published in French and English)

Barnes, C. (2003) 'What a difference a decade makes: reflections on doing "emancipatory" disability research', *Disability and Society*, vol 18, no 1, pp 3–17.

Bar On, B.A. (1993) 'Marginality and epistemic privilege', in L. Alcoff and E. Potter (eds) *Feminist Epistemologies*, London: Routledge, pp 83–100.

Barry, M. (2006) 'Dispensing [with?] justice: young people's views of the criminal justice system', in K. Gorman, M. Gregory, M. Hayles and N. Parton (eds) *Constructive Work with Offenders*, London: Jessica Kingsley.

Bauer, R.A. (1968) 'The study of policy formation: an introduction', in R.A. Bauer and K.J. Gergen (eds) *The Study of Policy Formation*, New York, NY: The Free Press, pp 1–26.

Bauman, Z. (1990) *Thinking Sociologically*, Oxford: Basil Blackwell.

Beck, U. and Lau, C. (2005) 'Second modernity as a research agenda: theoretical and empirical explorations in the "meta-change" of modern society', *British Journal of Sociology*, vol 56, no 4, pp 525–59.

Belenky, M.F., Clinchy, M.B., Goldberger, N.R. and Tarule, M.J. (1997) *Women's Ways of Knowing, The Development of Self, Voice And Mind*, New York, NY: Basic Books.

Bennett, C. (1991) 'How states utilize foreign evidence', *Journal of Public Policy*, vol 33, no 4, pp 31–54.

Benyon, J. and Solomos, J. (eds) (1987) *The Roots of Urban Unrest*, Oxford: Pergamon.

Beresford, P. (2001) 'Service users, social policy and the future of welfare', *Critical Social Policy*, vol 21, no 4, pp 494–512.

Beresford, P. (2003) *It's Our Lives: A Short Theory Of Knowledge, Distance And Experience*, London: Citizen Press in association with Shaping Our Lives.

Beresford, P. (2005) '"Service user": regressive or liberatory terminology?', *Disability and Society*, vol 20, no 4, pp 469–77.

Beresford, P. and Campbell, J. (1994) 'Disabled people, services users, user involvement and representation', *Disability and Society*, vol 9, no 3, pp 315–25.

Bernard, P. (1999) *Social Cohesion: A Critique*, CPRN Discussion Paper #F09, Ottawa: Canadian Policy Research Networks.

Berting, J. (2006) 'Uniting Europeans by values: a feasible experience?', *European Journal of Social Quality*, vol 6, no 1, pp 127–49.

Bhabha, H. (1995) 'Cultural diversity and cultural difference', in B. Ashcroft, G. Griffiths and H. Tiffin (eds) *The Post Colonial Studies Reader*, London: Routledge, pp 206–9.

Bhaskar, R. (1989) *Reclaiming Reality: A Critical Introduction To Contemporary Philosophy*, London: Verso.

Bichard, M. (2005) *The Bichard Inquiry, Final Report*, Report by Sir Michael Bichard's reconvened inquiry to establish progress on delivering the recommendations made in his original report published on 22 June 2004, London: HMSO.

Biestek, F. (1961) *The Casework Relationship*, London: Allen & Unwin.

Birch, M., Miller, T., Mauthner, M. and Jessop, J. (2002) 'Introduction', in M. Mauthner, M. Birch, J. Jessop and T. Miller (eds) *Ethics in Qualitative Research*, London: Sage, pp 1–13.

Black, N. (2001) 'Evidence based policy: proceed with care', *British Medical Journal*, vol 323 (7307), pp 275–9.

Block, F. (1977) 'The ruling class does not rule: notes on the Marxist theory of the state', *Social Revolution*, vol 7, no 3, pp 6-28.

Block, F. (1990) 'Political choice and the multiple "logics" of capital', in S. Zukin and P. DiMaggio (eds), *Structure of Capital*, Cambridge: Cambridge University Press, pp 293–310.

Boas, M. and McNeill, D. (2004) *Global Institutions and Development*, Basingstoke: Palgrave Macmillan.

Bocock, B.J. (1986) *Hegemony*, London: Tavistock.

Bond, S. and Jenkinson, T. (1996) 'The assessment: investment performance and policy', *Oxford Review of Economic Policy*, vol 12, no 2, pp 1–29.

Bonnet, K. (1985) 'Corporatism and industrial policy', in A. Cawson (ed) *Organized Interests and the State: Studies in Meso-corporatism*, London: Sage, pp 85–105.

Bonoli, G. (1997) 'Classifying welfare states: a two-dimension approach', *Journal of Social Policy*, vol 26, no 3, pp 352–72.

Bourdieu, P. ([1984]1988) *Homo academicus*, Paris: Les Éditions de Minui, trans by Peter Collier, Cambridge: Polity Press in association with Basil Blackwell.

Bourdieu, P. and Wacquant, L. (1992) *An Invitation to Reflexive Sociology*, Chicago, IL: Polity Press.

Bowker, G.C. and Star, S.L. (1999) *Sorting Things Out: Classification and its Consequences*, London and Cambridge, Mass: MIT Press.

Boxall, K., Carson, I. and Docherty, D. (2004) 'Room at the academy? people with learning difficulties and higher education', *Disability and Society*, vol 19, no 2, pp 99–112.

Branfield, F. and Beresford, P. with contributions from others (2006) *Making User Involvement Work: Supporting Service User Networking and Knowledge*, York: Joseph Rowntree Foundation.

Britton, N.J. (2000) *Black Justice? Race, Criminal Justice and Identity*, Stoke-on-Trent: Trentham Books Ltd.

Brown, K. (2000) 'CBI chief's valediction is upbeat about Euro: industry could cope with the single currency at an exchange rate of DM2.85 Sir Clive Thompson tells Kevin Brown', London: *Financial Times*, 10 July.

Brown, M. (2005) 'The "*nutty*" professor', *AutLOOK*, January.

Brown, H. and Smith, H. (1989) 'Whose "ordinary life" is it anyway?', *Disability, Handicap and Society*, vol 4, no 2, pp 105-19.

Burawoy, M. (2000) 'Grounding globalization', in M. Burawoy, J. Blum, S. George, Z. Gille, T. Gowan, L. Haney, M. Klawiter, S. Lopez, S. Riain and M. Thayer (eds) *Global Ethnography: Forces, Connections and Imaginings in a Postmodern World*, Berkeley, CA: University of California Press, pp 337–50.

Burr, V. (1995) *An Introduction to Social Constructionism*, London: Routledge.

Bytheway, B. (1995) *Ageism*, Buckingham: Open University Press.

Cahill, M. (2001) *The Environment and Social Policy*, London: Routledge.

Callon, M. (1986) 'Some elements of a sociology of translation: domestication of the scallops and the fishermen of St Brieuc Bay', in J. Law (ed) *Power, Action and Belief – A New Sociology of Knowledge?*, Sociological Review Monograph 32, London: Routledge & Kegan Paul, pp 196–34.

Campbell, J. and Oliver, M. (1996) *Disability Politics: Understanding our Past, Changing our Future*, London: Routledge.

Campbell, P. (1996) 'The history of the user movement in the United Kingdom', in T. Heller, J. Reynolds, R. Gomm, R. Muston and S. Pattison (eds) *Mental Health Matters: A Reader*, Basingstoke: PalgraveMacmillan.

Carr, S. (2004) *Has Service User Participation Made a Difference to Social Care Services?*, London: Social Care Institute for Excellence.

Carr, H. (2005) '"Someone to watch over me": making supported housing work', *Social and Legal Studies*, vol 14, no 3, pp 387-408.

CCETSW (Central Council for Education and Training in Social Work) (1972) *Values in social work*, London: CCETSW.

CCETSW (1991) *Rules and Requirements for the Diploma in Social Work*, CCETSW Paper 30, London: CCETSW.

Cerny, P. (1997) 'Paradoxes of the competition state: the dynamics of political globalization', *Government and Opposition*, vol 32, no 2, pp 251–74.

Chamberlayne, P. and King, A. (2000) *Cultures of Care: Biographies of Carers in Britain and the Two Germanies*, Bristol: The Policy Press.

Chartered Institute of Personnel and Development (2004) *Employing Ex-offenders: A Practical Guide*, London: Chartered Institute of Personnel and Development.

Chau, A. (2004) *World on Fire: How Exporting Free-Market Democracy Breeds Ethnic Hatred and Global Instability*, London: Heinemann.

Chau, R. (2007) *The Involvement of Chinese Older People in Policy and Practice: Aspirations and Expectations*, York: Joseph Rowntree Foundation.

Chau, R. and Yu, S. (2001) 'Social exclusion of Chinese people in Britain', *Critical Social Policy*, vol 21, no 1, pp 103–25.

Choi, B., Pang, T., Lin, V., Puska, P., Sherman, G., Goddard, M., Ackland, M., Sainsbury, P., Stachenko, S., Morrison, H. and Clottey, C. (2005) 'Can scientists and policy makers work together?', *Journal of Epidemiology and Community Health*, vol 59, pp 632–7.

Clarke, J. (1999) 'Coming to terms with culture' in H. Dean and R. Woods (eds) *Social Policy Review 11*, Luton: Social Policy Association, pp 71–89.

Clarke, J. (2004) *Changing Welfare, Changing States: New Directions in Social Policy*, London: Sage.

Clarke, J. (2005a) 'Welfare states as nation states: some conceptual reflections', *Social Policy and Society*, vol 4, no 4, pp 407–15.

Clarke, J. (2005b) 'What's culture got to do with it?', Paper presented to Research Seminar 'Anthropological Approaches to Studying Welfare', University of Aarhus, Denmark, 16–18 November.

Clarke, J. and Newman, J. (1997) *The Managerial State: Power, Politics and Ideology in the Remaking of Social Welfare*, London: Sage.

Clegg, S. (1989) *Frameworks of Power*, London: Sage.

Clifford, J. (1997) *Routes: Travel and Translation in the Late Twentieth Century*, Cambridge, MA: Harvard University Press.

Clough, P. (1995) 'Problems of identity and method in the investigation of special educational needs', in P. Clough and L. Barton (eds) *Making Difficulties: Research and the Construction of Special Educational Needs*, London: Paul Chapman.

Clough, P. and Barton, L. (eds) (1995) *Making Difficulties: Research and the Construction of Special Educational Needs*, London: Paul Chapman.

Clough, P. and Barton, L. (eds) (1998) *Articulating with Difficulty: Research Voices in Inclusive Education*, London: Paul Chapman.

Cohen, S. (2004) *Searching for a Different Future: The Rise of a Global Middle Class*, Durham, London: Duke University Press.

Colebatch, H.K. (2002) *Policy* (2nd edn), Buckingham: Open University Press.

Collier, S. and Ong, A. (2005) 'Global assemblages, anthropological problems', in S. Collier and A. Ong (eds) *Global Assemblages: Technology, Politics, and Ethics as Anthropological Problems*, Oxford: Blackwell, pp 3–21.

Collins, P.H. (1997) 'Comment on Hekman's "Truth and method: feminist standpoint theory revisited": where's the power?', *Signs: Journal of Women in Culture and Society*, vol 22, no 2, pp 375–81.

Collins H.M. and Evans, R. (2002) 'The third wave of science studies: studies of expertise and experience', *Social Studies of Science*, vol 32, no 2, pp 235–96.

Coppel, J. and Durand, M. (1999) *Trends in Market Openness*, Economics Department Working Papers no 221, Paris: OECD.

Cormie, J. and Warren, L. (2001) *Guidelines for Running Discussion Groups and Influencing Practice*, Bristol: The Policy Press.

Cornwall, A. and Gaventa, J. (2000) 'From users and choosers to makers and shapers: repositioning participation in social policy', *IDS Bulletin*, vol 31, no 4, pp 50–62.

Cowburn, M. (1998) 'A man's world: gender issues in working with male sex offenders in prison', *Howard Journal*, vol 37, no 3, pp 234–51.

Cowburn, M. (2004) 'Confidentiality and public protection: ethical dilemmas in qualitative research with adult male sex offenders', *Journal of Sexual Aggression*, vol 11, no 1, pp 49–63.

Cowburn, M. (2005) 'Hegemony and discourse: reconstruing the male sex offender and sexual coercion by men', *Sexualities, Evolution and Gender*, vol 7, no 3, pp 215–31.

Cowburn, M. and L. Dominelli (2001) 'Masking hegemonic masculinity: reconstructing the paedophile as the dangerous stranger', *British Journal of Social Work*, vol 31, no 3, pp 399–414.

Croft, S. and Beresford, P. (1989) 'User-involvement, citizenship and social policy', *Critical Social Policy*, vol 9, no 5, pp 5–17.

Cutler, T. and Waine, B. (2000) *Managing the Welfare State: The Politics of Public Sector Management* (2nd edn), London: Berg.

Dahl, R. (1961) *Who Governs? Democracy and Power in an American City*, New Haven, CT: Yale University Press.

Dahl, R. and Lindblom, C. (1976) *Politics, Markets and Welfare*, Chicago, IL: University of Chicago Press.

Dale, A., Dex, S. and Lindley, J.K. (2004) 'Ethnic differences in women's demographic, family characteristics and economic activity profiles, 1992–2002', *Labour Market Trends*, vol 112, no 4, pp 153–65.

Davey Smith, G., Ebrahim, S. and Frankel, S. (2001) 'How policy informs the evidence', *British Medical Journal*, vol 322 (7280), pp 184–5.

Deacon, B. (1992) 'The future of social policy in Eastern Europe', in *The New Eastern Europe*, London: Sage, pp 167–91.

Deacon, B. (2000) 'Eastern European welfare states: the impact of the politics of globalisation', *Journal of European Social Policy*, vol 10, no 2, pp 146–61.

Deacon, B. (2007) *Global Social Policy and Governance*, London: Sage.

Defra (2007) 'About Defra', www.defra.gov.uk/corporate/index.asp

Denzin, N.K. and Lincoln Y.S. (2003) *The Landscape of Qualitative Research: Theories and Issues*, Thousand Oaks, CA, and London: Sage.

Department for Education and Skills (2005) *The Protection of Children Act 1999: A Practical Guide to the Act for all Organisations Working with Children*, London: Department for Education and Skills.

Department for Education and Skills and Department of Health (2006) *Vetting and Barring Scheme: Policy Briefing Pack*, London: DfES.

Department of Health (2001) *Valuing People: A New Strategy For Learning Disability For The 21st Century*, London: DH.

Department of Health (2004) *Protection of Vulnerable Adults Scheme in England and Wales for Care Homes and Domiciliary Care Agencies: A Practical Guide Including Changes to the Requirement for Criminal Records Bureau Disclosures in Certain Circumstances*, London: DH.

Department of Health (2006) *Vulnerable Adults*, London: DH, www.dh.gov.uk/PolicyAndGuidance/HealthAndSocialCareTopics/SocialCare/POVA/fs/en

Desai, R. (1994) 'Second-hand dealers in ideas: think-tanks and Thatcherite hegemony', *New Left Review*, 203, Jan/Feb, pp 27–64.

Diamond, I. (1999) 'The census', in D. Dorling and S. Simpson (eds) *Statistics in Society: The Arithmetic of Politics*, London: Arnold, pp 9–18.

Docherty, D., Hughes, R., Phillips, P., Corbett, D., Regan, D., Barber, A., Adams, M., Boxall, K., Kaplan, I. and Izzidien, S. (2005) 'This is what we think', in D. Goodley and G. Geert Van Hove (eds) *Another Disability Reader? Including People with Learning Difficulties*, Antwerp: Garant Publishers, pp 29–49.

Dolowitz, D. and Marsh, D. (1996) 'Who learns what from whom: a review of the policy transfer literature', *Political Studies*, vol 44, no 2, pp 343–57.

Dolowitz, D. and Marsh, D. (2000) 'Learning from abroad: the role of policy transfer in contemporary policy-making', *Governance*, vol 13, no 1, pp 5–24.

Dominelli, L. (1988) *Anti Racist Social Work*, London: Macmillan.

Dominelli, L (2002) *Anti-oppressive Social Work: Theory and Practice*, London: Palgrave Macmillan Press.

Dominelli, L. (2006) 'Dangerous constructions: black offenders in the criminal justice system', in K. Gorman, M. Gregory, M. Hayles and N. Parton, *Constructive Work with Offenders*, London: Jessica Kingsley.

Dowding, K. (2001) 'There must be an end to confusion: policy networks, intellectual fatigue and the need for political science methods courses in British universities', *Political Studies*, vol 49, issue 1, pp 89–105.

Downes, D. and Morgan, R. (1994) 'Hostages to fortune'? The politics of law and order in post-war Britain', in M. Maguire, M. Morgan and R. Reiner, *The Oxford Handbook of Criminology* (3rd edn), Oxford: Oxford University Press, pp 183–232.

Downes, D. and Morgan, R. (2002) 'The skeletons in the cupboard: the politics of law and order at the turn of the millennium', in M. Maguire, M. Morgan and R. Reiner, *The Oxford Handbook of Criminology* (3rd edn), Oxford: Oxford University Press, pp 286–321.

Drinkwater, C. (2005) 'Supported-living and the production of individuals', in S. Tremain (ed) *Foucault and the Government of Disability*, Ann Arbor, MN: University of Michigan Press, pp 229–44.

Dunleavy, P. and O'Leary, B. (1987) *Theories of the State: The Politics of Liberal Democracy*, London: Macmillan.

Dunleavy, P.J. and Hood, C. (1994) 'From old public administration to new public management', *Public Money and Management*, vol 14, no 3, pp 9–16.

Dwyer, P. (2004) *Understanding Social Citizenship: Themes and Perspectives From Policy and Practice*, Bristol: The Policy Press.

Dyer, R. (1997) *White*, London: Routledge.

Eggar, T. (1994) 'Debate on inward investment', *House of Commons*, 29 October.

Erskine, A. (1998) 'The approaches and methods of social policy', in P. Alcock, A. Erskine and M. May (eds) *The Student's Companion to Social Policy*, Oxford: Blackwell, pp 11–16.

Esping-Andersen, G. (1990) *The Three Worlds of Welfare Capitalism*, Cambridge: Polity Press.

Etzioni, A. (1995) *The Spirit of Community*, London: Fontana Books.

Etzioni, A. (1997) *The New Golden Rule*, London: Profile Books.

Etzioni, A. (2000) *The Third Way to a Good Society*, London: Demos.

Falconer, P. and McLaughlin, K. (2000) 'Public-private partnerships and the "New Labour" government in Britain', in S. Osborne (ed) *Public–Private Ppartnerships in International Perspective*, London: Routledge, pp 120–33.

Farnsworth, K. (1998) 'Minding the business interest: the CBI and social policy, 1980-1996', *Policy Studies*, vol 19, no 1, pp 19-38.

Farnsworth, K. (2004) *Corporate Power and Social Policy in Global Context: British Welfare under the Influence*, Bristol: The Policy Press.

Farnsworth, K. (2005) 'International class conflict and social policy', *Social Policy and Society*, vol 4, no 2, pp 217–26.

Farnsworth, K. (2006) 'Capital to the rescue? New Labour's business solutions to old welfare problems', *Critical Social Policy*, vol 26, no 4, pp 817–42.

Farnsworth, K. and Gough, I. (2000) 'The enhanced structural power of capital: a review and assessment', in I. Gough, *Global Capital, Human Needs and Social Policies*, Basingstoke: Palgrave, pp 77–102.

Faulkner, A. (2004) *Capturing the Experiences of those Involved in the TRUE Project: A Story of Colliding Worlds*, Eastleigh: INVOLVE.

Faulkner, D. (2004) 'Taking citizenship seriously', *Criminal Justice*, vol 3, no 3, pp 287–315.

Feeley, S. and Simon, J. (1992) 'The new penology: notes on the emerging new criminal law', in D. Nelken (ed) *The Futures of Criminology*, London: Sage.

Felske, A. W. (1994) 'Knowing about knowing: margin notes on disability research', in M. Rioux and M. Bach (eds) *Disability is Not Measles, New Research Paradigms in Disability*, North York Ontario: Roeher Institute, pp 181–99.

Ferge, Z. (1997) 'The changed welfare paradigm: the individualization of the social', *Social Policy and Administration*, vol 31, no 1, pp 20–44.

Ferge, Z. (2001) 'European integration and the reform of social security in the accession countries', *European Journal of Social Quality*, vol 3, no 1/2, pp 9–25.

Ferrera, M. (1996) 'The "southern" model of welfare in social Europe', *Journal of European Social Policy*, vol 6, no 1, pp 17–37.

Fine, G. (2003) 'Towards a peopled ethnography: developing theory from group life', *Ethnography*, vol 4, no 1, pp 41–60.

Finkelhor, D. and Lewis, I.S. (1988) 'An epidemiologic approach to the study of child molestation', in R.A. Prentky and V. Quinsey (eds), *Human Sexual Aggression: Current Perspectives (528)*, New York, NY: New York Academy of Sciences.

Fischer, F. (2003) *Reframing Public Policy: Discursive Politics and Deliberative Practices*, Oxford: Oxford University Press.

Fisher, J. (1994) 'Why do companies make donations to political parties', *Political Studies*, xii, pp 690–9.

Fitzpatrick, T. (1996) 'Postmodernism, welfare and radical politics', *Journal of Social Policy*, vol 25, no 3, pp 303–20.

Fook, J. (2002) *Social Work: Critical Theory and Practice*, London: Sage.

Foucault, M. (1984) *The History of Sexuality: An Introduction*, London: Peregrine.

Foucault, M. (1989) *The Archaeology of Knowledge*, London and New York, NY: Routledge.

Freeman, R. (2004) 'Research, practice and the idea of translation', consultation paper, University of Edinburgh, www.pol.ed.ac.uk/freeman/healthpolicy.html#working

Furby, L., Weinrott, R.M., and Blackshaw, L. (1989) 'Sex offender recidivism: a review', *Psychological Bulletin*, vol 105, no 1, pp 3–30.

Gamble, A. (1990) *Britain in Decline: Economic Policy, Political Strategy and the British State*, Basingstoke: Macmillan.

Garfinkel, H. (1967) *Studies in Ethnomethodology*, Englewood Cliffs: Prentice Hall.

Garland, D. (2000) 'The culture of high crime societies', *British Journal of Criminology*, vol 40, no 3, pp 347–75.

Garland, D. (2001) *The Culture of Control: Crime and Social Order in Contemporary Society*, Oxford: Oxford University Press.

Gebhardt, E. (1982) 'Introduction to Part III: a critique of methodology', in A. Arato and E. Gebhardt (eds) *The Essential Frankfurt School Reader*, New York, NY: Continuum, pp 81–95.

Gergen, K.J. and Gergen, M.M. (1986) 'Narrative form and the construction of psychological science', in T.R. Sarbin (ed) *Narrative Psychology: The Storied Nature of Human Conduct*, New York, NY: Praeger, pp 22–44.

Giddens, A. (1990) *The Consequences of Modernity*, Cambridge: Polity Press.

Giddens, A. (1998) *The Third Way: The Renewal of Social Democracy*, Cambridge: Polity Press.

Giddens, A. (2000) *The Third Way and its Critics*, Cambridge: Polity Press.

Gieryn, T. (1983) 'Boundary work and the demarcation of science from non-science', *American Sociological Review*, vol 48, no 6, pp 781–95.

Gieryn, T. (1999) *Cultural Boundaries of Science: Credibility on the Line*, Chicago, IL: University of Chicago Press.

Ginsburg, N. (1992) *Divisions of Welfare*, London: Sage.

Ginsburg, N. (2004) 'Structured diversity: a framework for critically comparing welfare states?', in P. Kennett (ed) *A Handbook of Comparative Social Policy*, Cheltenham: Edward Elgar, pp 201–16.

Glasius, M., Kaldor, M. and Anheier, H. (2006) *Global Civil Society 2005/6*, London: Sage.

Goodley, D. and Moore, M. (2000) 'Doing disability research: activist lives and the academy', *Disability and Society*, vol 15, no 6, pp 861–82.

Goodman, A. (2003) 'Probation into the millenium: the punishing service?', in R. Matthews and M. Young (eds) *The New Politics of Crime and Punishment*, Cullompton: Willan, pp 199–222.

Gorman, K. (2001) 'Cognitive behaviouralism and the Holy Grail: the quest for a universal means of managing offender risk', *Probational Journal*, vol 48, no 1, pp 3–9.

Gorman, K., O'Byrne, P. and Parton, N. (2006) 'Constructive work with offenders: setting the scene', in K. Gorman, M. Gregory, M. Hayles and N. Parton, *Constructive Work with Offenders*, London: Jessica Kingsley, pp 13–31.

Gould, J. (2004) 'Positionality and scale: methodological issues in the ethnography of aid', in J. Gould and H. Secher Marcussen (eds) *Ethnographies of Aid: Exploring Development Texts and Encounters*, Roskilde University IDS Occasional Paper 24, pp 263–90.

Gould, J. (2005) 'Timing, scale and style: capacity as governmentality in Tanzania', in D. Mosse and D. Lewis (eds) *The Aid Effect: Giving and Governing in International Development*, London: Pluto, p 65.

Gough, I. (1979) *The Political Economy of the Welfare State*, London: Macmillan.

Gough, D. and Elbourne, D. (2002) 'Systematic research synthesis to inform policy, practice and democratic debate', *Social Policy and Society*, vol 1, no 3, pp 225-36.

Gramsci, A. (1971) *Selections from Prison Notebooks*, London: Lawrence and Wishart.

Grant, W. (1993) *Business and Politics in Britain*, Basingstoke: Macmillan.

Grant, W. and Marsh, D. (1977) *The CBI*, London: Hodder & Stoughton.

Greaves, I. (2006) *Disability Rights Handbook, 31st Edition, April 2006– April 2007*, London: Disability Alliance.

Greer, C. (2003) *Sex Crime and the Media: Sex Offending and the Press in a Divided Society*, Cullompton: Willan Publishing.

Gregory, M. (2006) 'The offender as citizen: socially inclusive strategies for working with offenders in the community', in K. Gorman, M. Gregory, M. Hayles and N. Parton, *Constructive Work with Offenders*, London: Jessica Kingsley, pp 49–66.

Gregory, M. and Holloway, M. (2005) 'Language and the shaping of social work', *British Journal of Social Work*, vol 35, no 1, pp 37–53.

Guillen, A. and Palier, B. (2004) 'Introduction: does Europe matter? Accession to EU and social policy developments in recent and new member states', *Journal of European Social Policy*, vol 14, no 3, p 204–9.

Haahr, J.-H. (2004) 'Open co-ordination as advanced liberal governmentality', in *Journal of European Public Policy*, vol 11, no 2, pp 209–30.

Haas, P. (1992) 'Introduction: epistemic communities and international policy coordination', *International Organisations*, vol 46, no 1, pp 1–35.

Hall, S. (1991) 'Old and new identities, old and new ethnicities', in A. King (ed) *Culture, Globalisation and the World System: Contemporary Conditions for the Representation of Identity*, Basingstoke: Macmillan, pp 19–40.

Hall, P.A. and Soskice, D. (eds) (2001) 'Introduction', in *Varieties of Capitalism: The Institutional Foundations of Comparative Advantage*, Oxford: Oxford University Press, pp 1–68.

Hall, R. and Biersteker, T. (2002) *The Emergence of Private Authority in Global Governance*, Cambridge: Cambridge University Press.

Hammersley, R. and Atkinson, P. (1995) *Ethnography: Principles in Practice* (2nd edn), London: Routledge.

Hanley, B. (2005) 'Research as empowerment?' Report of a series of seminars organised by the Toronto Group, York: Joseph Rowntree Foundation, www.jrf.org.uk/bookshop/eBooks/1859353185.pdf

Hanson, R. and Bussiere, M.T. (1998) 'Predicting relapse: a meta-analysis of sexual offender recidivism studies', *Journal of Consulting and Clinical Psychology*, vol 66, no 2, pp 348–62.

Harding, S. (1991) *Whose Science? Whose Knowledge? Thinking from Women's Lives*, Milton Keynes: Open University Press.

Hardt, M. (2002) 'Porto Alegre: today's Bandung', *New Left Review*, 14 March–April, pp 112–18.

Harrison, S. and Mort, M. (1998) 'Which champions, which people? public and user involvement in health care as a technology of legitimation', *Social Policy and Administration*, vol 32, no 1, pp 60–70.

Hayek, F. (1944) *The Road to Serfdom*, London: Routledge & Kegan Paul.

Healey, K (2000) *Social Work Practices: Contemporary Perspectives on Change,* London: Sage.

Healey, K. (2006) *Social Work Practices,* London: Sage.

Hearn, J. (1998) 'Theorizing men and men's theorizing: varieties of discursive practices in men's theorizing of men', *Theory and Society,* vol 27, no 6, pp 781–816.

Heidenheimer, A.J. (1986) 'Politics, policy and police as concepts in English and continental languages: an attempt to explain divergences', *The Review of Politics,* vol 48, pp 3–30.

Hein, W. and Kohlmorgan, L. (2005) 'Global health governance: conflicts on global social rights', German Overseas Development Institute, www.duei.de/workingpapers

Hekman, S. (1997) 'Truth and method: feminist standpoint theory revisited', *Signs: Journal of Women in Culture and Society,* vol 22, no 2, pp 341–65.

Held, D., McGrew, A., Goldblatt, D. and Perraton, J. (1999) *Global Transformations,* Cambridge: Polity Press.

Herbert-Cheshire, L. (2003) 'Translating policy: power and action in Australia's country towns', *Sociologica Ruralis,* vol 43, no 4, pp 454–73.

Hersak, E. (2003) 'Globalization and the Croatian code', in M. Mestrovic (ed) *Globalization and its Reflections on (in) Croatia,* New York, NY: Global Scholarly Publications, pp 131–48.

Hill, M. (ed) (1993) *The Policy Process: A Reader,* London: Harvester Wheatsheaf.

Hill, M. (1997) *The Policy Process in the Modern State,* London: Prentice Hall.

Hill, M. (2005) *The Public Policy Process* (4th edn), Harlow: Pearson Longman.

Hillyard, P. and Watson, S. (1996) 'Postmodern social policy: a contradiction in terms?', *Journal of Social Policy,* vol 25, no 3, pp 321–46.

HMSO (Her Majesty's Stationery Office) (1982) *Corporation Tax,* Cmnd 8456, London: HMSO.

HMSO (2003) *Explanatory notes to Sexual Offences Act 2003,* London: HMSO, www.opsi.gov.uk/ACTS/en2003/2003en42.htm

Hodge, S. (2005) 'Participation, discourse and power: a case study in user involvement', *Critical Social Policy,* vol 25, no 2, pp 164–79.

Hogwood, B. and Gunn, L. (1984) *Policy Analysis for the Real World,* Oxford: Oxford University Press.

Holmes, D. and Marcus, G. (2005) 'Cultures of expertise and the management of globalization: toward the re-functioning of ethnography', in A. Ong and S. Collier (eds) *Global Assemblages: Technology, Politics and Ethics as Anthropological Problems*, Oxford: Blackwell, pp 235–52.

Holy, L. and Stuchlik, M. (1983) *Actions, Norms and Representations: Foundations for Anthropological Inquiry*, Cambridge: Cambridge University Press.

Home Office (1984) *Probation Service in England and Wales: Statement of National Objectives and Priorities*, London: Home Office.

Home Office (1988) *Punishment, Custody and the Community*, London: HMSO.

Home Office (1992) *National Standards for the Supervision of Offenders in the Community*, London: Home Office.

Home Office (1998) *Joining Forces to Protect the Public: Prisons–Probation. A Consultation Document*, London: Home Office.

Home Office (2000) *National Standards for the Supervision of Offenders in the Community*, London: Home Office.

Home Office (2001) *Criminal Statistics: England and Wales 2000*, Cm 5312, London: Home Office.

Home Office (2002) *Criminal Statistics: England and Wales 2001*, Cm 5606, London: Home Office.

Howard League Working Party (1985) *Unlawful Sex: Offences, Victims and Offenders in the Criminal Justice System of England and Wales. The Report of Howard League Working Party*, London: Waterlow Publishers Ltd.

Howe, D. (1993) *On Being a Client: Understanding the Process of Counselling and Psychotherapy*, London: Sage.

Hudson, B. (1987) *Justice Through Punishment: A Critique of the Justice Model of Corrections*, London: Macmillan.

Hudson, B. (2001) 'Human rights, public safety and the probation service: defending justice in the risk society', *The Howard Journal*, vol 40, no 2, pp 103–13.

Hudson, J. and Lowe, S. (2004) *Understanding the Policy Process*, Bristol: The Policy Press.

Hughes, B. (2002) 'Disability and the body', in C. Barnes, M. Oliver and L. Barton (eds) *Disability Studies Today*, Cambridge: Polity Press, pp 58–76.

Hulme R. (2004) 'Borrowing or learning? The role of policy transfer in assessing the impact of American ideas on British social policy', Paper presented to GASPP seminar 'The Rise and Fall (?) of the International Influence of US American Social Policy', McMaster University, Canada 10–11 September, www.gaspp.org/seminars/papers/7/rhulme.pdf

Hunt, P. (1998) 'A critical condition', in T. Shakespeare (ed) *The Disability Reader: Social Science Perspectives*, London: Cassell.

Hurst, A. (1995) 'The seed-time and the harvest: towards the development of a community of scholars', *Disability Research Archive UK*, www.leeds.ac.uk/disability-studies/archiveuk

IDS (1993) *IDS Quarterly*, London: Incomes Data Services, no 66, 8 April.

Ignatieff, M. (2000) *The Rights Revolution*, Toronto: House of Anansi Press.

Innes, J. (2002) *Knowledge and Public Policy* (2nd edn), New Brunswick, NJ: Transaction Books.

Irving, Z., Yeates, N. and Young, P. (2005) 'What can global perspectives contribute to curriculum development in social policy?', *Social Policy and Society*, vol 4, no 4, pp 475–84.

Ivekovic, R. (2005) 'Transborder translating', *Eurozine*, 14 January, www.eurozine.com/articles/2005-01-14-ivekovic-en.html

Jackson, M. (1984) 'Sexology and the social construction of male sexuality (Havelock Ellis)', in L. Coveney, M. Jackson, S. Jeffreys, L. Kaye and P. Mahony (eds) *The Sexuality Papers*, London: Hutchinson, pp 45–68.

Jacobson, M.F. (2000) 'Looking Jewish, seeing Jews', in L. Back and J. Solomos (eds) *Theories of Race and Racism*, London: Routledge, pp 238–52.

Jasanoff, S. (2005) *Designs on Nature*, Princeton and Oxford: Princeton University Press.

Jasanoff, S. (ed) (2006) *States of Knowledge: The Co-production of Science and the Social Order*, Abingdon: Routledge.

Jasanoff, S., Markle, G., Petersen, J. and Pinch, T. (eds) (1995) *Handbook of Science and Technology Studies*, London and Thousand Oaks, CA: Sage.

Jenkins, R. (1986) *Racism and Recruitment: Managers, Organisations and Equal Opportunity in the Labour Market*, Cambridge: Cambridge University Press.

Jenkins, R. (1996) *Social Identity*, London: Routledge.

Jenkins, R. (1997) *Rethinking Ethnicity: Arguments and Explorations*, London: Sage.

Jenkins, R. (2002) *Foundations of Sociology: Towards a Better Understanding of the Human World*, Basingstoke: Palgrave Macmillan.

Jenkins, R. (2004) *Social Identity* (2nd edn), London: Routledge.

Jenkins, R. (2006) 'Telling the forest from the trees: local images of national change in Denmark', *Ethnos*, vol 71, pp 367–89.

Jenkins, J.C. and Brents, G.B. (1989) 'Social protest, hegemonic competition, and social reform: a political struggle interpretation of the origins of the American welfare state', *American Sociological Review*, no 54, Dec, pp 891–909.

Jepson, M. and Pascual, A. (2005) 'The European Social Model: an exercise in deconstruction', *Journal of European Social Policy*, vol 15, no 3, pp 231–45.

Jones, C. (1996) 'Anti-intellectualism and the peculiarities of British social work education', in N. Parton (ed) *Social Theory, Social Change and Social Work*, London: Routledge, pp 190–210.

Jones, R. and Gnanapala, W. (2000) *Ethnic Minorities in English Law*, Stoke-on-Trent: Trentham Books Ltd.

Jordan, G. (1991) *The Commercial Lobbyists: Politics for Profit in Britain*, Aberdeen: Aberdeen University Press.

Josselin, D. and Wallace, W. (2001) *Non-state Actors in World Politics*, Basingstoke: Palgrave.

Juhasz, G. (2006) 'Exporting or pulling down? The European Social Model and eastern enlargement of the EU', *European Journal of Social Quality*, vol 6, no 1, pp 82–108.

Kaldor, M. (2003) *Global Civil Society*, Cambridge: Polity Press.

Kant, I. (1964) *Groundwork of the Metaphysic of Morals*, New York, NY: Harper and Row Publishers, Inc.

Katrougalos, G. (1996) 'The southern European welfare model: the Greek welfare state in search of an identity', *Journal of European Social Policy*, vol 6, no 1, pp 39–60.

Kelly, L. (1988) *Surviving Sexual Violence*, Oxford: Polity Press.

Kelly, R. (2006) 'Ruth Kelly: full statement on school vetting', *Times Online*, London: www.timesonline.co.uk/article/0,,2-2000841,00.html

Kemshall, H. (1998) *Risk in Probation Practice*, Aldershot: Ashgate.

Kerr, C. (1962) *Industrialism and Industrial Man: the Problem of Labour and Management in Economic Growth*, London: Heinemann.

Kiberd, D. (1995) *Inventing Ireland: Literature of the Modern Nation*, London: Vintage Press.

Kirkup, J. and Peev, G. (2006) 'How many sex offenders in schools? No idea', *The Scotsman*, Edinburgh, Glasgow and London: thescotsman.scotsman.com/index.cfm?id=52612006

Kitzinger, J. (1999) 'The ultimate neighbour from hell: media framing of paedophiles', in B. Franklin (ed) *Social Policy, the Media and Misrepresentation*, London: Routledge, pp 207–21.

Knowles, C. (2005) 'Making whiteness: British lifestyle migrants in Hong Kong', in C. Alexander and C. Knowles (eds) *Making Race Matter: Bodies, Space and Identity*, Basingstoke: Palgrave Macmillan, pp 90 –110.

Koenig-Archbugi, M. (2002) 'Mapping global governance', in D. Held and A. McGrew (eds) *Governing Globalization*, Cambridge: Polity Press, pp 46–69.

Korpi, W. (1983) *The Democratic Class Struggle*, London: Routledge & Kegan Paul.

Korpi, W. (1989) 'Power, politics and state autonomy in the development of social citizenship: social rights during sickness in eighteen OECD countries since 1930', *American Sociological Review*, no 54, pp 309–28.

Korver, T. and Oeij, P. (2006) 'Covenants, external effects and employability', *European Journal of Social Quality*, vol 6, no 1, pp 50–82.

Kovics, J. (2002) 'Approaching the EU and reaching the US? Rival narratives on transforming welfare regimes in East-Central Europe', *West European Politics*, vol 25, no 2, pp 175–204.

KPMG (2003) *Global Corporate Tax Rate Survey: Emerging Trends Pinpointed*, London: KPMG: www.kpmg.co.uk/kpmg/uk/press/detail. cfm?pr¼1669

Kuhn, T.S. (1970) *The Structure of Scientific Revolutions*, 2nd edn, London, Chicago, IL: University of Chicago Press.

Kvale, S. (1996) *Interviewing: An Introduction to Qualitative Research Interviewing*, London: Sage.

Kvist, J. (2004) 'Does EU enlargement start a race to the bottom? Strategic interaction among EU member states in social policy', *Journal of European Social Policy*, vol 14, no 3, pp 301–18.

Labour Party (2001) *The Best Place to do Business, The Labour Party's 2001 Business Manifesto*, London: The Labour Party.

Latour, B. (1987) 'The power of association', in J. Law (ed) *Power, Action and Belief: A New Sociology of Knowledge?*, London: Routledge, pp 262–80.

Latour, B. (2000) 'When things strike back: a possible contribution of "science studies" to the social sciences', *British Journal of Sociology*, vol 51, no 1, pp 107–23.

Latour, B. (2004) *Politics of Nature: How to Bring the Sciences into Democracy*, Cambridge, MA and London: Harvard University Press.

Latour, B. (2005) *Reassembling the Social: An Introduction to Actor-network Theory'*, Oxford: Oxford University Press.

Law, J. (1992) 'Notes on the theory of the actor-network: ordering, strategy, and heterogeneity', *Systems Practise*, vol 5, no 4, pp 379–93.

Lee, R.M. (1993) *Doing Research on Sensitive Topics*, London: Sage.

Lee, R.E., Martin, W.J., Sonntag, H.R., Taylor, P.J., Wallerstein, I. and Wieviorka, M. (2005) *Social Science and Social Policy: From National Dilemmas to Global Opportunities*, Paris: UNESCO.

Leibfried, S. (1992) 'Towards a European welfare state? On integrating poverty regimes into the European Community', in Z. Ferge and J. Kolberg, *Social Policy in a Changing Europe*, Frankfurt: Campus Verlag, pp 245–280.

Leisering, L. (2003) 'Nation state and welfare state: an intellectual and political history', *Journal of European Social Policy*, vol 13, no 2, 175–86.

Lendvai, N. and Stubbs, P. (2006) 'Translation, intermediaries and welfare reforms in South Eastern Europe', Paper prepared for the 4th ESPANET conference: 'Transformation of the welfare state: Political regulation and social inequality', 21–23 September 2006, Bremen.

Lewis, G., Gewirtz, S. and Clarke, J. (eds) (2000) *Rethinking Social Policy*, London: Sage.

Leys, C. (1989) *Politics in Britain: From Labourism to Thatcherism*, London: Verso.

Lindblom, C.E. (1959) 'The science of "muddling through"', *Public Administration Review*, vol 19, pp 78–88.

Lindblom, C.E. (1977) *Politics and Markets*, New York, NY: Basic Books.

Lipsky, M. (1980) *Street-level Bureaucracy: Dilemmas of the Individual in Public Services*, New York, NY: Russell Sage Foundation.

Lister, R. (2003) *Citizenship: Feminist Perspectives* (2nd edn), Basingstoke: Palgrave Macmillan.

Longino, H. E. (1990) *Science as Social Knowledge: Values and Objectivity in Scientific Inquiry*, Princeton, NJ: Princeton University Press.

Loomba, A. (1998) *Colonialism/Postcolonialism*, London: Routledge.

Lukes, S. (1974) *Power: A Radical View*, London: Macmillan.

Lupton, C. (1992) 'Feminism, managerialism and performance measurement', in M. Langan and L. Day, *Women, Oppression and Social Work: Issues in Anti-discriminatory Practice*, London: Routledge, pp 92–111.

Lynch, M. (2000) 'Against reflection as an academic virtue and source of privileged knowledge', *Theory, Culture, Society*, vol 17, no 3, pp 26–54.

MacClancey, J. (2002) 'Introduction: taking people seriously', in J. MacClancey (ed) *Exotic No More: Anthropology on the Front Lines*, Chicago, IL: Chicago University Press, pp 1–14.

MacNaghten, P., Kearnes, M., and Wynne, B. (2005) 'Nanotechnology, governance and public deliberation: what role for the social sciences?', *Science Communication*, vol 27, no 2, pp 268–91.

McCarty, R. (2002) 'Science, politics and peer review: an editor's dilemma', *American Psychologist*, vol 57, issue 3, pp 198–201.

McGuire, J. and Priestly, P. (1995) 'Reviewing "what works": past, present and future', in J. McGuire (ed) *What Works: Reducing Reoffending*, Chichester: Wiley.

McLaughlin, E. and Muncie, J. (2000) 'The criminal justice system: New Labour's new partnerships', in J. Clarke, S. Gewirtz and E. McLaughlin (eds), *New Managerialism, New Welfare*, London: Open University/Sage, pp 169–85.

Mair, G. (1997) 'Community penalties and probation', in M. Maguire et al (eds) *The Oxford Handbook of Criminology* (2nd edn), Oxford: Clarendon Press, pp 1198–231.

Mair, G. (2004) 'The origins of what works in England and Wales: a house built on sand?', in G. Mair, *What matters in probation*, Cullompton: Willan, pp 12–33.

Mann, M. (1993) *The Sources of Social Power, Vol II: The Rise of Classes and Nation-states, 1760–1914*, Cambridge: Cambridge University Press.

Mann, K. (1998) 'The welfare state and postmodernity', *Critical Social Policy*, vol 18, no 1, pp 85–93.

Manning, N. (2004) 'Diversity and change in pre-accession Central and Eastern Europe since 1989', *Journal of European Social Policy*, vol 14, no 3, pp 211–32.

Marcus, G. (1995) 'Ethnography in/of the world system: the emergence of multi-sited ethnography', *Annual Review of Anthropology*, vol 24, no 1, pp 95–117.

Marinetto, M. (2003) 'Who wants to be an active citizen? The politics and practice of community involvement', *Sociology*, vol 37, no 1, pp 103–20.

Marmot, M.G. (2004) 'Evidence based policy or policy based evidence?', *British Medical Journal*, vol 328 (7445), pp 906–7.

Marsh, D. (1995) 'The convergence between theories of the state', in D. Marsh and G. Stoker (eds) *Theory and Methods in Social Science*, Basingstoke: Macmillan, pp 248–69.

Marshall, T.H. (1972) 'Value problems of welfare capitalism', *Journal of Social Policy*, vol 1, pp 15–32.

Marston, S.A. (2000) 'The social construction of scale', *Progress in Human Geography*, vol 24, no 2, pp 219–42.

Martin, J. (1984) *Hospitals in Trouble*, Oxford: Blackwell.

Martinson, R. (1974) 'What works? Questions and answers about prison reform', *Public Interest*, vol 35, Spring, pp 22–54.

Maruna, S., Immarigeon, R. and LeBel, T. (2004) 'Reintegration and restorative justice: towards a theory and practice of informal social control and support', in S. Maruna and R. Immarigeon (eds) *After Crime and Punishment: Pathways to Offender Re-integration*, Cullompton: Willan, pp 3–26.

Means, R., Richards, S. and Smith, R. (2003) *Community Care: Policy and Practice* (3rd edn), Basingstoke: Palgrave Macmillan.

Merton, R.K. (1957) *Social Theory and Social Structure* (2nd edn), Glencoe: Free Press.

Meyer, J., Frank, D., Hironaka, A. and Tuma, N. (1997) 'The structuring of a world environmental regime 1870–1970', *International Organisations*, vol 51, no 4, pp 623–51.

Miles, R. and Brown, M. (2003) *Racism* (2nd edn), London: Routledge.

Milewa, T., Valentine, J. and Calnan, M. (1999) 'Community participation and citizenship in British health care planning: narrative of power and involvement in the changing welfare state', *Sociology of Health and Illness*, vol 21, no 4, pp 445–65.

Miliband, R. (1969) *The State in Capitalist Society*, London: Quartet Books.

Miliband, R. (1973) 'The power of Labour and the capitalist enterprise', in J. Urry and J. Wakeford (eds) *Power in Britain*, London: Heinemann Educational Books.

Miliband, D. (2006) Speech at the launch of Natural England, London, 11 October, www.defra.gov.uk/corporate/ministers/speeches/daiv-miliband/dm061011.htm

Mirza, H.S. (2006) '"Race", gender and educational desire', *Race, Ethnicity and Education*, vol 9, no 2, pp 137–58.

Modood, T. (1990) 'British Asian Muslims and the Rushdie affair', *Political Quarterly*, vol 61, pp 143–60.

Monaci, M. and Caselli, M. (2005) 'Blurred discourses: how market isomorphism constrains and enables collective action in civil society', *Global Networks*, vol 5, no 1, pp 49–69.

Moran, M. (2006) 'Interdisciplinarity and political science', *Politics*, vol 26, no 2, pp 73–83.

Morris, J. (1991) *Pride Against Prejudice*, London: Women's Press.

National Probation Service for England and Wales (2001) *A New Choreography: An Integrated Strategy for The National Probation Service for England and Wales – Strategic Framework 2001–2004*, London: Home Office.

Naughton, M. (2005) '"Evidence-based policy" and the government of the criminal justice system – only if the evidence fits', *Critical Social Policy*, vol 25, no 1, pp 47–69.

Naughton, P. (2006) 'Kelly says no sex offenders in schools', *Times Online*, London, www.timesonline.co.uk/article/0,,2-1999956,00.html

Nazroo, J. (1999) 'The racialisation of ethnic inequalities in health', in D. Dorling and S. Simpson (eds) *Statistics in Society: The Arithmetic of Politics*, London: Arnold, pp 215–22.

Nellis, M. (1995) 'Probation values for the 1990s', *The Howard Journal*, vol 34, no 1, pp 19–44.

Nellis, M. (2000) 'The new probation training', *Criminal Justice Matters*, no 39, Spring, pp 22–3.

Nellis, M. (2001a) 'The new probation training in England and Wales, realising the potential', *Social Work Education*, vol 20, no 4, pp 415–31.

Nellis, M. (2001b) 'Community values and community justice', *Probation Journal*, vol 48, no 1, pp 34–8.

Nellis, M. and Gelsthorpe, L. (2003) 'Human rights and the probation values debate', in W.C. Hui and M. Nellis (eds) *Moving Probation Forward*, Harlow: Pearson Education.

Nellis, M. (2005) Speech to NAPO Annual General Meeting, www.napo2.org.uk/agm2005/archives/2005/10/probation_value.html

Newman, J. (2002) 'Putting the "policy" back into social policy', *Social Policy and Society*, vol 1, no 4, pp 347–54.

Newton, T. (1996) 'Agency and discourse: recruiting consultants in a life insurance company', *Sociology*, vol 30, no 4, pp 717–39.

Nicolson, P. (1995) 'Feminism and psychology', in J.A. Smith, R. Harré and L. Van Langenhove (eds), *Rethinking Psychology*, London: Sage, pp 122–42.

Niranjana, T. (1992) *Siting Translation: History, Post-structuralism and the Colonial Context*, Berkeley, CA: University of California Press.

Noll, H. (2002) 'Towards a European system of social indicators: theoretical framework and system architecture', *Social Indicators Research*, vol 58, pp 47–87.

O'Brien, R., Goetz, A.M., Scholte, J. and Williams, M. (2000) *Contesting Global Governance: Multilateral Economic Institutions and Global Social Movements*, Cambridge: Cambridge University Press.

O'Connor, J. (2003) 'Policy coordination, social indicators and the social policy agenda of the European Union', *Journal of European Social Policy*, vol 15, no 4, pp 345–61.

O'Malley, P. (1996) 'Indigenous governance', *Economy and Society*, vol 25, no 3, pp 310–36.

Oatley, N. (1998) 'Cities, economic competition and urban policy', in N. Oatley (ed) *Cities, Economic Competition and Urban Policy*, London: Paul Chapman, pp 3–20.

Offe, C. and Weisenthal, H. (1980) 'Two logics of collective action: theoretical notes on social class and organisational form', in M. Zeitlin (ed) *Political Power and Social Theory*, Greenwich, CT: JAI Press, pp 67–115.

Offe, C. and Ronge, V. (1982) 'Theses on the theory of the state', in A. Giddens and D. Held (eds) *Classes, Power and Conflict*, Basingstoke: Macmillan.

Oldfield, M. (1994) 'Talking quality, meaning control: McDonalds, the market and probation service', *Probation Journal*, vol 411, no 4, pp 186–92.

Oliver, M. (1990) *The Politics of Disablement*, Basingstoke: Macmillan.

Oliver, M. (1992) 'Changing the social relations of research production', *Disability, Handicap and Society*, vol 7, no 2, pp 101–14.

Oliver, M. and Barnes, C. (1998) *Social Policy and Disabled People: From Exclusion to Inclusion*, London: Longman.

Oliver, M. and Sapey, B. (2006) *Social Work with Disabled People*, Basingstoke: Palgrave Macmillan.

Ong, A. and Collier, S.J. (eds) (2004) *Global Assemblages: Technology, Politics and Ethics as Anthropological Problems*, Oxford: Blackwell Publishing.

Orenstein, M. (2005) 'The new pension reform as global policy', *Global Social Policy*, vol 5, no 2, pp 175–202.

Osler, D. (2002) *Labour Party Plc: New Labour as a Party of Business*, Edinburgh: Mainstream Publishing.

Pakaluk, M. (2005) *Aristotle's Nicomachean ethics: An introduction*, Cambridge: Cambridge University Press.

Parkinson, J. (2004) 'Hearing voices: negotiating representation claims in public deliberation', *British Journal of Politics and International Relations*, vol 6, no 3, pp 370–88.

Parton, N. and O'Byrne, P. (2000) *Constructive Social Work*, London: Macmillan.

Pascoe-Watson, G. (2006) '150 paedos in your schools', *Online Sun*, London, www.thesun.co.uk/article/0,,2-2006030317,00.html

Pateman, C. (1989) 'Feminist critiques of the public/private dichotomy', in C. Pateman (ed) *The Disorder of Women*, Cambridge: Polity Press, pp 118–40.

Patomaki, H. and Teivainen, T. (2005) 'The post-Porto Alegre World Social Forum: an open space or a movement of movements', www.forumsocialmundial.org

Pawson, R. (2002a) 'Evidence-based policy: in search of a method', *Evaluation*, vol 8, no 2, pp 157–81.

Pawson, R. (2002b) 'Evidence-based policy: the promise of "realist synthesis"', *Evaluation*, vol 8, no 3, pp 340–58.

Pembroke, L.R. (1994) *Self-harm: Perspectives from Personal Experience*, London: Survivors Speak Out.

Penna, S. and O'Brien, S. (1996) 'Postmodernism and social policy: a small step forwards?', *Journal of Social Policy*, vol 25, no 1, pp 39–61.

Percy, A. and Mayhew, P. (1997) 'Estimating sexual victimisation in a national crime survey: a new approach', *Studies on Crime and Crime Prevention*, vol 6, no 2, pp 355–62.

Pfau-Effinger, B. (2005) 'Culture and welfare state policies: reflections on a complex interrelation', *Journal of Social Policy*, vol 34, no 1, pp 1–18.

Phillips, D. (2006) *Quality of Life: Concept, Policy and Practice*, London: Routledge.

Phillpotts, G.O. and L. Lancucki (1979) *Previous Convictions, Sentence, and Reconvictions*, London: Home Office, HMSO.

Pickering, A. (ed) (1992) *Science as Practice and Culture*, Chicago, IL: University of Chicago Press.

Pierson, P. (1995) 'Fragmented welfare states: federal institutions and the development of social policy', *Governance*, vol 8, no 4, pp 447–8.

Piven, F.F. and Cloward, R.A. (1979) *Poor People's Movements*, New York, NY: Pantheon.

Pollock, A.M. (2004) *NHS plc,* London: Verso.

Poulantzas, N. (1973) 'The problem of the capitalist state', in J. Urry and J. Wakeford (eds) *Power in Britain*, London: Heinemann Educational Books.

Powell, M. and Barrientos, A. (2004) 'Welfare regimes and the welfare mix', *European Journal of Political Research*, vol 43, no 1, pp 83–105.

Pratt, M. (1992) *Imperial Eyes: Travel Writing and Transculturation*, London: Routledge.

Przeworski, A. and Wallerstein, M. (1988) 'Structural dependence of the state on capital', *American Political Science Review*, vol 82, no 1, pp 11–29.

Purvis, T. and A. Hunt (1993) 'Discourse, ideology, discourse, ideology, discourse, ideology ...', *The British Journal of Sociology*, vol 44, no 3, pp 473–99.

Quinsey, V. (1986) 'Men who have sex with children', in D. Weisstub (ed) *Law and Mental Health: International Perspectives*, New York, NY: Pergamon Press, pp 140–72.

Quinsey, V., Chaplin, T. and Upfold, D. (1984) 'Sexual arousal to nonsexual violence and sadomasochistic themes among rapists and non-sex offenders', *Journal of Consulting and Clinical Psychology*, vol 52, no 4, pp 651–7.

Race, D. (1995) 'Historical development of service provision', in N. Malin (ed) *Services for People with Learning Disabilities*, London: Routledge, pp 46–78.

Race, D. (2002) *Learning Disability – A Social Approach*, London: Routledge.

Radford, J. (1994) 'Intellectual disability and the heritage of modernity', in M. Rioux and M. Bach (eds) *Disability is Not Measles, New Research Paradigms in Disability*, North York Ontario: Roeher Institute, pp 9–27.

Ray, K. (2003) 'Constituting "Asian women": political representation, identity politics and local discourses of participation', *Ethnic and Racial Studies*, vol 26, no 5, pp 854–78.

Rapaport, K. and Burkhart, B.R. (1984) 'Personality and attitudinal characteristics of sexually coercive college males', *Journal of Abnormal Psychology*, vol 93, pp 216–21.

Reason, P. and Bradbury, H. (2001) *Handbook of Action Research: Participative Inquiry and Practice*, London: Sage.

Rhodes, R.A.W. (1997) *Understanding Governance: Policy Networks, Governance, Reflexivity and Accountability*, Buckingham: Open University Press.

Rhodes, M. (2000) 'Restructuring the British welfare state: between domestic constraints and global imperatives', in F.W. Scharpf, and V.A. Schmidt (eds) *Welfare and Work in the Open Economy*, Oxford: Oxford University Press, pp 19–69.

Rhodes, R.A.W. and D. Marsh (1992) 'New directions in the study of policy networks', *European Journal of Political Research*, vol 21, pp 181–205.

Roediger, D. (1994) *Towards the Abolition of Whiteness*, London: Verso.

Rose, R. (1991) 'What is lesson drawing?', *Journal of Public Policy*, vol 11, no 1, pp 1–22.

Rosenstock, L. and Lee, L. J. (2002) 'Attacks on science: the risks to evidence-based policy', *American Journal of Public Health*, vol 92, no 1, pp 14–18.

Rustin, M. and Freeman, R. (1999) 'Introduction: welfare, culture and Europe', in P. Chamberlayne, A. Cooper, R. Freeman and M. Rustin (eds) *Welfare and Culture in Europe. Towards a New Paradigm In Social Policy*, London: Jessica Kingsley, pp 1–31.

Ryan, J. and Thomas, F. (1987) *The Politics of Mental Handicap*, London: Free Association Books.

Sakai, N. (2006) 'Translation', *Theory, Culture, Society*, vol 23, nos 2–3, pp 71–8.

Scholte, J. (2005) *Globalizations: A Critical Introduction*, Basingstoke: Palgrave.

Schön, D. and Rein, M. (1994) *Frame Reflection*, New York, NY: Basic Books.

Schutz, A. (1944) 'The stranger: An essay in social psychology', *American Journal of Sociology*, vol 49, pp 499–507.

SCIE (2003) *Commission: Information Review – Structuring Electronic Access to Knowledge about Transition for Young People with Learning Disabilities and their Families and Supporters*, London: Social Care Institute for Excellence, June.

Scott, J. (1991) *Who Rules Britain*, Oxford: Polity Press. Scott, J.W. (2002) 'A networked space of meaning? Spatial politics as geostrategies of European integration', *Space and Polity*, vol 6, no 2, pp 147–67.

Scott, R. and Crooks, A. (2005) *Polls Apart 4: Campaigning for Accessible Democracy*, London: Scope.

Scruggs, L. and Allan, J. (2006) 'The material consequences of welfare states – benefit generosity and absolute poverty in 16 OECD countries', *Comparative Political Studies*, vol 39, no 7, pp 880–904.

Seller, A. (1988) 'Realism versus relativism: towards a politically adequate epistemology', in M. Griffiths and M. Whitford (eds) *Feminist Perspectives in Philosophy*, Basingstoke: Macmillan, pp 169–86.

Sen, G. (2006) 'The quest for gender equality', in P. Utting (ed) *Reclaiming Development Agendas*, Basingstoke: Palgrave, pp 128–43.

Sen, J., Anand, A., Escobar, A. and Waterman, P. (2004) *World Social Forum: Challenging Empires*, New Delhi: Viveka Foundation.

Shaw, M. and Hannah-Moffatt, K. (2004) 'How cognitive skills forgot about gender and diversity', in G. Mair (ed) *What Matters in Probation*, Cullompton: Willan.

Shepherd, A. and Whiting, E. (2006) *Re-offending of Adults: Results from the 2003 Cohort (report 20/06)*, London: Home Office.

Shore, C. and Wright, S. (1997) 'Policy: a new field of anthropology', in C. Shore and S. Wright (eds) *Anthropology of Policy: Critical Perspectives on Governance and Power*, London: Routledge, pp 3–39.

Shore, C. and Wright, S. (eds) (1997) *Anthropology of Policy: Critical Perspectives on Governance and Power*, London: Routledge.

Siaroff, A. (1994) 'Work, welfare and gender equality: a new typology', in D. Sainsbury (ed) *Gendering Welfare States*, London: Sage, pp 82–100.

Sklair, L. (2002) *Globalization: Capitalism and its Alternatives*, Oxford: Oxford University Press.

Skocpol, T. (1979) *States and Social Revolutions*, Cambridge: Cambridge University Press.

Skocpol, T. (1985) 'Bringing the state back in: current research', in P. B. Evans, D. Reuschemeyer and T. Skocpol (eds) *Bringing the State Back in*, Cambridge: Cambridge University Press.

Smith, M.J. (1993) *Pressure, Power and Policy*, Hemel Hempstead: Harvester Wheatsheaf.

Soederberg, S. (2006) *Global Governance in Question*, London: Pluto Press.

Solomon, E. (2005) *Recycling Offenders Through Prison*, London: Prison Reform Trust.

Solomos, J. (1988) *Black Youth, Racism and the State: The Politics of Ideology and Policy*, Cambridge: Cambridge University Press.

Solomos, J. and Back, L. (1995) *Race, Politics and Social Change*, London: Routledge.

Soothill, K. and Gibbens, T. (1978) 'Recidivism of sex offenders: a reappraisal', *British Journal of Criminology*, vol 18, no 3, pp 267–76.

Soothill, K., Francis, B. and Ackerley, E. (1998) 'Paedophilia and paedophiles', *New Law Journal* (12 June), pp 882–3.

Spencer, J. (1995) 'A response to Mike Nellis: probation values for the 1990s', *The Howard Journal*, vol 34, no 4, pp 344–9.

SSI (1998) *They Look After Their Own, Don't they?* London: Social Services Inspectorate/DoH.

St Clair, A. (2006) 'Global poverty: the co-production of knowledge and politics', *Global Social Policy*, vol 6, no 1, pp 57–78.

Stainton, T. (2001) 'Reason and value: the thought of Plato and Aristotle and the construction of intellectual disability', *Mental Retardation*, vol 39, no 6, pp 452-60.

Stanley, L. and Wise, S. (1993) *Breaking out Again: Feminist Ontology and Epistemology*, London: Routledge.

Stermac, L.E., Segal, Z.V., and Gillis, R. (1990) 'Social and cultural factors in sexual assault', in W.L. Marshall, D.R. Laws and H.E. Barbaree (eds) *Handbook of Sexual Assault: Issues, Theories and Treatment of the Offender*, New York, NY: Plenum, pp 143–59.

Stern, S. and Seligmann, E. (2004) *The Partnership Principle: New Forms of Governance in the 21st Century*, London: Archetype.

Stone, D. (2002) *Policy Paradox: The Art of Political Decision Making* (revised 2nd edn), New York, NY: WW Norton and Company.

Stone, D. (2003) 'Public knowledge in the global agora', in A. Krizsan and V. Zentai (eds) *Reshaping Globalization: Multilateral Dialogues and New Policy Initiatives*, Budapest: Central European University Press, pp 41–62.

Stone, D. (2005) 'Knowledge networks and global policy', in D. Stone and S. Maxwell (eds) *Global Knowledge Networks and International Development*, London: Routledge, pp 89–105.

Stone, D. and Maxwell, S. (2005) *Global Knowledge Networks and International Development*, London: Routledge.

Strang, H. and Braithwaite, J. (eds) (2000) *Restorative Justice: Philosophy to Practice*, Aldershot: Ashgate.

Straw, J. (1999) Home Secretary's preface to the government's crime reduction strategy, London: Home Office, www.crimereduction.gov. uk/archive/0401/crsdoc1.htm

Stubbs, P. (2003) 'International non-state actors and social development policy', *Global Social Policy*, vol 3, no 3, pp 319–48.

Stubbs, P. (2005a) 'Stretching concepts too far?: Multi-level governance, policy transfer and the politics of scale in South-Eastern Europe', *South Eastern European Politics*, vol 6, no 2, pp 66–87, www.seep.ceu. hu/archives/issue62/stubbs.pdf

Stubbs, P. (2005b) 'Multi-level governance and policy transfer in South Eastern Europe', SEERC workshop, Zagreb 4–5 February.

Stubbs, P. (2006) 'Towards an ethnography of welfare reform', Baltics to Balkans seminar, Bristol, 8 February.

Tarpey, M. (2006) *Why People Get Involved in Health and Social Care Research: A Working Paper*, Eastleigh: INVOLVE.

Taylor, D. (1998) 'Social identity and social policy: engagements with postmodern theory', *Journal of Social Policy*, vol 27, no 3, pp 329–50.

Taylor-Gooby, P. (1981) 'The empiricist tradition in social administration', *Critical Social Policy*, vol 1, no 2, pp 6–21.

Taylor-Gooby, P. (1994) 'Postmodernism and social policy: a great leap backwards', *Journal of Social Policy*, vol 23, no 3, pp 385–404.

Taylor-Gooby, P. (1997) 'In defence of second best theory: state, class and capital in social policy', *Journal of Social Policy*, vol 26, no 2, pp 171–92.

Therborn, G. (2001) 'On the politics and policy of social quality', in W. Beck, L. Van der Maesen and A. Walker (eds) *Social Quality: A Vision for Europe*, The Hague: Kluwer Law International, pp 19–30.

Therborn, G. and Therborn, M. (2005) 'Social quality in Sweden', *European Journal of Social Quality*, vol 5, nos 1/2, pp 244–61.

Thompson, S. and Hoggett, P. (1996) 'Universalism, selectivism and particularlism: towards a post–modern social policy', *Critical Social Policy*, vol 16, no 1, pp 21–43.

Thomson, M. (1998) *The Problem of Mental Deficiency: Eugenics, Democracy and Social Policy in Britain c. 1870–1959*, Oxford: Clarendon Press.

Tickell, A. and Peck, J. (2003) 'Making global rules: globalisation or neoliberalisation?', in J. Peck and H. W.-C. Yeung (eds) *Remaking the Global Economy: Economic–Geographical Perspectives*, London: Sage, pp 163–81.

Timms, N. (1968) *The Language of Social Casework*, London: Routledge & Kegan Paul.

Titmuss, R.M. (1974) *Social Policy*, London: George Allen & Unwin.

Tonry, M. (2004) *Punishment and Politics: Evidence and Emulation in the Making of English Crime Control Policy*, Cullompton: Willan.

Townsend, P. (1976) *Sociology and Social Policy*, Harmondsworth: Penguin Books Ltd.

Tronto, J. (1993) *Moral Boundaries: A Political Argument for an Ethic of Care*, New York and London: Routledge.

Turner, M. and Beresford, P. (2005a) *User Controlled Research: Its Meanings and Potential*, Final Report, Eastleigh: INVOLVE.

Turner, M. and Beresford, P. (2005b) *Contributing on Equal Terms: Service User Involvement and the Benefits System*, London: Social Care Institute for Excellence.

UKTI (2007) 'UK inward investment', London: UK Trade and Investment, www.ukinvest.gov.uk/2/d/10128/en/GB/1.0.html

UNCTAD (2002) *World Investment Report*, New York, NY: United Nations Conference on Trade and Development.

UNRISD (2005) *Gender Equality: Striving for Justice in an Unequal World*, Geneva: UNRISD.

Useem, M. (1990) 'Business and politics in the United States and the United Kingdom', in S. Zukin and P. DiMaggio (eds) *Structures of Capital: The Social Organisation of the Economy*, Cambridge: Cambridge University Press, pp 263–92.

Valdes, J. (1995) *Pinochet's Economists: The Chicago School in Chile*, Cambridge: Cambridge University Press.

Van der Maesen, L., Walker, A. and Keizer, M. (2005) *European Network Indicators of Social Quality – ENIQ – 'Social Quality': The Final Report*, Amsterdam: European Foundation on Social Quality.

Van Langenhove, L. (1995) 'The theoretical foundations of experimental psychology and its alternatives', in J. A. Smith, R. Harré and L. Van Langenhove (eds) *Rethinking Psychology*, London: Sage, pp 10–23.

Venn, C. (2006) 'Translation: politics and ethics', *Theory, Culture and Society*, vol 23, nos 2–3, pp 82–4.

Vuori, M. and Gissler, M. (2005) 'Social quality in Finland', *European Journal of Social Quality*, vol 5, nos 1/2, pp 67–85.

Wade, R. (2004) 'On the causes of widening world income inequality', *New Political Economy*, vol 9, no 2, pp 163–88.

Walker, A. (1981) 'Social policy, social administration and the social construction of welfare', *Sociology*, vol 15, no 2, pp 225–50.

Walker, R. (2004) *Social Security and Welfare: Concepts and Comparisons*, Buckingham: Open University Press.

Ward, D. (1996) 'Probation training: celebration or wake', in M. Preston-Shoot and S. Jackson (eds) *Educating Social Workers in a Changing Policy Context*, London: Whiting and Birch.

Warren, L. (1990) 'Doing, being, writing: research on home care for older people', *Feminist Praxis*, monograph no 31, pp 1–59.

Warren, L. (1999) 'Empowerment: the path to partnership', in M. Barnes and L. Warren (eds) *Paths to Empowerment*, Bristol: The Policy Press.

Warren, L. and Maltby, T. (2000) 'Averil Osborn and participatory research: involving older people in change', in T. Warnes, L. Warren and M. Nolan (eds) (2000) *Care Services for Later Life: Transformations and Critiques*, London: Jessica Kingsley, pp 291-310.

Warren, L. and Cook, J. (2005) 'Working with older women: benefits and challenges of involvement', in L. Lowes and I. Hulatt (eds) *Involving Service Users in Health and Social Care Research*, London: Routledge.

Warren, L., Cook, J., Clarke, N., Haywood-Reed, L. M., Parkinson, M., Robinson, J. and Winfield, W. (2003) 'Working with older women in research', *Quality in Ageing*, vol 4, no 4, pp 24–31.

Watson, S. (2000) 'Foucault and the study of social policy', in G. Lewis, S. Gewirtz and J. Clarke (eds) *Rethinking Social Policy*, London: Sage, pp 66–77.

Webb, S. (2001) 'Some considerations on the validity of evidence-based practice in social work', *British Journal of Social Work*, vol 31, no 1, pp 57–79.

Weber, M. (1978) *Economy and Society: An Outline of Interpretive Sociology*, edited by G. Roth and C. Wittich, Berkeley, CA: University of California Press.

Wedel, J. (2004) 'Studying through a globalizing world: building method through aidnographies', in J. Gould and H. Secher Marcussen (eds) *Ethnographies of Aid: Exploring Development Texts Encounters*, IDS Occasional Paper 24, pp 149–74, Roskilde University.

Wedel, J. (2005) 'US foreign aid and foreign policy', *International Studies Perspectives*, vol 6, no 1, pp 35–50.

Wenger, E. (1998) *Communities of Practice: Learning, Meaning, Identity*, Cambridge: Cambridge University Press.

West, D. (1987) *Sexual Crimes and Confrontations. A Study of Victims and Offenders*, Aldershot: Gower.

Whitehead, S.M. (2002) *Men and Masculinities: Key Themes and New Directions*, Cambridge: Polity Press.

Whitfield, D. (2001) *Public Services or Corporate Welfare: Rethinking the Nation State in the Global Economy*, London: Pluto Press.

Wilding, P. (1982) *Professional Power and Social Welfare*, London: Routledge and Kegan Paul.

Williams, F. (1989) *Social Policy; A Critical Introduction*, Cambridge: Polity Press.

Williams, B. (1992) *Probation Values*, Birmingham: Venture Press.

Williams, F. (1992) 'Somewhere over the rainbow: universality and diversity in social policy', in N. Manning and R. Page (eds) *Social Policy Review 4*, Canterbury: Social Policy Association, pp 200–19.

Williams, F. (2001) 'Race/ethnicity, gender and class in welfare states: a framework for comparative analysis', in D. Fink, G. Lewis and J. Clarke (eds) *Rethinking European Welfare*, London: Sage, pp 131–62.

Williams, M. (2004) 'Discursive democracy and new labour: five ways in which decision-makers manage citizen agendas in public participation initiatives', *Sociological Research Online*, vol 9, no 3 www.socresonline.org.uk/9/3/9/3/williams.html

Willis, P. and Trondman, J. (2000) 'Manifesto for ethnography', *Ethnography*, vol 1, no 1, pp 5–16.

Wilson, A. and Beresford, P. (2002) 'Madness, distress and postmodernity: putting the record straight', in M. Corker and T. Shakespeare (eds) *Disability/Postmodernity: Embodying Disability Theory*, London: Cassell, pp 143–58.

Wistow, G. (2005) *Developing Social Care: The Past, the Present and the Future*, London: Social Care Institute for Excellence.

Wolfensberger, W. (2000) 'A brief overview of social role valorization', *Mental Retardation*, vol 38, no 2, pp 105–23.

Woolgar, S. (2000) 'Social basis of interactive social science', *Science and Public Policy*, vol 27, no 3, pp 165–73.

Worrall, A. (1992) 'Equal opportunity or equal disillusion? The probation service and anti-discriminatory practice', in B. Williams (ed) *Probation Values*, Birmingham: Venture Press.

Yanow, D. (1996) *How Does a Policy Mean?*, Washington DC: Georgetown University Press.

Yanow, D. (2004) 'Translating local knowledge at organizational peripheries', *British Journal of Management*, vol 15, no 1 (special issue), pp 9–25.

Yearley, S. (2005) *Making Sense of Science: Understanding the Social Study of Science*, London and Thousand Oaks, CA: Sage.

Yeates, N. (1999) 'Social politics and policy in an era of globalization: critical reflections', *Social Policy and Administration*, vol 33, no 4, pp 372–93.

Young, J. (1999) *The Exclusive Society*, London: Sage.

Young, K., Ashby, D., Boaz, A. and Grayson, L. (2002) 'Social science and the evidence-based policy movement', *Social Policy and Society*, vol 1, no 3, pp 215–24.

Zielonka, J. and Mair, P. (2002) 'Introduction: diversity and adaptation in the enlarged European Union', *West European Politics*, vol 25, no 2, pp 1–18.

Index

Note: Page numbers in *italic* refer to figures and tables

Nicolson, P. 140
Niranjana, T. 177
Noll, H. 49
non-governmental organisations
    (NGOs) 104, 123, 129-30
'non-white' 70, 71
Norway, welfare regime 38, *46*

O
Oatley, N. 112
O'Brien, R. 119
O'Byrne, P. 96
O'Connor, J. 50, 51
OECD 120, 128, 130
Oeij, P. 51, 52
Offe, C. 101, 102
older people as service users 157, 158,
    159
O'Leary, B. 99
Oliver, M. 157, 160, 164, 166, 167, 168
O'Malley, P. 177
'one planet living' 193, 199
Ong, A. 183, 206
Orenstein, M. 121, 122
organ retention scandals 162
Osler, D. 103
Oxfam 129
Oxford English Dictionary (OED) 30

P
paedophiles 144, 145, 146
    see also male sexual violence
Pakaluk, M. 97
Palier, B. 51, 52, 55-6
Parkinson, J. 161
participatory democracy 42
Parton, N. 96
Pascual, A. 50, 51
Pateman, C. 169, 170
Patomaki, H. 131
Pawson, R. 11
Peck, J. 183
Pembroke, L.R. 157
Percy, A. 147
Phillips, D. 42
Phillpotts, G.O. 146
phronesis 97
Pickering, A. 196
Pierson, P. 103
Piven, F.F. 104, 105
pluralism 99-100
pluralist democracy 43, 44
Poland, welfare regime *48*
policy
    changing meanings of 29-31
    and culture 29

definition of 22-6
and ethnography 32-5
historical uses of 30
as meaning-making 174-6
and politics relationship 26-8
Policy English 178
policy formulation 26
policy formulation and implementation
    26, 27, 28, 29, 32, 34, 35
policy implementation 26
policy spaces 123-4
policy studies 3-4
policy transfer 178-81
    and sociology of transfer, vocabulary
    differences *180*
political donations 103
political lobbying 102
politics and policy relationship 26-8
politics of scale 123-4
Portugal, welfare regime 45, *47*
post-structural approaches to power
    141-2
Poulantzas, N. 101
Pratt, M. 181
preventive partnership in crime control
    81
Priestly, P. 93
principle-based approaches to ethics
    138-9, 150-1
privileged interest 99-100
Probation Boards Association 96
probation, definition 89
probation practice
    cognitive behavioural methodology
    92-3
    language change 83-6, 88-9
    managerialisation and marketisation
    88-9
    National Standards 89-90
    punitive managerialism 88-92
    value future 94-7
    values 82-6
    see also criminal justice
Przeworski, A. 100-1
public services
    change in language 87-9
    managerialisation and marketization
    86-9
punitive managerialism 88-9, 90-2
Purvis, T. 82, 141, 142

R
'race' 67-8
Race, D. 160
Race Relations Act (1976) 69